EXILED IN AMERICA

STUDIES IN TRANSGRESSION

Studies in Transgression

EDITOR: David Brotherton
FOUNDING EDITOR: Jock Young

The Studies in Transgression series will present a range of exciting new crime-related titles that offer an alternative to the mainstream, mostly positivistic approaches to social problems in the United States and beyond. The series will raise awareness of key crime-related issues and explore challenging research topics in an interdisciplinary way. Where possible, books in the series will allow the global voiceless to have their views heard, offering analyses of human subjects who have too often been marginalized and pathologized. Further, series authors will suggest ways to influence public policy. The editors welcome new as well as experienced authors who can write innovatively and accessibly. We anticipate that these books will appeal to those working within criminology, criminal justice, sociology, or related disciplines, as well as the educated public.

OTHER BOOKS IN THIS SERIES

Terry Williams and Trevor B. Milton,
The Con Men: Hustling in New York City, 2015

EXILED IN AMERICA
LIFE ON THE MARGINS
IN A RESIDENTIAL MOTEL

Christopher P. Dum

Columbia University Press   New York

Columbia University Press
Publishers Since 1893
New York   Chichester, West Sussex
cup.columbia.edu
Copyright © 2016 Columbia University Press
All rights reserved

Library of Congress Cataloging-in-Publication Data
Names: Dum, Christopher P., author.
Title: Exiled in America : life on the margins
in a residential motel / Christopher P. Dum.
Description: New York : Columbia University Press, 2016. |
Series: Studies in transgression |
Includes bibliographical references and index.
Identifiers: LCCN 2016009591 | ISBN 9780231176422 (cloth : alk. paper) |
ISBN 9780231542395 (e-book)
Subjects: LCSH: Sex offenders—Housing—United States. |
Marginality, Social—United States. | Social isolation—United States. |
Motels—United States.
Classification: LCC HV6592 .D86 2016 |
DDC 365/.34—dc23
LC record available at
https://lccn.loc.gov/2016009591

∞

Columbia University Press books are printed on permanent
and durable acid-free paper.
Printed in the United States of America

c 10 9 8 7 6 5 4 3 2 1

Jacket design: Noah Arlow

For Kim Gwang Soo and Kim Young Sook,
who brought me into this world, and for
Donna Hoffman and Richard Dum,
who gave me the chance to explore it.

Not like the brazen giant of Greek fame,
With conquering limbs astride from land to land;
Here at our sea-washed, sunset gates shall stand
A mighty woman with a torch, whose flame
Is the imprisoned lightning, and her name
Mother of Exiles. From her beacon-hand
Glows world-wide welcome; her mild eyes command
The air-bridged harbor that twin cities frame.
"Keep, ancient lands, your storied pomp!" cries she
With silent lips. "Give me your tired, your poor,
Your huddled masses yearning to breathe free,
The wretched refuse of your teeming shore.
Send these, the homeless, tempest-tost to me,
I lift my lamp beside the golden door!"
　　　　　—Emma Lazarus, "The New Colossus" (1883)

CONTENTS

PREFACE

In 1993 National Public Radio (NPR) reporter David Isay arrived in the South Side of Chicago with a remarkable idea. His mission was to find two kids growing up in public housing and, in his words, "hire them as reporters for a week and give them a chance to tell their stories."[1] Isay's methodology was brilliant in its simplicity. He would give his young reporters tape recorders to carry as they went about their daily lives, chronicling their thoughts and experiences as they happened. It was in the Ida B. Wells housing project that Isay found his young and insightful correspondents; thirteen-year-old LeAlan Jones and fourteen-year-old Lloyd Newman. For seven days in 1993 and a year from 1994 to 1995, the pair used the simple power of their voices to capture the realities of inner-city life. They also reported on the aftermath of the death of Eric Morse, who died at the age of five after he was dropped from the fourteenth floor of an apartment building by two other young boys. Using over a hundred hours of audio, Isay, Jones, and Newman produced two award-winning NPR segments and the book *Our America: Life and Death on the South Side of Chicago*. I read this book as a first-year doctoral student and it made me wonder, what other voices were waiting to be heard?

Many voiceless individuals are battling some sort of stigma that they feel they cannot reveal. According to sociologist Erving Goffman, stigma is "an attribute that is deeply discrediting."[2] There is perhaps no other class of criminal more stigmatized or scrutinized in the United States than sexual offenders, especially those who offend against children. In fact, one study found that individuals would prefer to have a murderer in their neighborhood over a child molester.[3] Fears of recidivism have led to the passage of numerous federal, state, and local laws designed to keep convicted sex offenders away from potential child victims. They include sex-offender registration laws, such as the Jacob Wetterling Act, community notification laws, such as Megan's Law, and residence restrictions, which limit the areas where sex offenders may live. Research suggests, however, that many legal measures may not be effective; sex-offender registries are filled with inaccuracies, and residence restrictions show little impact on recidivism.[4]

Yet the laws do have a tremendous impact on released sex offenders who try to reenter their communities. In surveys and interviews, many sex offenders report trouble finding jobs and securing housing, as well as the psychological effects of losing friends, feeling alone and isolated, being harassed in public, and fearing for their safety.[5] These experiences may have distinct effects on the ability of sex offenders to reintegrate successfully into society. As I studied the lives of sex offenders, I wondered what it was like for them to live with these policies and the social stigma that surrounds their presence in the community. If someone empowered them to be the reporters of their lives, as Isay did with Jones and Newman, what would they say?

My initial explorations into the state sex-offender registry alerted me to the presence of the Boardwalk Motel (figure 1), located in the largely white and middle-class suburban town of Dutchland.[6] This motel held a dubious reputation in the community because government agencies used it to house registered sex offenders who would otherwise be homeless. It was the subject of many community debates concerning where sex offenders could live and how many should be allowed to live in one location. Adding to the concerns, a local legislator found through her own investigation that social services had placed families with children at the Boardwalk at the same time that registered sex offenders were living there. She also uncovered a plethora of code violations that included "no up-to-date fire alarm certifications, raw sewage, structural damage to roof, interior water damage, mold throughout entire rooms, exposed wiring, gas leak, missing bathroom tiles, rooms missing smoke detectors, bug infestation, bathroom mold, debris piled outside rooms, electric socket falling from wall, spliced wiring, cracked toilets."[7] In the fallout from this investigation, social services stopped housing families with children at the Boardwalk but continued to place adult clients there.

These revelations about the Boardwalk made it clear to me that the motel was not just a home for sex offenders. Rather, it housed a variety of marginalized populations (such as people who were mentally ill, disabled, struggling addicts, or working poor) who lived hidden from the public eye, in squalid conditions that many of us would consider unfit for habitation. I had found not only an interesting group of potential reporters but a unique location where they were socially embedded. The focus of my study then moved from a more general interest in how sex offenders lived in the community to a much more specific inquiry into how marginalized populations lived at this motel. Inspired by classic and contemporary ethnographic works, including Elliot Liebow's *Tally's Corner*, Philippe Bourgois's *In Search of Respect*, David Snow and Leon Anderson's *Down on Their Luck*, Elijah Anderson's *Code of the Street*, and Mitch Duneier's *Sidewalk*, I set out for the Boardwalk Motel to capture the voices of its residents.[8] I ended up living there for a year, witnessing firsthand the small triumphs and many indignities that the residents faced every day.

This book is an exploration of the Boardwalk Motel told through the perspective of those most qualified to tell it: the residents themselves. I conceptualize these residents as "social refugees"— persons who have been impelled to relocate within their own country of citizenship because of the influence of social context and/or social policy. By recounting their experiences, often in their own voices, I analyze what it was like to live in the intimate world of the motel, as well as in the surrounding community. Motel residents faced stigma and stereotype not only from the citizens of Dutchland, who feared for the safety of their homes and children, but also from one another. My goal is to show how these social contexts influenced resident status, identity, and behavior.

Ultimately, I argue that their experiences at the Boardwalk Motel strongly affected motel residents in ways that were unique to the setting. These residents represented some of the most vulnerable individuals in society, and their living situation exacerbated their vulnerabilities. They were often precariously close to living on the street, a fact that was largely ignored in the public discussions of the motel.

While the dynamics of homelessness are outside the scope of this work, writer Jonathan Kozol provides a simple lens through which to understand its root causes. In his book *Rachel and Her Children*, Kozol writes, "The cause of homelessness is lack of housing."[9] The following chapters examine how various social forces created a lack of housing that necessitated the existence of the Boardwalk Motel.

Toward the end of my research project, the motel was forced to close and its residents needed new housing. Once again, societal forces pushed them to other, similar locations on the margins and out of the public eye. In this respect, the story of the Boardwalk is the story of society's response to marginalization and inequality as manifested through the outcome of homelessness.

The introduction that follows provides the historical contexts for studying the Boardwalk Motel. I examine the rise and fall of the American motel industry, as well as the impact of America's criminal justice system and the recent Great Recession on residential instability. I then describe my research methods and introduce the residents who were key informants in my research. Chapter 1 paints an in-depth portrait of the Boardwalk Motel, its history, and the living conditions encountered there. In chapter 2 I analyze how residents viewed the motel's conditions relative to their previous housing environments. Residents also share their life histories, often featuring characteristics of vulnerability and instability that predated their arrival at the Boardwalk. Chapter 3 explores the issue of stigma and uses narratives to illustrate how residents formed identities and boundaries as a resistance to stigma. In chapter 4 I dive into the subculture of the motel that revolved around what I call the cycle of community, conflict, and fragility. Specifically, I examine the ways in which residents sought to address their deprivations through social interaction, and how the consequences of interactions gone wrong often left residents more vulnerable than when they arrived. Chapter 5 then turns its eyes toward the ways in which concerns about "quality of life," "civility," and "order" dominated perceptions about the motel, and how these concerns were, or were not, realized through resident behavior in the local community.

Finally, the conclusion examines the historical and political significance of the Boardwalk Motel's existence. By examining what happened after I left the field, I show how meaningful policy changes can be made in order to address the many societal failures that plagued life at the Boardwalk. It is a call for action and for a new way of looking at the many forms of marginalization, not just of homelessness but of class and social structure, wielded by powerful groups in attempts to "sanitize" their social space.

Ethnographers find themselves in a unique position to observe the lives of others in deeply intimate ways. This gives us the power to show the other side of the coin, so to speak. My goal in this book is to tell the motel's story in the words of those who know it best. It is an "alternative history" in a sense, because without it, the only record of the Boardwalk would be the accounts written by those who did not even live there. Throughout the book I attempt to present a counter-force to the stereotypes and stigmas that often plague marginalized populations such as those living at the Boardwalk. Such stereotypes often fail to take into account the social forces that affect human behavior. Goffman writes, "Persons in the same social position tend to possess a similar pattern of behavior. Any item of a person's behavior is, therefore, a sign of his social position."[10] The social forces that drive behavior and social position cannot be considered when stereotypes and stigma prevail. Ultimately, I believe that by presenting the perspectives and experiences of motel residents, I allow them to lay claim to their significance as distinct and valid human beings.

ACKNOWLEDGMENTS

In the future, over the course of what I hope is a long and fulfilling life, this book will be referred to over and over again as "mine." While that would not be a false narrative, it would mask the important contributions of those who helped guide this work. Because I view this study as part of a larger literature that attempts to uncover hidden worlds, I think it is fitting that I take the time to pull back the curtain and express my gratitude to those whose support made this possible.

Throughout this project, I have tried to remain conscious of the fact that my life is largely the result of good fortune. I entered foster care at a very young age, and were it not for the loving actions of my adoptive parents, Donna Hoffman and Richard Dum, I would not be where I am today. Any sense of duty that I have to fellow human beings stems from their early efforts to expose me to people from different circumstances, and I am grateful for the values that they instilled. I am also thankful for my incredible extended families. Your love and strength is nothing short of amazing. I am so fortunate to have you all in my life.

I am indebted to my mentor Jamie Fader. She placed more trust in me than I ever should have asked her to, advocated tirelessly for me, and never lost faith in my abilities. Frankie Bailey, Jeff Ferrell, and Alissa Worden deserve my gratitude as well. Their enthusiastic support and constructive critiques allowed me to fill the shell of my original idea.

Jennifer Perillo and Stephen Wesley at Columbia University Press have been amazing partners and collaborators since we first met, and I owe them a great deal for giving this book a home. Furthermore, this research could not have been completed without the generous support from the National Science Foundation, the American Society of Criminology, the Association of Doctoral Programs in Criminology and Criminal Justice, and the University at Albany Benevolent Association. I would like to thank Allison Redlich and Heather Washington for their insights into applying for this funding.

My friends in Albany offered incredible support and helped convince me that writing this book was something I could actually achieve. Kelly Socia and Robert Norris deserve particular recognition for their willingness to lend an ear, although I am sure our mutual appreciation for beer made my self-doubt much more tolerable. Thanks to Caitlyn O'Donnell, Vicky Schall, Chris Nelson, Chris Cutler, and Eric Fowler for our Friday nights at the Pump Station. To the wonderful friends that I made through countless soccer teams, I am thankful for the games, weddings, trips, and amazing experiences that I had with you all. Having a group that never wanted to talk about anything related to criminal justice was a life saver when I needed to get away. And to Jennifer Masa, thank you for never complaining or wavering in your belief in me, as I spent days upon days away in the field.

Finally, the most important contributors to this book are the men and women of the Boardwalk Motel. I met you simply wanting to understand you, and as we faded in and out of one another's lives, I was overwhelmed by your courage, care, and perseverance in the face of incredible odds. After all that you endured, there was little reason to open up and trust me with your life stories, but you did, and you have my upmost respect. I would not trade my time with you for anything, and my greatest hope is that you feel I have told your stories in ways that acknowledge the richness of who you are. This is for your hopes and dreams: may they forever flourish.

EXILED IN AMERICA

Introduction

Why are you hanging out here with these guys?
—Natalie

The run-down, "no-tell" motel is a classic symbol of tattered Americana, a staple in old-fashioned horror movies and alongside busy highways.[1] In contrast to chain hotels, which stand tall and pristine, struggling motels conjure up visions of empty swimming pools and neon "vacancy" signs flickering in thunderstorms. After a recent period of economic upheaval, the independent American motel industry struggles to stay afloat, with many motels relying on a marginalized clientele to survive.[2]

These motels can trace their origins to ancient Rome, an epicenter of commerce and travel. Inns were constructed to house visitors coming into the city on foot or horseback. Initially, innkeepers in Rome held the same lowly social status as gamblers and thieves. As the world evolved, so did inns, which eventually became a respected source of lodging for stagecoach travelers and nobles across the world.[3] As American cities grew, so did the need to provide accommodations for city residents and travelers ("hotel" derives from the French word for host). Many early hotels were located in the downtown areas of cities or towns, and the time period between 1880 and 1930 is regarded as the most vibrant period of downtown hotel living.[4] In 1910 there were ten thousand hotels in the United States, and in 1920 construction of hotels reached an all-time high, with overall occupancy rates of 85 percent.[5]

As an improving highway system made America more accessible to travelers, a system of lodging was needed to meet the demand for hospitality on the road. Thus the first road hotels were born. The word "motel" was coined in 1925 when a California architect named Arthur Heineman built a lodge near San Luis Obispo that allowed guests to drive up to the door of their rooms.[6] He decided to call it a "motor hotel" and then shorted it to "motel." At the time of its opening, rooms at Heineman's Mo-tel Inn cost $2.50 a night.[7] Motels differed from hotels in both purpose and design. Whereas downtown hotels were designed to provide tourists with lodging in bustling city centers, motels provided highway travelers with a place to stay briefly before continuing on their journey. Motels attracted motor tourists because they provided better parking than downtown hotels and were located outside congested downtown areas. Motels also deliberately eschewed the formality of hotels, in that they lacked public meeting spaces such as lobbies, dining rooms, and ballrooms, which often required particular codes of dress and social conduct.[8]

In the mid-1930s, about a decade after Heineman built his motel, the American Automobile Association estimated that forty million people took car trips that required lodging each year.[9] Then the post–World War II increase in prosperity, coupled with the emergence of armies of traveling salesmen, caused a boom in motel construction. The number of motels rose from 9,848 in 1935 to 25,874 in 1948.[10] In 1950 overall hotel and motel lodging occupancy was at 80 percent; now-familiar chains such as Marriott, Ramada, Howard Johnson, and Holiday Inn were all established during that decade.[11] By 1961 there were 60,951 motels in the United States, a substantial increase from 29,426 in 1954.[12]

The boom for independent motel operators was somewhat short-lived. By the late 1960s concerns with safety and reliability caused travelers to choose chain hotels, and as a consequence, small motels began going out of business.[13] Further competition arose in 1988, when Residence Inns and Homewood Suites opened extended-stay chain hotels.[14] These were designed to house businesspeople whose frequent travel often required stays of between five and thirty nights, and they subsequently drew even more business away from independent motels.[15] In November 2000 the American Hotel & Lodging Association removed the word "motel" from its title after marketing research advised the change. An industry spokesperson acknowledged that the reputation of motels factored into the decision, saying, "They all have these negative associations with them."[16] With this move came the death of the motel that Arthur Heineman and millions of American travelers once knew. These formerly respectable and thriving businesses were reanimated as low-end residential motels that catered not to tourists but to those on the margins of society in need of shelter.[17]

The use of motels as last-ditch housing for the socially and financially marginalized actually has a long history in the world of American lodging. Early forms of cheap lodging found in major U.S. cities during the late 1880s and early 1900s catered to the urban labor force, made up of single males who had migrated to the city from more rural areas. These lodging houses provided minimal amenities and were known for poor maintenance, pest infestations, and other unsanitary conditions.[18] In 1905 Raines Law hotels in New York City were viewed as a public nuisance and targeted by activist groups in an effort to clean up the city. At the time, hotels were allowed to sell alcohol on Sundays, while saloons could not. Because hotels were defined as any location with a restaurant and ten bedrooms, saloon owners began serving lunch and adding ten bedrooms, which they rented to prostitutes, in order to serve alcohol.[19] In his book *Hotel Life* (1936), sociologist Norman Hayner saw hotels as indicative of the evils of city life, stating, "problems of urban culture such as the decline in home life, the increasing freedom of and independence of women and children, the challenges of the new leisure, the disintegration of the mores—all of these are found in an accentuated form in the hotel."[20] After Elliot Ness's famous encounters with Al Capone, the government hired the prohibition agent to mount an effort against prostitution in hotels around military bases in the 1940s. Hotels offered the "ideal locale" for prostitution, and their policies of "hear no evil, see no evil, speak no evil" created a culture where clandestine encounters led to high rates of venereal disease among American servicemen.[21] Around the same time, J. Edgar Hoover voiced his concerns about motels fostering criminality and immorality.[22]

In the 1950s and 1960s attention focused on "skid rows" in major American cities, which sociologist Donald Bogue described as "a district in the city where there is a concentration of substandard hotels and rooming houses charging very low rates and catering primarily to men with low incomes."[23] These skid rows were the remnants of city areas that had served and housed the transient, single, poor workers in the early 1900s.[24] Many rooms on skid row in the mid-1900s were cheap single-room occupancy (SRO) units.[25] Single-room occupancy is a term that originated in New York City to refer to tenement apartment buildings that were converted to individual living quarters for the urban poor.[26] SRO units may come with or without kitchens or sanitary facilities, and it is common for unit residents to share bathrooms and kitchens on a floor. "SRO" is mostly reserved for hotels that have been either designed as or refurbished into single-room units. Unlike motels, SRO locations are not intended to rent to tourists.

The majority of residents in SRO housing are what medical sociologist Harvey Siegal calls the "socially terminal," or people whom mainstream society deems problematic.[27] They are often poor and transient, with histories of drug abuse, mental illness, and criminal behavior. After spending eighteen months observing residents in a variety of SRO locations, Siegal found that the SRO was more than just a building for the poor: it was a social system with a variety of residents who had distinct orientations toward life in SROs.

Similar studies by Norman Hayner, J. Kevin Eckert, Robert C. Prus, Steve Vassilakopoulos, and Styllianoss Irini have looked past the stereotypes associated with low-end residential lodging to focus on the people who live there and the social worlds they inhabit.[28] For the most part, these dwellings provide autonomy for their residents. Because identification is rarely requested and privacy is respected, it is easy to blend in and do whatever one pleases.[29] Residents are free to engage in drug activity, sexual behavior, and gambling, or live completely reclusive lives with few barriers from staff. However, that is not to say that owners and desk clerks are unaware of those to whom they rent. Some managers instruct their staff on how to screen potential customers, and staff often know many details about the lives of long-time residents.[30] At one particular motel that rented specifically for sexual trysts, clerks asked potential customers if they were staying for a few hours or overnight, and if the answer was overnight, the customer was informed that there were no available rooms.[31] Architecturally, some locations have large lobbies that encourage socializing, while others are devoid of furniture to discourage any sort of public interactions.[32] Owners and managers walk a fine line between protecting their clients from too much exposure and encouraging some sort of community.

Customers, although diverse in many respects, are drawn to low-end residential lodging for several common reasons. First and foremost, the alternative for many of these impoverished individuals would be homelessness, or some sort of institutionalization.[33] Others arrive because locations cater to their needs, an example being older people with few social supports who find that some hotels and motels provide easy access to other elderly residents, affordable nutrition, and services such as laundry and barbershops.[34] In other cases, residential lodging provides the privacy needed to do drugs, turn tricks, or run numbers. Finally, because the markers of success and respect are different in residential lodging locations from those in the middle-class world, life there provides important opportunities to establish social status for those who lack the means to achieve status in a typical middle-class environment.[35]

However, the hidden aspect of residential lodging is not always a benefit. In 1995 a heat wave ravaged the city of Chicago, with heat indexes reaching into the 120s.[36] Sociologist Eric Klinenberg found that in one area of Northeast Chicago, 16 of 26 heat-related deaths occurred in SROs, while 62 of the 160 death reports at the Public Administration Office used the word "room" (a code word for hotel residence) to signify the location where the resident died.[37] Although SROs can offer the privacy and isolation that some residents crave, these very same qualities led to their abandonment and eventual death.

Because there are so many forms of low-end lodging in the United States, it is difficult to gather comprehensive data on their numbers, cost, and use. Therefore my data come from a variety of sources. Leslie Brownrigg provides a collection of this information in her report *People Who Live in Hotels* (2006). The National Housing Survey conducted by Fannie Mae in 1981 found that the average monthly cost for a bedroom and bathroom in a transient hotel was $180. In 2002 the New York City Housing and Vacancy Survey estimated that 6,777 housing units in the city were used for SRO purposes.[38] According to the American Hotel & Lodging Association, in 2012 there were 342 properties supplying 34,498 rooms at the rate of $30 or under per night.[39]

This long-standing need for cheap lodging has created a fascinating historical record of housing locations and their cultures. What these locations have in common is that they provide shelter for a wide variety of residents who, for one reason or another, experience residential instability on the margins of society. Often these reasons are linked to broad social forces (such as the changing labor landscapes in the 1920s and deinstitutionalization of the mentally ill in the 1970s). More recently, when I began my research for this book, a punitive criminal justice policy and an economic recession were increasing residential instability and social marginalization for millions of people in the United States.

In the years between 1978 and 2009, the number of federal and state prisoners rose from 294,400 to 1,555,600, an increase of almost 430 percent.[40] At the end of 2012 the total number of U.S. adults under correction supervision was 6,937,600 offenders, meaning that 1 in every 35 adult residents in the United States was under some form of correctional supervision in 2012.[41] One consequence of the punitive turn in criminal justice policy has been an increase in residential instability among previously incarcerated individuals. Ninety-three percent of prisoners eventually leave prison.[42] In 2012, 637,411 individuals were released from state and federal prison, saddled with the many challenges of returning to society.[43]

Prisoner reentry has become an undeniably important issue for our justice system. Reentering prisoners face difficulties finding employment, establishing (or reestablishing) strong relationships with romantic partners and children, and securing stable housing.[44] While all these challenges are related, a lack of stable housing may prevent individuals from securing and maintaining employment as well as isolate them from important social networks and reentry services. In extreme cases, an individual may fall off the grid after becoming homeless.

Finding reentry housing is even more difficult for registered sex offenders released from prison and jail. In 2012 it is estimated that 21,800 sex offenders were released from prison to the community.[45] Upon release, sex offenders face residence restrictions that affect their access to stable housing. They are designed to prevent recidivism by barring registered sex offenders from living within certain distances (often 500 or 1,000 feet) from schools, daycare facilities, parks, and other locations where children congregate. These policies may limit sex offenders' access to affordable housing, which could lead to financial and emotional hardship, which in turn could lead to new offenses.[46] At the aggregate level, it has been found that many sex offenders live in impoverished neighborhoods that lack informal social control or reactive and proactive behaviors that encourage conformity to the law.[47] Restricting sex offenders to these neighborhoods may decrease the chances of successful reentry by surrounding them with neighbors who offer little social support and often engage in drug use and criminal behavior.[48] Residence restrictions may also force sex offenders out of urban areas, and living in rural areas may limit their opportunities for employment and access to treatment.[49]

In addition, the recent Great Recession increased residential instability among the poor. According to the U.S. Census Bureau, in 2010 there were 46.2 million people living in poverty, which represented the fourth consecutive annual increase and the largest number recorded in the fifty-two years that poverty estimates have been published.[50] In 2012 that number increased to 46.5 million. Many individuals attempted to consolidate their living situations in the hope of saving money. From 2007 to 2013 the number of adults living in shared households increased from 61.7 million to 71.5 million.[51] However, this strategy was not an option for those with limited or nonexistent social networks. In the face of increasing poverty, those who already came from low socioeconomic status with no family or friends to move in with were likely to turn to alternative locations.

In addition to increasing residential instability among poor minorities, the recession affected formerly middle-class individuals as well. From 2008 to 2010 at least 3.5 million home foreclosures were completed, and at the end of 2010, 2.2 million more homes were in the foreclosure process.[52] Without places to live, many evicted families turned to the types of motels that have long provided homes for the chronically impoverished.[53] In a 2009 survey conducted by the National Coalition for the Homeless, 26 percent of the newly evicted homeless reported living in motels or hotels.[54] Professor and social worker Terri Lewinson interviewed families living in extended-stay motels and found that residents experienced a variety of feelings toward low-end residential lodging. Residents felt trapped by their inability to leave the motel; some reported depression and even suicidal thoughts.[55] However, they also admitted that in some ways the motel afforded them "family independence, social engagement, a sense of safety and a connection to a community context."[56]

Policies intended to manage homelessness have also aided the transition of independent motels to low-budget lodging. Welfare agencies in New York City placed poor and homeless individuals in hotels as early as the 1960s.[57] In the face of rising numbers of homeless individuals in the 1980s and 1990s and a lack of available shelter space, social service agencies in cities such as New York, San Francisco, and Boston paid commercial hotels to house the homeless. For some owners, these contracts provide their most significant source of year-round income, while for others they act as a financial cushion during winter months when tourist traffic is low and shelter need is high.[58] Using motels to shelter the homeless is now a widespread practice among social services agencies. States such as Vermont, Massachusetts, California, New Jersey, Missouri, and Oregon, along with the District of Columbia, have used or considered using motels to house the homeless. Massachusetts spent $48.1 million in 2013 to house nearly two thousand families in motels.[59] Portland, Maine, placed families in motels for 198 nights in 2013, compared to 68 nights in 2012, an increase of 191 percent.[60] Children are also affected by the use of motels, and statistics show that from 2008 to 2009, 892 children lived in motels or hotels in Orange County, California.[61]

A YEAR AT THE BOARDWALK

This book examines the impact of these social and criminal justice policies on marginalized individuals by using a year of ethnographic research at one such repurposed location, the Boardwalk Motel. Built in 1960 in the town of Dutchland, the Boardwalk saw its reputation decline in the 1980s when locals grew concerned about the type of clients that the motel's new owner rented to. In the early 2000s the county Department of Social Services began to pay the motel's owner to shelter the homeless. This government-assigned clientele included parolees, individuals with disabilities, and registered sex offenders.

Of particular note was the stigma that the local Dutchland community attached to the motel. In his study, Siegal referred to the typical SRO as "an outpost of the poor located in a comfortable middle and upper-class area which is actively hostile to its presence."[62] The Boardwalk Motel was a target of similar concern. Dutchland community members complained that the motel residents wandered around their neighborhoods and diminished their quality of life.[63] Others voiced similar concerns about behavior, "They create an unsafe situation. They are continually partying every night."[64] In response to someone defending the presence of sex offenders at the Boardwalk, a resident wrote on a local newspaper's online website: "If you don't think people have a right to be concerned with housing that fosters such a dense concentration of rapists and child molesters in the middle of a community otherwise characterized by families and single family homes then you are absolutely correct. . . . This country is going down the tubes, I tell you what."[65] During a town meeting, an elderly Dutchland resident suggested that her tax dollars should not have to pay for any ambulances and police who responded to incidents at the motel.

The Boardwalk Motel offered a unique opportunity for me to study the powerful social forces of inequality as they were shaped by cultural issues and social institutions. The motel represented a location of last resort for poor individuals in search of affordable housing. It was also home to registered sex offenders and other parolees in need of shelter. Finally, the motel was a refuge for many individuals with mental and physical disabilities who were placed there by social services because they lacked the ability to secure more stable residences. In short, the Boardwalk Motel was symbolic of the larger social issue of homelessness and the cyclical ways in which homelessness creates a new underclass while also exacerbating conditions among the existing underclass.[66]

The Boardwalk also represented the increasingly dystopian cultural response to inequality, what sociologist Jeff Ferrell calls "the regulation of public interaction, the restoration of exclusionary community, the reencoding of cultural space along lines of order and privilege." As Ferrell documents, those in power have made concerted efforts to "sanitize" urban public space by removing those deemed unsightly and unwanted (including the homeless) from the streets. The local response to the Boardwalk Motel suggested that the "insidious sanitization of urban life" extended far beyond city streets, as powerful suburban communities attempted to "round up and neutralize as many undesirables, outsiders, and subversives as possible."[67] Fueled by the desire to sanitize social space, the public discourse on locations like the Boardwalk lacks insight into who motel residents are, how they behave, and how social forces influence their lives.

The Boardwalk's confluence of "problematic" residents created a stigmatized community whose members were similarly situated on the outskirts of society but who were also wildly different in many respects. This book explores how residents of the Boardwalk went about their daily lives in the context of the social forces that created the very need for the motel in the first place, and, at the same time, the cultural resistance to its existence. This framework is driven by the following questions:

1. How did residents arrive at the motel?
2. How are residents affected by the stigma attached to their residence?
3. What survival strategies do residents employ in daily life?
4. How do motel residents interact with a local community opposed to their presence?
5. What types of societal changes are required to best address the issues of culturally situated marginalization?

With these questions in mind, my next step was to figure out how to make contact with and recruit motel residents to participate in the study. Putting flyers or business cards under doors or on car windshields seemed invasive and out of the question, as did going over to the motel as a complete stranger to knock on doors or try to approach people who I saw out and about. After I spent some time considering and discarding various ideas, a solution became clear. I would move in.

RESEARCH DESIGN AND CONSIDERATIONS

I maintained a rented room at the Boardwalk from June 6, 2012, through June 5, 2013, at the rate of $205 a week. Renting a room enabled me to conduct an in-depth examination of the social setting of the motel. A social setting can be viewed as the interaction of one or more actors engaging in activity at a particular time in a particular place.[68] Immersing myself in the social setting of the motel allowed me to capture what inhabitants viewed as meaningful and important by observing daily conversations and activities.[69] Many social scientists have employed this ethnographic technique to shed light on hidden groups and locations, such as Italian immigrants, unemployed black men in the nation's capital, public drunks, poor black communities, working people in the ghetto, homeless people living in the streets, crack dealers in Harlem, street youth in Canada, sidewalk vendors in Greenwich Village, inner-city youth in Philadelphia, black middle-class families, working poor in the inner city, and urban youth transitioning to adulthood.[70]

While works of investigative journalism involve reporters going undercover in order to walk in the shoes of others, my renting a motel room was never about becoming a motel resident.[71] I never considered creating a cover story to portray myself as a sex offender, an individual on welfare, or someone down on his luck. To do so would have been unethical because those we study have the right to know they are being studied. As a social scientist, I had to decide what sort of membership role I would take in the field, once I had disclosed my purpose to participants. After considering the pros and cons of full participation, I decided to focus not on my experience but on the experiences of true residents of the motel. There are two reasons why I took this approach.

First, I acknowledged early on that the ethnomethodologist approach would be to put most of my belongings in storage and move into the motel as if I were a new resident, making "a total commitment to becoming the phenomenon in order to study it."[72] This would require me to sever all connections to my former world, something that even the best ethnographers admit is almost impossible to accomplish.[73] Reminded by these scholars to be aware of my beliefs and abilities, I knew that this sort of immersion was beyond my limits.

My second reason for not going underground was purely logistical. Full commitment to the motel as a primary residence would require some set of rules governing how I would live. How much money could I spend each week? Would I give up my car? If many residents struggled without health insurance, would I do the same? Could I stay overnight with friends, and, if so, how often? The only way to come up with guidelines about how to live as a motel resident would be to first understand how motel residents lived. It seemed to me that this understanding was precisely the point of the study, so total commitment would be putting the cart before the horse.

Looking back on this decision, I am confident that it was the correct one. I am a Korean American, highly educated, from a middle-class family. As I will show later in this chapter, once I made my presence as a researcher known, residents were quite aware of our differences. If I had tried to hide that aspect of my life and residents found out, it would have been met with disastrous results. More important, having an apartment to return home to during the study was a real blessing. On several occasions I felt the need to disengage from my research and reflect on events that had occurred. In some instances I simply retreated to my room, but when something particularly striking or exciting or stressful happened, I headed home to my apartment and the other social world that I inhabited. By not using the motel as a primary residence, I created sanctuaries of respite that relieved the stresses of my fieldwork.

PROTECTING RESEARCH PARTICIPANTS

Ethnographic research could not exist without the cooperation of those who live in the social settings under study. This participation largely depends on the relationships that a researcher builds with his or her human subjects. Establishing these relationships requires the researcher to respect potential subjects during the recruitment process. Maintaining the relationships requires protection of what they choose to share. I developed several ways of respecting and protecting residents of the motel. The population for this study included all motel residents and workers, as well as those with substantial connections to these individuals (such as friends and family). The caveat was that I did not view anyone under the age of eighteen as a potential participant. (See appendix 1 for a complete listing of participants and selected demographic information.)

I provided potential subjects with, and read aloud from, an Institutional Review Board–approved Informed Consent form that summarized the purpose of the study and reiterated the protections in place. I also made it clear to residents that (1) participation was entirely voluntary, (2) there would be no benefits or compensation provided for participation, (3) they could withdraw at any time, and (4) all identifying information would remain confidential. When participants agreed to be a part of the study, they were not asked to sign this consent form because any link between their real name and illegal behavior would have created undue risk to them.

Once residents agreed to participate, I recorded observations in the form of written field notes. Participants were not asked for their full names, and their real names were never recorded in my field notes. Instead, I used code names to mask their identities. These names were not street names, nicknames, or any other names that they used in daily life. Furthermore, all attempts were made to mask details of their lives, to the extent that their stories could still be preserved. For example, if a person worked at a particular fast-food establishment, I recorded it as another such establishment to provide additional protection.

When residents became comfortable with my presence as a researcher, I employed a digital audio recorder in certain situations with their permission. Using the recorder improved the validity of my observations in several ways. First, I used it to record field notes in spoken form. Using the recorder allowed me to take note of events that had just transpired much more quickly than I could have done if I were writing. Second, as sociologist Robert Weiss states, note taking without audio accompaniment "tends to simplify and flatten respondents' speech patterns," and the "vividness of speech disappears." Because audio recording captured the actual words, phrases, and speaking patterns of residents, the data reflect what Weiss describes as "respondents' false starts and stray thoughts and parenthetic remarks."[74] The recording of conversations actually benefited the residents who participated because their words were not filtered through my memory. I kept the notebooks containing these field notes on my person or locked them in my motel room. After I finished my research, I kept physical copies of field notes in a locked desk in a locked office. All forms of electronic data were stored on a password-protected computer.

KEY INFORMANTS

The first person I encountered at the Boardwalk was Elizabeth, the manager who worked afternoon and overnight and also managed the nearby Park Place Motel, which was also owned by the Boardwalk's owner. He allowed her to live in the small house that sat on the Park Place's property. Some residents called her "Ms. Elizabeth." She was a short, chubby white woman pushing seventy, with a round face and scratchy voice. When she was not wearing a reddish/brown wig, she wore a knitted cap, and she often shuffled slowly around the property with her twelve-year-old brown pit bull, Mocha. As I got to know Elizabeth, I learned that her moods oscillated between friendly and negative. Her greeting to residents who walked into the office was often a raspy, "Whaddya want?" However, I got along well with her because I rarely caused trouble, and although she was reluctant to share many details about herself, she took my presence as a researcher in stride.

I was quite nervous when I first moved into my room. Luckily, I encountered a friendly face in my neighbor, Roy, which calmed my nerves. Roy was a black male in his forties who had been living with his girlfriend at the Boardwalk for a month when I moved in. He had a shaved head and a laugh that sounded like he was pushing the last bit of air out of his chest. I had a particular affinity for him because he engaged me immediately and loved to talk. After his girlfriend left him a few weeks later, Roy was evicted for falling behind on his rent, although the fact that he dealt drugs may have had something to do with his eviction as well.

My worries about establishing relationships with residents were eased even more when I met Biggie and Deirdre on my second day at the motel. They were a middle-aged couple who lived in a chaotic and cluttered room on the first floor, largely owing to Biggie's habit of scrapping metal. He was a forty-four-year-old black male, with a large belly and a scar running down the middle of his chest from heart surgery. Easily excited, he was prone to talking so loudly that some assumed he was yelling. Deirdre was a white woman with thick glasses, who told me she was in her fifties, although some people claimed that she was much older. She spoke slowly and quietly in comparison to her partner and often told the same stories over and over. They moved out in fall 2012 to a trailer, but rumors abounded that they lost it soon after.

Biggie and Deirdre introduced me to Steve, a chain-smoker in his fifties who lived a few doors down from Biggie with a roommate who he had met at the motel. I enjoyed talking with Steve because he often asked me questions about my own life, such as what dishes my mother cooked that I really loved. However, because of what many thought was an unspecified mental illness, Steve found it tough to care for himself, and I often saw him wearing dirty clothes. Other residents worried about him, and he was eventually removed in summer 2012 to an assisted living facility.

My relationship with Biggie and Deirdre also put me in contact with Avery and Elisha. They were a young white couple in their late twenties who stayed at the Boardwalk for four weeks on the recommendation of a friend. Elisha had a baby who occasionally lived in the motel with them (Avery was not the baby's father). They interacted often with Biggie and Deirdre and then eventually moved into a trailer down the street that Avery purchased with money from a worker's compensation case. Elisha returned in the winter when her mother, father, and teenaged brother, Clive, moved in after her father lost his job. They moved out in the cold months of early 2013.

Biggie's outgoing personality put him in contact with many other residents, such as Dee and Toby. Dee was a white, thirty-something ex-stripper/escort and recovering drug addict who had lived with her boyfriend Toby at the Boardwalk for almost a year when I met them. She used a bike to get around until it was stolen while she was shopping. When she got excited she spoke with a distinct New York accent. Toby was a quiet white man in his forties and also a recovering addict. I found it hard to get to know Toby, so most of my data about them comes from Dee. Guy was a middle-aged white male who was Dee's friend and former client, and he continued to visit and help pay some of her rent while she lived at the motel, although they did not engage in sexual activity. Dee and Toby moved out of the motel with the financial help of family in early spring 2013.

I first heard about Reg during a conversation with Steve, who commented on Reg's physical prowess and ability to "take care of the place." Reg was a hulking Irish giant in his early thirties. He and his partner, Sky, had lived at the Boardwalk for a year and a half when I met them. Reg became a central figure in my study because his personality and tenure made him a feared and respected figure at the motel. Once he had a clear understanding of my research he became one of my closest friends. Sky was in her mid-twenties and loved reading and the television show *Family Guy*. She suspected that she was bipolar because she was very depressed some days and bright and cheerful on others. Sky and Reg had a complicated relationship that underwent much stress during my time at the Boardwalk. I helped them move out of the motel in August 2013.

A lover of Metallica, Jake was close friends with Reg and Sky and lived next door to them for much of the study. Jake and I shared a love of movies, so he and I bonded by reminiscing about our favorite films, especially those in the horror and action genres. He was tall and skinny and in his mid-thirties. He often wore t-shirts referencing cartoons or movie characters. It was hard to get to know much about his life before the motel, but I always enjoyed hanging out with him. He moved with Reg and Sky when they left the motel.

Fran was a friend of Sky's who moved in with Sky when Reg was sent to jail in December 2012. She was in her early forties, considerably obese, and admitted to having bipolar disorder. Fran told me that she had lost custody of her thirteen-year-old son several years ago because of her alcohol and drug addiction. One of her goals was to secure an apartment and stable lifestyle that would allow her to regain custody sooner rather than later, because she worried that as he grew older he would cease to recognize her as his mother. In the summer of 2013 she left the Boardwalk to spend a few days with a boyfriend and never returned to the motel.

At almost 6'9" and quite thin, Sam was hard to miss. A black veteran in his fifties who grew up in Chicago, he became one of my closest friends after Reg introduced us. We spent many hours sitting outside, and I enjoyed listening to him rant about the treatment of blacks in America and his goal of leaving the motel. His wife, Justine, did not live at the motel with him, choosing instead to live with her daughter in an apartment that was close to her job at a girls' residential facility. Sam refused to join her because he felt that dependency was an affront to his pride. Justine visited him often and they came to view me as a good friend, who could also provide an occasional loan. When Sam moved out in November 2012 we made plans to keep in touch, but he eventually stopped returning my calls and I worried that he had fallen back into selling and using drugs.

Natalie began working at the motel in late June 2012 as a desk worker and housekeeper. After speaking with other residents who knew her, I learned that Natalie was Elizabeth's daughter. She was in her late forties, with a raspy New York accent. Her boyfriend Mike worked as a maintenance man at the Boardwalk for a time and also drove a cab in the evenings. In his mid-forties with a beer gut, Mike spoke loudly and had a deep laugh. Both of them struggled with drug addiction. Natalie and Mike disappeared for several months in fall 2012 after it was rumored that they stole from the motel. They returned in spring 2013 to live with Elizabeth in the house at the Park Place.

Ed can best be described as an enigma, as he did not share much about his personal life with me or other residents, although Natalie claimed that she had known him for years. He was a white man in his fifties who arrived in late June 2012. Other residents worried about his well-being because he was often drunk or high. Ed had a lower lip that stuck out, giving him a grumpy resting face, but he was always friendly with me and I enjoyed speaking with him, especially about his views on ghosts and the paranormal. He disappeared in

November 2012, and many suspected he had simply gone off the grid and died.

While I knew that the motel was home to vulnerable populations, Curtis's situation was particularly troubling. Curtis was a skinny male in his early thirties with yellow teeth and pale skin who came to the motel in early July 2012. He walked around without shoes or socks, and his gaunt face and sunken eyes made him look like a zombie. He had mental health issues that were rumored to have been caused by a car accident or drug use. Curtis was unique in that several members of his family came to check on him periodically, as did a case worker, but the sentiment among residents was that Curtis needed go to somewhere where his behavior could be monitored. He was moved out by his family and case worker at the end of October 2012.

Trim moved in with his on-again, off-again girlfriend Ellen in late June 2012 and made a show of strutting shirtless to his room to show off his heavily tattooed upper body. Despite this aggressive performance, Trim was incredibly friendly with me. He was a white male in his sixties and claimed to work a construction job that sometimes took him out of town. In the fall his ex-wife from Utah arrived for a few days with her young son. This caused a problem because the motel was not supposed to allow children. Trim left in September 2012 to find a place for them.

Marc was a young Guatemalan in his twenties with a limited command of English who arrived in late July 2012. Fortunately, I possessed a limited command of Spanish, so we were able to communicate. He moved from New Jersey to work at a car dealership near the motel and sent the money back to his family. Marc was very friendly, liked to do cocaine, and was quick to share beer and food. I tried to repay this by taking him to the store and buying his beer since he lacked a license. He eventually moved to the Park Place and was still living there when I left.

I met Ramòn when he showed up one summer day in 2012 to hang out with Jake and Reg. He was a Puerto Rican man in his thirties who used to live at the motel and worked with Jake at KFC. He often visited on his bike and made jokes about being "Spic-tacular." He and I hit it off immediately because of his easygoing nature, and

I felt sorry for him when I learned from Jake that he had fallen at another motel in the winter and broke his leg in several places.

Cinque had a stocky build and large dreadlocks that Sam joked made him look like the Predator. He was in his thirties and arrived in August 2012 on parole from prison. Although he never admitted it to me, Cinque was a registered sex offender. He was one of the few at the motel to have an on-the-books job (at Waste Management), although he grew frustrated with it and was sent back to jail for selling marijuana in October 2012.

Randy was a white male in his fifties and one of several sex offenders who lived at the Park Place Motel. Because of his skills as a handyman, he served as a maintenance man for both the Park Place and the Boardwalk. Residents were dependent on his skills, so they were always friendly with him. His room at the Park Place was significantly larger than others and more like an apartment. He kept two gas grills out back, as well as a tent and his pickup, which either caught or was set on fire late one summer night. Randy was still living at the Park Place when I finished my study.

Darryl arrived at the motel in September 2012 when he was paroled as a registered sex offender. In his late forties, Darryl became quite enthusiastic about the project and we spent a lot of time talking about the challenges he faced, such as finding a job, finding an actual apartment, and dealing with stomach- and back-related health issues. He was a white man who identified as bisexual and fell in love with a black man in his late thirties named Digital. Even after Darryl moved out in January 2013, I spent a lot of time with them; Darryl later served as a guest speaker in a class at my university.

Larry was a self-identified drifter who arrived at the motel in early October 2012. He was an ex-marine in his fifties and made a concerted effort to keep in shape by running around the area and doing pushups in his room. Larry's story was unique because he went from resident to part-time desk worker/maintenance man, and this gave him an interesting perspective on life at the motel. When I left, he was living at the Park Place at a discount and still working at both motels.

I first met Noonan early on because he lived next door to me when I arrived, but we did not get to know each other well until later in my fieldwork. Noonan was a white parolee in his forties, tall and stocky, and worked with a union. After a few weeks he moved out of the Boardwalk to do union work, but he returned in October 2012 and moved down to the Park Place shortly thereafter. He and I were friendly when we saw each other, and from what I gathered, he was still living at the Park Place when I ended my study.

Burt bore a striking resemblance to Noonan and was referred to as "Mr. Clean" by residents. When he arrived in September 2012 he immediately annoyed the others by asking them to turn down their music and be quiet in the evening, because he said he needed to work via phone in his room. Sam claimed that Burt was a liar and a pedophile, but I could find no records of this. I returned to the motel one day in November to find that Burt was gone; rumor was he got kicked out for failing to pay rent.

I first encountered Eric in the office in October 2012 when he tried to sell me and Elizabeth a North Face jacket that I suspected was stolen. Like Randy, Eric lived at the Park Place but was close with several residents of the Boardwalk. Eric was a tiny white male in his twenties, who often wore a baseball cap and had small bug tattoos under his eyes, which I first mistook for tears. He had a habit of annoying residents by constantly asking for handouts, although they often put up with his presence. Eric was arrested in December 2012 when he tried to punch Elizabeth after an altercation with Noonan at the Park Place.

It was hard not to notice Dale when he first walked into the motel parking lot wearing aviator sunglasses and sporting brown hair down to his shoulders. Dale was a registered sex offender in his early forties and enjoyed chewing tobacco. He was also a divorced army veteran of the first Iraq War. We made plans to move some of his belongings out of his father's house nearby, but he moved out in December 2012 before we could. One of my most vivid memories was of him sitting on the landing one fall day in his sunglasses, jeans, and a cut-off white t-shirt, strumming an acoustic guitar. I stood for several minutes to watch him because the moment seemed to transport both of us away from the motel and the dire situation that it represented.

The motel housed several residents with physical disabilities, but Vito's situation was the most pronounced. Vito was an overweight resident in his late thirties who used an electric wheelchair because he was bitten by a brown recluse spider on his birthday seven years prior and it damaged the nerves in his legs. He moved in with his friend Slash, also in his thirties, in March 2013. Slash was on parole so he made an effort to avoid drugs and alcohol. His goal was to become a tattoo artist, and he claimed he had done several tattoos in prison. The first time I saw Slash he was sitting outside his room, drinking a Pepsi, and working on a Sudoku. He and Vito still lived in the motel when I left the field, but I followed up with Vito and he told me that Slash was arrested for violating his parole and sent to prison in December 2013.

Spike was a Puerto Rican man in his late thirties who moved into the motel with his girlfriend, Mary Anne, in April 2013. Mary Anne was in her late twenties and became friends with Sky. Although he was quite muscular and imposing, Spike spoke very calmly and we had a good rapport. He wore several bracelets that promoted condom use because an uncle and several friends had succumbed to complications from AIDS. Spike and Mary Anne moved out at the end of May 2013.

Tat was a registered sex offender in his mid-thirties who knew Reg and Sky from a previous stint at the motel. He returned from prison in early April 2013 and, like Slash, wanted to be a tattoo artist. Tat was up-front about his sex-offender status and eager to speak with me. He was kicked out in early May for playing his music too loudly, and I suspect it may have had something to do with the fact that his neighbors, Spike and Mary Anne, were aware of his sex-offender status and unhappy with his presence.

Most of the residents who moved into the motel during my fieldwork had very little in the way of possessions. Love, Ben, and Lisa were an exception, arriving in a pickup truck full of belongings in early May 2013. Love was a white female in her sixties, and her makeshift family unit consisted of her son Ben and his girlfriend Lisa, both of whom were in their late twenties. Love immediately began to aggravate residents by complaining about the conditions of the curtains and bathroom and seeking out assistance with repairs. Although he laughed at Love's aura of helplessness, Slash extended a helping hand by replacing broken light bulbs that were out of her reach. Love, Ben, and Lisa were still living at the motel when I concluded my fieldwork, but they eventually left in a depressing turn of events that I will describe later.

DEVELOPING RAPPORT

The challenge facing any ethnographer is to gain entrance into a new social setting and establish relationships with those who compose it. One of my early encounters with Biggie offers a prime example of how I met residents at the start of my research. Although I technically gained entrance into the social world of the motel simply by renting a room there, making connections with residents was not as easily done. After I moved my belongings into room 34, I spent my first night simply observing behavior from the landing outside my room. The next day was gorgeous and sunny so I decided to take advantage of the weather and try to engage some of the residents who were outside. Biggie was sitting shirtless outside of his room and waved me over as I walked by, almost commanding with his deep voice, "Come down here with me, I need some company!"

Biggie sat with a woman who he introduced as his girlfriend, Deirdre. Between them was a metal cabinet covered with a plate of two cheeseburgers, a few ears of corn, a bottle of Heineken, and a ceramic pipe. He spoke loudly, unabashedly, and dominated the conversation. At one point we got to talking shoes and he said, "I got wide feet, just like my cock, it is wide. And it is juicy!" As he talked, Deirdre attempted to get a few words in, but Biggie looked over at her and said, "Oh, I'm sorry, I'm finished," or, "Oh, was you finished?"

Eventually he asked if I was in school, which was a logical assumption, given my age and appearance. I told Biggie that I was studying sociology and social inequality and that I wanted to write a book about motel life.[75] He got excited and asked if he was going to be in it. I explained that I would like him to be, but it was entirely his decision and he could change his mind at any time. I gave him and Deirdre consent forms, and they both agreed to participate. Biggie continued to talk about how much money we were going to make, and how we could go to parties and drink champagne together. I emphasized that I surely was not in it for the money but rather to share the stories of people like him.

This form of disclosure occurred often when I interacted with strangers in my early days of fieldwork. My goal was to not only observe as much activity as possible but make myself as visible as possible. When I passed residents in the parking lot or on the stairways or landings, I made a conscious effort to make eye contact and greet them. I found that most residents responded in kind. However, this was not always the case, and several individuals refused to acknowledge me. In such cases I left the ball in their court for future engagement.

In other instances, residents made it clear that they would not welcome any interaction. One afternoon I noticed a man walking into the parking lot and started to walk toward him. As I approached he began to rap, "I catch you in my fucking house, I leave your body on the cement. That's a fuckin' promise, and a fuckin' threat." I mentioned this later to Roy and he got very excited and exclaimed, "He's crazy. Stay away from that dude. You see him at the bus stop, he shadowboxes the air, like [Muhammad] Ali. I see him at the bus stop. Fighting the air, he's knocking out the air, he's fucking the air up!"

During initial conversations, I tried to keep things casual, talking about simple subjects like the weather (nice days were highly valued at the motel). Then I steered the conversation by asking how long someone had been at the motel and what they thought of it. I disclosed my role and asked for consent when the other person began opening up to me or asked a question that could easily lead to my disclosure. Sometimes the question was simple, such as, "So do you go to school?" Other times it was more direct, as in the case of Natalie, who asked when I went to pay my rent one morning:

NATALIE: Hey, let me ask you something, serious.
ME: Yeah?
NATALIE: Nah.
ME: You gonna ask if I'm a cop? No, tell me. What?
NATALIE: You seem pretty intelligent. Why are you hanging out here with these guys?

Early on several residents joked about whether I was a cop, or maybe someone sent by the owner to investigate people. One day a resident pointed at me and said, "Policio. He's policio. Let me see your badge. Bend over, let me see your badge!" However, I never felt that residents were truly suspicious of me, and people quickly realized that I had no affiliation with law enforcement when drug use and drug sales occurred around me without repercussion. It then became a running joke with Reg, who would occasionally introduce me as an "undercover brother" and tell people, "He's investigating us!" or, "Don't mind him, he's the neighborhood cop." This continued public portrayal of me as a cop, even if it was in jest, helped participants retain their power as research subjects.

In these early stages of involvement and disclosure I treaded slowly and carefully for several reasons. First, it was obvious that the motel had established social circles, and I wanted to ingratiate myself into them through invitation rather than intrusion. Fortunately, those with whom I became close were quick to put me at ease. One day I saw Jake and Reg sitting outside of Jake's room, listening to music. I decided to break the ice by asking for a light. Jake gave me one and said, "Take a seat, man." I made a comment about not wanting to intrude, and Reg said, "You're not intruding, we're hanging out. If we wanted privacy we'd go in our rooms."

Second, there was evidence that not everyone at the motel got along, as Biggie stated when I first met him: "Some people here are good and some you wanna stay away from. Some people come from the right side of the tracks and some people come from the wrong side, you know what I mean? But others are cool, if you need something to eat or drink or anything you just knock on the door. All the people from me down, they are good." Not wanting to put myself immediately in the middle of any feuds (although that proved unavoidable in the long run) or in danger, I tried to be wary of who I talked to and what we talked about.[76]

REG: THE BULL AND THE GATEKEEPER

The turning point in my project came one evening at the end of July. I was drinking beer with Reg and Marc as we sat at the base of the second staircase. Reg seemed like an ideal contact for several reasons. First, he had lived at the motel for over a year, which was quite a long time relative to other residents. This tenure made him an expert on the motel's culture. Second, he was the most social resident; I noticed that when there were instances of community and conflict, Reg was often involved. Third, he had an imposing physical presence. If there was one person who I did not want to aggravate, it was him. These factors made it clear to me that in order to successfully carry out my study, Reg was someone I needed to get to know.

It was this evening that I decided to disclose my criminal justice background. Reg exclaimed, "I knew it! I knew it was criminal psychology!" He said he knew I was holding back, that he was not stupid and knew something was up from the start. Fearing that I was about to get either beat up or blacklisted from the motel, I told him that I meant no disrespect and simply did not think it was wise to walk into the motel and announce that I was interested in speaking with sex offenders. He looked at me and spread his arms wide, disclosing his status as a sex offender by declaring, "Who do you think you've been talkin' to all this time?" My worry increased as he made what could be perceived as a threat: "I'm the bull around this place. You shouldn't forget that." I apologized and he instructed me not to, saying that he hated it when people did because it meant you did something wrong. He said I had seen his world and now he wanted to see mine. We made plans to "talk sober" over the next few days because I was completely overwhelmed by this turn of events, and we had all been drinking a fair amount.[77]

After meeting with my dissertation adviser, I headed back to the motel with a plan to strengthen my relationship with Reg. We sat outside and I gave him a peace offering: a copy of Elliot Liebow's *Tally's Corner*. I told him that not only was it considered a classic, but it was what I hoped my book could be. He assured me that he had been "messing with me" because I was drunk and he thought it was funny that I kept apologizing. He understood why I did not want to tell people I was studying criminal justice and said that he liked me since we first met. In response to his request to see my world, I invited him and his partner, Sky, to come see my campus office and have lunch with my adviser.

In early August I picked up Reg and Sky at the motel to bring them to campus. Reg was admittedly nervous, saying he needed a few beers to calm down. I had a rule about not smoking in my car, but I made an exception on this trip because Reg kept mentioning his nerves. At one point he told me that he did not want to be just part of the project and that when the research was done he wanted to hang out and go camping. I told him that I viewed him as a friend and that we would hang out after my research was complete.

When we got to campus Reg commented again about his nervousness. I told him to just be himself and he replied, "When am I not?" I first took him into my office and showed him some copies of the journal *Criminology*. He looked through them and said, "Now I have a better idea of what you do and I believe that you're really a student." We walked over to a lab where my adviser was sitting with another professor. I introduced Reg and Sky to them, and my adviser told Reg about her ethnographic work with active drug sellers.

What happened next was almost a blur. Reg quickly took control of the conversation and called me out on the mistakes I had made in the field so far: that he had called me on "my bullshit," how I would come and go, which made people think I was a cop, and how I was interested in sex offenders and did not know that I was talking to one all along. He commented several times that he knew what I was about, that something was not quite right, and that he had me figured out. This was the second time Reg dressed me down, but it was much more embarrassing because it occurred in front of my adviser and another professor. I could do nothing but stand sheepishly silent as he continued to assert himself in front of his audience as a smart, perceptive person who was always in control. He finished by saying, "People at the motel look to me as a leader and gravitate towards me. I don't know why 'cause I'm not a leader!" I brought myself back into the conversation by saying it was my job to find out why.

After Reg had said his piece, we all headed to lunch at a local tavern. During lunch, my adviser made it clear that she was treating everyone, and Reg asked if ordering the $10 French Dip was okay. After she assured him that it was, he made a show of taking out several bills from his wallet and choosing some music on the jukebox.

When we left the tavern, Reg went out of his way to give money to a black man sitting in the grass near campus. The man did not explicitly ask for it or even look particularly destitute, but Reg later mentioned to me that he hoped my adviser was not offended by this gesture and that he liked to "help out people who don't have much." In some ways this behavior seemed like a performance for my adviser, but I learned over time that Reg exerted a great amount of effort to improve the lives of others.

THE RESEARCHER ROLE

After this experience with Reg, my life at the motel took quite a turn. Reg shared the details of his visit with others, and people accepted my role as a researcher. Several residents took it on themselves to actively recruit others for my study. Reg introduced me to Mike, telling him that I was in college and writing a book with the goal of telling people's stories. He further explained that I did not use real names and that I was a "good kid." After Sam and I had established a good rapport, he recruited Larry for the study: "I went up there and asked him. I said, I said Chris don't force it on nobody, it's all voluntarily. He said, what's in it for me? I said nothin', shit in it for you. He said, yeah Sam, I'm interested in tellin' my story." People began viewing me as both a researcher who respected them and a friend with whom they enjoyed spending time. Sometimes our behaviors reflected my role as a college student conducting a research project. Other times they were more oriented toward friendship and my role as a part of the community.

My role as a college student led to several behaviors on the part of residents and myself. When greeting me, Biggie would say something like, "What's up, college kid?" Others commented on my career path, such as Ed, who told me one day, "Well, I'm impressed man. You're doin' good." Sitting nearby, Jake chimed in, "You're goin' places, Chris, lemme tell ya." Residents kept tabs on me, and Larry would ask, "You getting everything you need for your, uh, project?" Sam sometimes started rants by saying, "Write this shit down, Chris," and when Eric found out about the book, he got excited: "Write a book about me. Here's this little white kid. There's this little kid named Eric. There's this crazy kid Eric, he's always drinkin', he's always doin' crazy shit."

Some residents often asked about my connections to the college party scene and Asian women. After Eric asked me to take him to a party and hook him up with "a hot Asian chick," Reg piped in with, "Why does everyone around here ask you the same question over and over again?" He then turned to Eric and asked, "What is a good, well-to-do college girl gonna want with someone like you? No job." Similarly, one night Biggie called out, "Hey, you! One of these days you take me to one of your college parties, man!" Sam tried to explain that those kids were fresh out of high school and that at age twenty-nine, I did not party. Biggie responded, "What? Wait a minute, wait a minute. You lie! What kind of hookup is you then? You can't hook me up with no college chicks? I thought you had some connections." Later Sam said to me, "Could you imagine taking Biggie to a college party? Don't you ever do that!"

While my role as a researcher was perhaps my most prominent (as it distinguished my social position from true residents of the motel), most of the time I spent at the motel consisted of simply hanging out as a friend. I was invited to birthday parties and barbecues, was introduced to family members, enjoyed a communal meal on Thanksgiving, and was given gifts on Halloween and Christmas. I tried to reciprocate by exchanging gifts on Christmas, making food for Thanksgiving, and taking residents out to dinner in the community. One day I took Sam to the movies to watch a documentary about pickup basketball games held in a local park, and he was excited to see some people he knew up on screen.

Most residents lacked the money or transportation to engage in activities away from the motel, so their days consisted of watching television and, during warmer days, sitting outside talking, drinking, listening to music, and doing drugs. I often joined in, and while I did not partake in illegal drug use, residents were comfortable discussing, buying, selling, and using drugs in front of me. However, I did make it clear that I would not be involved with handling or storing drugs, or using my car to transport them knowingly or unknowingly. This first arose when Reg texted me one day asking for a ride to a town about twenty miles away and I responded with, "How long will it take and for what exactly? I can't facilitate anything illegal, no offense intended." He texted me back, saying that he needed to pick up his disability check and that nothing illegal was involved. On the ride there I explained my position and he said, "Just so you know so you can always ease your mind, I would never get into a car with drugs on me with you. I would never put drugs in your car, I would never have you bring anything to do with drugs or anything illegal. 'Cause I respect the fact of what you are. You're a clean, good working, fricken studying whatever, you're good people altogether. And I'd never do that to ya."

Another day Cinque asked me for a ride downtown and Reg spoke up, saying that I would not drive him and I would not "have it" in my car. He then said, "I put a stop to that for you before he even asked. I wouldn't let that happen to you, and if I knew someone was askin' you for a ride for that I'd tell you in a heartbeat. Your career ain't worth fuckin' up over drugs." Later I had to clarify to Cinque when he asked half-joking if he could store "something" in my room if parole came by and what I would do if he threw drugs in my room and walked out. I told him in no uncertain terms that we would not talk anymore and that I would not be involved.

Because I had a car, people often asked me for rides.[78] On most occasions it was to the grocery store and back, but occasionally I was asked to venture further from the motel. I was careful about this and attempted to get to know an individual before I drove him or her somewhere. However, there were occasions when I did drive relative strangers because I believed it would be useful for my research. When I became close with several residents, I drove them to unemployment hearings, other housing locations, and family residences. I never asked for anything in return, but when I was offered beer, food, or a few bucks, I accepted graciously.[79]

Residents also asked me for loans, which I expected but was not sure how to deal with until it came up. I wish I could say that I had hard-and-fast rules, but borrowing money was common among residents, and often I had to decide fairly quickly whether I would help them. If I had a few dollars on me I obliged (I did not keep much cash on me for this reason). My biggest decisions came when residents asked for more substantial sums, as Sam did when he asked to borrow thirty dollars. No one asked to borrow that much unless we had grown close, and I often decided that it was in my best interests to avoid the possible fractures in our relationships that could come from not loaning. In these instances I always asked residents to not share the fact that I was loaning them money. While I did not hound anyone to pay me back, I made it clear that I could not loan more money until earlier loans were paid back, as I did not want to be seen as a walking ATM. The largest amount I ever loaned out was forty dollars to Sam, and I never felt that residents were trying to take advantage of my resources. In every instance that residents received a loan, they paid me back in full. Cell phones with minutes were also highly valued at the motel, so I consciously did not use my phone in front of residents I did not know, and it was rare that I let a stranger use my phone.

Ultimately, my role and relationship with residents most closely resembled what sociologists Patricia and Peter Adler refer to as a "peripheral" membership role. This role was a result of the limitations I imposed on myself by not fully committing to the motel experience. Peripheral roles are "the most marginal and least committed to the social world," and in these roles, researchers often refrain from "participating in activities that stand at the core of group membership and identification."[80] Like many researchers who take on peripheral roles, I used gatekeepers such as Reg and Sam, who came to trust me and then sponsored my project among other members. Participants came to regard me as a "researcher-member" and interacted with me on those terms. The most apparent aspect of this role was that I was free to come and go from the field whenever I wanted or needed to, a facet of the experience that sometimes made me feel guilty and awkward.

One day in September I was driving with Reg and apologized in advance for an absence due to a family reunion. He replied, "Dude, we don't worry about you, we know you have a life. Unlike the rest of us, we know you have a life." This made me uncomfortable and I said, "You guys got lives, come on." Reg tilted his head, smirked, and exclaimed, "Dude, really? We drink, we hang there, we live there. You think we have a life? You get out, you go do things, you go to college, you go to work, you go do things. You have a life. I don't take it offensively, I know I don't have a life, man." Despite my coming and going, I was able to form strong relationships and observe intimately the ways in which residents of the Boardwalk Motel went about their daily lives. For a deeper discussion of my research experience, please see appendix 2, "A Reflection on Method," at the end of the book.

LIMITATIONS OF THE STUDY

There are three key limitations to this study. The first concerns selection bias of those who were recruited. Although I spent a significant amount of time in the field, because the population of the motel was so transient, it is almost certain that some residents moved in and out while I was not there. Because of this, my data may lack accounts of some residents who lived at the motel for very short periods of time. Furthermore, of the residents who I did encounter at the motel, some remained strangers because they rebuffed my attempts to engage them, or the opportunity never arose for me to talk with them, or I avoided them because I suspected that they were dangerous or unstable. It is also quite possible that some residents chose not to participate because of who they observed me socializing with. In these respects, there may be a bias in the data due to my own behavior.

The second limitation revolves around the depth of data that I gathered from participants. Because of different life situations and personalities, I became closer to some residents than others. This led to an abundance of data for some and what could be viewed as an insufficient amount for others. I address this by attempting to give a voice to all residents when appropriate, while admitting up front that certain residents provided richer data than others because of our relationships.

The final limitation to this study involves the use of narratives. As sociologist Lois Presser writes, "Ethnographic or field researchers collect and analyze narrative data for the express purpose of understanding people's interpretations of their world." Narratives are inherently subjective because they are the public presentations of the narrator's perspective.[81] This is a concern because a good portion of this study consists of resident narratives concerning their lives before the motel and events that transpired out of sight of the researcher. To address this concern, I attempted to verify information about residents and their lives using public records, as well as gather multiple points of view and sources of data about particular incidents and residents. Whenever possible, data are presented using this triangulation. I also try to make it clear when I present resident accounts of unobserved and observed action.

There is another important consideration concerning the use of narratives, and that is their power to create and maintain identity and self. According to criminologist Shadd Maruna, the narratives that people form about themselves shape their present and future behavior.[82] These autobiographical narratives are verbal accounts of behavior that help form identity.[83] Identity is a dynamic sense of self that relies on the meaning attached to the roles that society attaches to a person and is the "lived social experience—the subjective past and present—as well as the desired future."[84]

While I am concerned with the "factual truth" about certain behaviors and incidents, the more important aspect of motel life is the "truth" that residents presented to me and one another. Regardless of whether residents presented the "truth" to me, they presented information that they wished to be viewed as true in the context of the motel and our mutual construction of knowledge about motel life. There were certainly instances when I felt like residents were exaggerating tales of behavior. However, I never felt that these presentations were for my sake only. Rather, they were exaggerations and modifications presented to the motel audience in general. Goffman reminds us that "when an individual appears before others, he knowingly and unwittingly projects a definition of the situation, of which a conception of himself is an important part."[85] Therefore the narratives in this book are dynamic constructions of conceptions and presentations of self. My goal is to examine these narratives, the motivations behind the presentation, and the effects on their audience. This facet of ethnography peels back complex layers of the culture being studied to reveal the cyclical interactions between residents, the social setting they constitute, and society at large.

1
Biography of a Residential Motel

You're only getting guys from social services,
they don't give a shit.
—Elizabeth

HOMECOMING

It is 11 AM as I drive out of the Riverfort County jail parking lot with Reg and his girlfriend, Sky. Reg's huge frame barely fits in my back-seat. He takes the pack of Newports I offer and mutters, "Get me outta here. Fuckin' A, it ain't real, man." He makes a phone call to secure marijuana: "It's me, Reg from the fucking Boardwalk Motel. I just got out, man, gimme a call." He looks at me in the rearview mirror and says, "I can taste the fuckin' beer already. I just wanna fuckin' beer, don't feel normal." Giddy to have him home after four months apart, Sky cuddles next to him as we make the fifteen-min-ute drive back to the Boardwalk Motel.

We pull into the parking lot of the two-story building, which is empty except for motel manager Elizabeth's purple Honda, and everyone bounds out of the car. Sky and Reg open the door to their first-floor room, and Sky announces to their roommates, Jake and Fran, "Look what I brought home! A stray puppy!" Reg immediately downs a hard cider that I brought, and Sky shows him how much cleaning she has done in the cramped space.

Fran's obese frame fills her chair at her usual spot at the room's only table. Jake lies on the worn black leather couch in front of the 60-inch projection TV, which is usually tuned to a reality television show or a cable movie. Reg tells them how life is going to be now that the four of them are sharing the crowded room:

> I just gotta wait to get my [Social Security disability] check before I can do anything, so it's gonna be tight quarters in here for about a month. Like I said, if I have to I can put half this shit in storage to give you guys a place to sleep. I don't give a fuck. We're gettin' outta here as soon as possible anyways. I just gotta get my check back, then we're out. Okay, Fran? I just gotta get my check and then once I get my check, we're all outta here. It's gonna be like a month or so before I get my check.

Curious about how Reg's return will affect the weekly rent payments, Fran asks, "What are we doin'?" and Reg cuts her off: "We'll talk about rent, fricken, tomorrow. It'll be cheaper on ya, so don't worry about it. We'll figure somethin' out here, we're gonna figure it out. We're gonna make this work."[1]

Reg grabs several hard ciders, and he and Sky walk up one of the three black metal staircases to the second floor to hang out with Sky's friend Mary Anne and her boyfriend, Spike. Jake and I go outside to talk to Larry, the resident-turned-manager who is built like a wrestler. Nolan, a frequent resident, walks by slowly from his room at the end of the first floor. I ask Larry if Nolan still carries a knife for protection and Larry says, "I dunno. He's loaded, he's been drinkin' brandy for the last day." Nolan saunters slowly over, mutters something through his white mustache, and gives Jake two dollars for a beer. Reg comes downstairs and says he is ready for some real food, so we walk to the nearby Home Cooking buffet.

After lunch, Reg is sated with "real meat," and we go back to the motel and hang out in the room with the door open, enjoying the nice weather. We hear Elizabeth yelling at a new resident in the parking lot, who yells back, "I ain't disrespect nobody. Fuck all that bullshit. I ain't no suck ass nigga. Sell that shit somewhere else." Reg wonders who it is, and I say it's someone new. He assumes the argument is over rent.

Later on, Reg asks if I can bring him and Sky to his storage unit to retrieve a grill and then to the Giant Foods so he can buy dinner.

I oblige, and they use $118 of their $200 monthly food stamp budget, buying mussels, sausage, burgers, and chicken. While this is a lot of food for a party, the leftovers will last them a while. Reg says, "That's enough food, freakin', to get us through a few days, four or five." He tells me that they also consistently supplement their food needs with pickups from a local food pantry.

Back at the motel, Jake has washed several pairs of blue jeans and hung them on the second floor railing to dry. I assemble the grill. The door opens to room 3, and Vito wheels his overweight frame out in his electric wheelchair. He welcomes Reg home, who tells him, "If you're around in an hour you can grab a burger."

Mary Anne comes downstairs with her sister, as well as Spike and her sister's boyfriend. She is still mad about the woman in room 23 calling the cops on her a few nights ago, "Fuckin' bitch is crazy. I told my boyfriend, what is up? Everywhere I go people call the cops on me." Vito's friend Slash comes out of their room in a white tank top, black pants, and red baseball cap. He brings several empty cans of Pepsi to the black trashcan near the middle staircase, and Jake quickly stops him: "Did you just throw empties away? Do you throw empties away?" Slash nods, and Jake says, "No, no, no, no, no, no. Put 'em in room 4." I tell Slash that cans are hot commodities because of the five-cent refund, and he says he will give them to us from now on. Slash then shows me several drawings of tattoos that he claims he did in prison for members of the Aryan Nation.

Reg puts burgers on the grill, and Jake regales us about one night in a motel up the road when all he had were burger patties and pancakes from Burger King so he ate them as a sandwich with mayonnaise. Elizabeth shuffles over from the office, taking her dog, Mocha, out for a walk. Slash tells her, "Nice sneakers!" and she says she got them for a dollar at the nearby drugstore. Reg offers her a burger, but instead she takes a hot dog for Mocha.

By 9 PM it is 48 degrees and clear. We have eaten our fill, and people are milling about outside their rooms. In room 3 Jake is drunk and Fran is on cloud nine because she had sex with Slash earlier, whom she had just met. "Nothing can put me in a bad mood right now. I'm fuckin' wired." Reg tries to cook meat in an electric skillet, but he and Jake keep blowing a breaker because Jake wants to watch the movie *Red Dawn* at the same time. Tat comes downstairs from his room looking for a beer, and Reg says, "It's right there, grab one."

Sometime after midnight things begin to wind down. Reg looks at Fran and Jake and says, "I don't care which one a you is sleeping where tonight, but fuckin', in the morning we're gonna figure this out for everybody." Jake tells Reg that he is not allowed to go to bed yet: "You're gonna fucking keep hanging out, and drinking." Reg and Sky's three cats are in heat, and their meowing is aggravating Jake to the point where he yells, "Stop it! Stop spraying!"

As everyone prepares for bed, Jake lies on the couch, which fits his skinny frame nicely, and says to Fran, "So this is like your new territory now right, again? So I got access to that chair and this is gonna be your shit." She replies, "Pretty much." Jake nods, "Alright, that's good to know. I gotta spray that down with fuckin' Febreze." Reg scolds him, "You're bein' too loud, Jake. You and Jake play nice, Fran." He heads into the back bedroom with Sky to watch the other TV and fall asleep. Their mattress sits directly on the floor, and as he lies down on it he mutters, "Fuck, I forgot how this bed was." Jake calls out drunkenly, "Yeah, that jailhouse bed is a lot better, right?"

A HISTORY OF THE BOARDWALK MOTEL

The Boardwalk Motel is located within the county of Riverfort, in the town of Dutchland. It sits on the edge of Main Street, occupying a rectangular parcel of land measuring 0.87 acre.[2] The Boardwalk is located almost at the midpoint of Main Street, about 7.5 miles northwest of Riverfort and 7 miles southeast of Pinewood. In 2011 this part of Main Street saw an average of twenty-three thousand daily trips, with peak evening rush hour traffic volumes of twenty-four hundred vehicles.[3]

Table 1.1 shows the demographics of the city of Riverfort and the town of Dutchland, drawn from 2013 U.S. Census data. While both localities have similar-sized populations, they differ in many key respects. Dutchland is mostly white, with a miniscule black population. Residents of Dutchland are also far wealthier than those of Riverfort, as indicated by Dutchland's high home ownership rate, high median household income, and low percentage of residents below the poverty line.

TABLE 1.1: Selected Demographics of Riverfort and Dutchland, 2013

	City of Riverfort	Town of Dutchland
Total population	98,142	81,908
Percentage of whites	56.2	84.7
Percentage of blacks	31.4	5.6
Home ownership rate	39.1	72.4
Median household income	$40,287	$72,642
Percentage of population below poverty line	25.2	6.9

Source: U.S. Census Bureau, 2013 ACS 5-Year Population Estimate.

According to an inventory study conducted by the town of Dutchland, Main Street was initially a gravel-covered stone road, called the Riverwood–Pinewood Turnpike, that connected downtown Riverfort and downtown Pinewood. It was completed in 1801 at a cost of $118,610. By 1803 it was a heavily traveled stretch of road, as evidenced by the twenty-eight taverns and inns that sprang up between the two cities. In 1901 a trolley was constructed, charging riders $0.25 for a forty-five-minute one-way trip. The turnpike was renamed Main Street in 1946 when the trolley was removed and the road was turned into five-lane, 40-mile-per-hour highway. According to the study, the same post–World War II economic and automobile boom that led to the rise of the American motel had a similar effect on Main Street, changing "the corridor from a major regional transportation link to one of the first American suburban auto strips."[4] The Boardwalk Motel was built in 1960 amid this period of local prosperity and was initially owned by Hans and Rachel Schurrle.

A postcard for the Boardwalk Motel from its early years advertises the Boardwalk as "Modern spacious rooms with individual climate control, & Color TV's. Commercial, & Weekly rates available. American Express, BankAmericard & Master Charge Accepted." The weekly rate sign is now gone, as well as all the lighted signs in the office, which looks open, well-lit, and inviting in the postcard. A local parole officer told me that at one time there was a dining and lounging area for guests. Certainly the lobby was once quite welcoming.

In 1967 ownership of the motel transferred to a local corporation called Orange Estates Inc. As of 1970 it was listed in local records as a two-story, twenty-nine-unit motel. A canopy was added in 1973, along with the sign on the roof and nine additional rooms. In 1977 ownership transferred to the Boardwalk Inn Corp. (which appears to be Orange Estates Inc. operating under a new name), owned by Emil and Judith Schonfeld. Ownership was fully transferred to Judith Schonfeld in 1978. In 1982 she sold the motel for $285,000 to the current owner, an Indian company called Tarsem Corp, run by a Mr. Singh, who also owns the local Park Place Motel and Home Cooking buffet restaurant.[5] A year after this purchase, a vehicle crashed into the portico of the motel, causing $9,000 worth of damage. Repairs took eight months to complete and were not initiated until over two months after the accident, after a town order. In retrospect, this attitude of neglect was a warning sign of things to come.

The motel was damaged by fire in March 1986, which led to the evacuation of all guests and the partial collapse of the second floor.[6] Later that year, a local newspaper published an unflattering portrayal of the direction that Mr. Singh was taking: "Obscenities are scrawled in the dust on the office windows and hand-lettered signs disclaiming liability are stapled to the wallpaper."[7] An industry expert explained that the rooms were renting at $22 to $28 a night because of low overhead, lamenting, "But often that is at the expense of the family-like coziness that was once the trademark of these motels." The owner of the nearby Paulson Motel commented, "This strip was simply much nicer before they bought in. The biggest problem is that they don't screen the people they rent to." This owner went on to say that the Boardwalk owner may "tolerate a bad element." In his defense, the owner of the Boardwalk stated, "Big hotels are tough to compete with." This evolution, or devolution, of the Boardwalk Motel continued in the years to come.

In April 1988 the Boardwalk was damaged by its third fire in two years, which displaced thirty guests and resulted in the arrest of one resident for drugs and weapons. The fire was deemed to be electrical, and investigators from the state fire investigation unit were called in to assess the issue.[8] Later that year police arrested a cat burglar who fled to the Boardwalk, while a resident of the Park Place was arrested for shoplifting.[9] In 1990 a Boardwalk resident was charged with raping a fourteen-year-old girl at the motel.[10] The year 1991 saw the arrest of another fugitive at the Boardwalk.[11] In 1993 several residents of the Park Place were arrested on drug charges stemming from a Grateful Dead concert, and five undocumented Polish asbestos workers from Brooklyn were arrested at the Boardwalk.[12] In 1995 the resident manager of the Park Place was arrested after stabbing her boyfriend—another resident—in a domestic dispute.[13]

The culture of these motels garnered increased attention in the local media, earning the name "desolation row" in a 1996 news story about one resident's death.[14] This article drew a stern rebuke from a local business owner, who claimed that the "second rate" motels were disappearing and that Main Street was slowly being revitalized, citing the fact that the buffet owned by the Boardwalk's owners used to be such a motel.[15] January 1997 brought about another controversy when local police cited an unwritten agreement with motel owners that encouraged them to report illegal activity without fear of gaining a reputation as a drug haven.[16]

THE SOCIAL SERVICES ERA

As early as 2002, the Riverfort County Department of Social Services (DSS) used the Boardwalk Motel to shelter individuals for $125 a week.[17] The Pinewood County DSS also used motels to house otherwise homeless individuals at this time. While some people viewed it as a misappropriation of public funds, the use of the Boardwalk as a home for displaced individuals went largely unnoticed by the public until summer 2007. That July a local legislator in Riverfort County released the details of an investigation she had conducted at the behest of her constituents. She found that the Riverfort County DSS had been housing families with children at the Boardwalk, which also housed registered sex offenders. This reliance on the Boardwalk was spurred by a Riverfort County residence restriction that forced sex offenders out of the city and into the suburbs. During a press conference outside of the Boardwalk, the legislator claimed that residents of the homes that bordered the motel's back lot were afraid to let their children outside to play.[18] The presence of sex offenders was not the only reason that placing children at the Boardwalk was ill-advised, as inspections uncovered a plethora of code violations that included "no up-to-date fire alarm certifications, raw sewage, structural damage to roof, interior water damage, mold throughout entire room, exposed wiring, gas leak, missing bathroom tiles, rooms missing smoke detectors, bug infestation, bathroom mold, debris piled outside rooms, electric socket falling from wall, spliced wiring, cracked toilets."[19]

In August 2007 the legislator proposed a resolution that instructed the Riverfort County DSS to (1) discontinue placing families with children or any other individuals at the Boardwalk or the Park Place, (2) remove any families with children or other individuals who were placed at the Boardwalk or the Park Place from these locations, and (3) cease placing families with children or any individuals at the Boardwalk or the Park Place until the code violations were addressed.[20] While county legislators defeated the resolution by 22–17, the group did pass an amendment to the resolution by 38–1 that required the Town of Dutchland Building Department and Department of Fire Services to make sure that the Boardwalk and the Park Place were made immediately code compliant. Nothing about the conditions of the Boardwalk and the Park Place was deemed so egregious in the ensuing inspections that residents were removed or the buildings shut down.[21]

A 2008 audit of the Riverfort County DSS by the county comptroller's office did nothing to quell concern over the Boardwalk's use.[22] The audit found that from 2005 to 2006, fourteen families with children were placed at the Boardwalk while sex offenders were living there, despite DSS claims that it did not house families with sex offenders. DSS also claimed that families were placed at the Boardwalk only in emergency situations and that the majority were moved the next day. The audit contradicted those claims as it found that twelve of the fourteen families were not moved the next day. While the Office of Temporary and Disability Assistance was required to carry out inspections of locations where families were placed every six months, these did not occur, and an August 2007 fire inspection of the Boardwalk found violations in each of the twenty-four inspected rooms. Even though the county lacked any sort of written contract with the motel, the DSS paid the Boardwalk $31,816 in 2005, $114,412 in 2006, and $157,164.60 in 2007, for a total of $303,392.60 over a three-year period. Records do not explain the exact reason for the increase from 2005; however, payments to the Park Place dropped from $8,847 in 2005 to $661 in 2006 and ceased in 2007. Therefore, it is possible that placements at the Boardwalk increased as the Park Place was phased out of use.

The results of the audit created a firestorm over where to place registered sex offenders in need of housing. In 2009, despite the fact that a 1,000-foot residence restriction existed within Riverfort County, a bill was proposed in the Town of Dutchland that would prevent level 2 or 3 sex offenders from living within 1,500 feet of one another.[23] This failed to pass, but local legislators grew increasingly concerned about the number of sex offenders within Dutchland Town limits who were not originally Dutchland residents. Police admitted that in July 2009 there were 125 sex offenders in the town, up from the 60 recorded eighteen months before.[24] In August 2009 Dutchland passed a law that limited the number of registered sex offenders who could stay in motels and required motel owners to purchase licenses in order to rent to sex offenders. At a board meeting, residents claimed that they and their children were in danger and felt like they were being watched.[25] The law forced a motel under fifty units, like the Boardwalk, to pay $1,500 a year in order to rent to sex offenders whose cumulative risk levels did not exceed 6 points (e.g., two level 3 offenders, three level 2 offenders, or similar combinations).[26] Specifically, the Town of Dutchland code stated in section 119–3:

> No person shall engage in the business of owning or operating a hotel or motel as defined herein that accepts placements, referrals or payment by or on behalf of any federal, state or local government or any subdivision thereof, or from any not-for-profit group, association or entity of any type or nature, on account of providing accommodations to one or more registered sex offenders without first obtaining a license therefor for each hotel or motel owned or operated by the said person from the Town Clerk of the Town of Dutchland as hereinafter provided.[27]

Furthermore, the law required any licensed motel to keep for a period of three years a register that detailed the name, residence, and date of arrival and departure for all persons who were given a room.

The passage of the law did reduce the number of sex offenders in the area. Two months later there were twenty fewer sex offenders within the Town of Dutchland, and within four months of passage only two motels, including the Boardwalk, had applied for the license.[28] In early 2010 the Boardwalk was the only motel in Dutchland that had a license to accept sex offenders, because the other motel owner received a refund when the license hurt his business.[29] Given that the Boardwalk received $45 a day to house sex offenders in 2009, it is likely that Mr. Singh felt that the guaranteed income was worth the price of the license.[30]

This is not to say that the law's passage resulted in a flawless execution of its intentions to reduce the number of sex offenders in Dutchland motels. The owner of the Boardwalk claimed that he was paid to specifically house sex offenders but that a separate stream of people on welfare might also include sex offenders that were unknown to him (a claim that DSS supported).[31] Additionally, the motel would only know the sex offender status of those sent by the state; sex offenders paying out of their own pocket would not be counted against the motel's tally.[32]

This crackdown did not satisfy the town.[33] In July 2010 Dutchland passed a moratorium on the building of new motels on Main Street that would run for two years, after officials raised concerns about the saturation of motels like the Boardwalk.[34] Town records show that in October 2010 the owner of the Boardwalk demolished a one-story portion of the motel containing rooms 16 to 22, which were deemed uninhabitable because of asbestos. At a May 2011 Dutchland Planning Board meeting, a local businessman requested that the moratorium be lifted so that he could refurbish an existing motel that had gone to ruin. Board members worried that it would include state-funded short-term rooms for homeless sex offenders and felons. Residents of the surrounding communities voiced concerns about the safety of their children, the presence of sex offenders, and the impact on property values, with one remarking, "I, too, am against sex offenders and all that."[35] Not surprisingly, this request was denied in a unanimous decision. The moratorium was supported by a June 2011 Main Street Corridor Inventory Study conducted by the Dutchland Planning and Economic Development Department. This study was a direct response to the controversy and found that the Main Street corridor was saturated with twenty motels. It advocated for increased zoning for single-family residences and recommended that land used for motels not be allowed to increase.[36] All this policy discussion ignored the simple fact that the Boardwalk Motel was a very attractive settlement for social refugees (persons who have been impelled to relocate within their own country of citizenship because of the influence of social context and/or social policy).

THE MAIN STREET ECOSYSTEM

The ecosystem of businesses and amenities within walking distance of the Boardwalk provided what urban sociologist Mitch Duneier would call a "sustaining habitat."[37] In his study of street vendors on New York's Sixth Avenue, Duneier argues that the avenue was able to sustain the lives of the homeless vendors because it offered a large pool of potential customers, as well as people willing to make donations, and access to cheap food and places to sleep. While the surrounding middle-class community publicly condemned the location of the Boardwalk, residents of the motel viewed its location as similarly sustaining because it was near businesses, services, and transportation. As Burt, also referred to as "Mr. Clean," told me, "If you're coming from jail or prison, this is a palace. You got a Giant Foods right here, you can jump on the bus right out front. Uh, you know, so you, you, you can't really complain too much."

Many motel residents lacked personal vehicles so they used public transit to travel to surrounding cities. A westbound bus stop to Pinewood is located on the sidewalk mere steps from the motel, and directly across the street is another for a bus that heads east into downtown Riverfort. There are also a variety of nearby businesses accessible by a short walk. A tenth of a mile west of the Boardwalk is the Save More Inn, a two-story motel that was once home to several current Boardwalk residents. According to these residents, the Save More is slightly more expensive for the week ($220 compared to $205 during the time of my research) but much nicer. Judging by its well-maintained exterior and the fact that it had a working website (which the Boardwalk lacked), this seems to be the case. Just past the Save More is a church that serves as a food pantry every Thursday. Many residents of the Boardwalk visit this food pantry on a regular basis. Between the Boardwalk and the Save More are an Indian restaurant (which sits directly next to the Boardwalk) and a Japanese restaurant.

Traveling east on Main Street from the Boardwalk, one will immediately encounter a trailer park with over a dozen trailers.[38] The trailer park and its residents serve multiple uses for the motel population. Biggie went through the trailer park looking for cans and scrap metal, while Reg sold drugs to residents, and other motel residents wandered over for company on nice days. Other times, relations between them got testy, as Reg claimed that someone at the trailer park called the cops on him during a fight, and someone called Sky a "bitch" over the fence. When we saw the police knocking on the door of a trailer one day, I asked what had happened, to which Reg scoffed, "Who knows, they're all fuckin' crazy."

Sam and Reg often talked about the trailers and how expensive it was to live there. Sam based his opinion on a conversation he had with the owner:

> I told him he was outta his rabid ass mind so he don't wanna talk to me no more. Who would give you $1,300 for any one of these goddamn trailer parks? He said all his appliances were new. I said, I wouldn't give a fuck if everything in that motherfucka was spic and span new. It still ain't worth no $1,300 a month. This ain't no goddamn condo. That's a damn trailer. And a stationary trailer at that. Ain't like I can pick it up and move around in it. I pay $1,300 I wanna travel in it.

About a tenth of a mile east of the trailer park is the Boardwalk's sister establishment, the Park Place Motel. The two motels share an owner, manager, and maintenance staff. The Park Place comprises two long, rectangular buildings separated by a parking lot in the middle. Attached to the rightmost building is a two-story house, painted blue, part of which serves as the office. This house is home to manager Elizabeth, her daughter Natalie, as well as maintenance crew members Mike and Larry, who all spent periods of time living there.

According to Elizabeth and Natalie, unlike the Boardwalk, the Park Place does not accept welfare payments so residents must pay cash. The Park Place is much less expensive than the Boardwalk, with a weekly rent of $150, compared to $205. This price cut does come with a downside, as the living conditions at the Park Place are much worse than those at the Boardwalk. The painted square mesh doors of the Park Place have an institutional feel. At the end of the parking lot is a pile of debris including mattresses and charcoal grills. During the winter I noticed a large coat stuffed in the window of one room for insulation. Noonan, the tall parolee who moved down to the Park Place from the Boardwalk, told me one night in December as we stood in the parking lot of the Boardwalk:

> I wanna come back here [the Boardwalk], because it's [the Park Place] really, it's not . . . it's awful. I was in the shower the other day, I burned my chest. The water went from absolutely warm to fuckin' scalding hot, like. I turned the hot water off, and it's still coming out boiling, scalding hot. I'm like, what the fuck? Turn the cold water off, water's still comin' outta the thing. I told Randy about it and he's like, pshhh. The first room I was in, it smelled like sewage. All the pipes under the ground are broken so when you flush the toilet, it just goes into the dirt underneath the building itself.

The residents of the Boardwalk and the Park Place interacted on a regular basis. Reg told me the two motels were "like this" and twisted his fingers together, even though, according to him, the sets of residents were not supposed to associate with each other at the behest of the owner, because of past verbal and physical confrontations. However, the Boardwalk residents did make a distinction between themselves and those at the Park Place, characterizing the latter as violent drunks and the location as "worse." As Reg told me, "They get drunk and fight over nonsense like a book of matches. They start drinking Milwaukee's Best in the morning and that makes them get wily." Natalie echoed this when she told me, "People at the Park Place are worse than up here. They're all drinkers. No drugs. They just drink from sunup to sundown." Sam commented one day,

"The people at the Park Place are alcoholic ass motherfuckers." I asked Ed if he liked hanging out at the Park Place and he replied, "No, they're crazy."

These sweeping statements were not entirely without merit. Late July 2012 saw a stabbing at the Park Place. As Biggie and Reg described it, two men were arm wrestling, and the loser decided to start a fight with the winner. The winner's wife came to his defense and slit the other man's throat with a box cutter. Reg and I walked down to the Park Place to speak with Randy about the incident. The rumor was that the victim was sent to the hospital after he was sliced from behind his ear, down the side of his neck, across his throat, and down his chest. Almost proud of his Park Place residency, Randy smiled and mused, "You come here, you leave in a body bag." While there was sporadic violence at the Boardwalk, this incident seemed to solidify the Park Place's reputation as the more rough and tumble of the two motels.

Across the street from the Park Place is the Paulson Motel. Residents of the Boardwalk claimed that DSS sent women and families to this location—as Sam stated, "Single ladies go to the Paulson." I asked him who came to the Boardwalk and he replied, "Everybody, all the fucked-up ones." Darryl echoed this when he said, "Say you and your girl have a kid, they're probably gonna put you over at the Paulson, 'cause they're not gonna put a child in one of those shelters."

Directly past the Park Place is the Home Cooking buffet, which serves a variety of American comfort food. The parking lot is consistently packed, in stark contrast to the parking lots of both motels. During my stay at the Boardwalk, Home Cooking was a de facto celebration spot where residents and I went to have an $8.99 all-you-can-eat lunch when we wanted to treat ourselves or each other. On one of these visits I noticed that the chairs in the rooms of the Boardwalk were the same as the chairs at Home Cooking.

Just past Home Cooking is an Asian hibachi and sushi restaurant, and about 50 yards further down Main Street is a Chinese buffet restaurant and motel.[39] This part of Main Street is home to the first traffic light and crosswalk that residents from all three motels encounter. There is a large shopping center across the street, home to a local pizza chain restaurant, laundromat, Big Sales discount store, dollar store, tobacco shop, Chinese take-out, and Giant Foods grocery store. Boardwalk residents frequently visited the mall. They bought loose tobacco and empty cigarette tubes at the tobacco shop for much less than packs of brand-name cigarettes.[40]

Proceeding down Main Street from the shopping center to the next intersection, at North Road, a person will encounter a McDonald's, Meijer discount department store, and a Getty gas station. If one walks from the Chinese buffet to North Road, Main Street offers a dance/ballet studio, pawn shop, and a CVS pharmacy. Across the street from the Getty is an Acme pharmacy. Further down Main Street past the North Road intersection is a small shopping plaza with a video game/movie trade-in store, and further down the street on the opposite side is another plaza with a Taco Bell, bagel shop, KFC, and other stores.

These commercial locations and city amenities allow residents of the Boardwalk to satisfy many of their material wants and needs. The dumpsters behind the businesses lining Main Street provide assorted treasures, such as scrap metal, cans, and discarded items that motel residents reuse. Potential residents considering the Boardwalk may be encouraged by the locations within walking distance, especially the commercial establishments that could provide a convenient place of employment. However, once residents move in, their enthusiasm may be dampened quite quickly.

A PORTRAIT OF THE BOARDWALK MOTEL

The Boardwalk is a two-story, L-shaped structure made of red brick and white horizontal siding, with the base of the L facing Main Street. An aerial view of the property (figure 2) shows a parking lot extending along the length of the motel, past the end of the structure, and ending at a thick grove of trees. Across the parking lot is a long, rectangular patch of grass nestled against a fading red wooden fence separating the motel property from the trailer park next door. In the height of summer, the dandelion-patched grass grew to around a foot high. This grassy knoll was a favorite of Elizabeth's pit bull Mocha, who used it as a restroom during warm weather, as well as a spot to sleep and roll around in. One day Spike and I watched Mocha in the grass and he said, "I guarantee you, when Mocha dies, they gonna bury her in the yard right here." I never saw any residents spend time there, although Larry built a snowman there during the winter.

The parking lot has faded white parking spaces, and in the wintertime a pickup truck with a plow drove into the lot and cleared the snow, while also taking huge chunks of concrete out of the ground. Over the course of the winter, these holes filled with water, froze, and then expanded into larger holes. I remember looking out my window at the end of winter and seeing a half dozen potholed puddles and a huge mound of snow. The snow melted in the coming months to reveal a black treasure of concrete nuggets. Larry attempted to fill some of these potholes with a concrete mixture, but the owner did not supply enough to fill all of them.

In the middle of the parking lot are two grapefruit-sized sewer pipes, which until quite recently were not capped off. Their exposure to the air created an awful stench that wafted throughout the parking lot so often that it was a frequent topic of residents who happened to be sitting outside, as illustrated by this exchange with enigmatic Ed and Jake, the movie buff:

ED: What is that smell? Is that smell from your bathroom?
JAKE: From my ass.
ED: What'd you eat?
JAKE: Your mom's pussy.
ED: (*smiles and laughs heartily*)

Finally, Larry decided to put an end to it by screwing bright red caps on the pipes, which did seem to help.

At the end of the parking lot sits a giant green metal dumpster that is emptied weekly by a waste management truck. On several occasions I saw Randy drive his rusty red pickup truck over from his home at the Park Place and toss trash in. I also observed the motel owner's wife do the same, albeit with a much nicer BMW. This was the location of what I call the "shopping cart graveyard." When residents returned from the local supermarket, dollar, and discount stores with shopping carts full of items, they rarely returned them; the carts were simply pushed to the end of the parking lot and left to rust (figure 3). Reg offered to bring them back to the local stores for a fee, but they hired someone else to come by in a pickup and return them to their rightful owners. This happened on a fairly irregular basis, so each time the man arrived, there were usually half a dozen carts awaiting him.

Behind the rear of the motel is another graveyard of sorts, home to a variety of items such as mattresses, tables, chairs, and a wheel barrel. These examples of disarray and decay overshadow the property's most startling feature, a garden along the back left fence. Reg told me that Kelly and Rudy from room 14 started it, and when they moved out, he and Natalie's boyfriend Mike started tending it. I went back there on several occasions and watched them pick large red tomatoes and small hot peppers. Reg and Mike claimed there were cucumber plants as well, but they never ended up producing. One day Reg gave me several small green hot peppers from the garden to take home. On another day he picked a yellow pepper and dared me to eat it, a challenge I accepted stupidly. Mike and Reg got a great laugh as they watched me cough and cry from the heat. When he decided I had suffered enough, Reg offered me a glass of milk, which I accepted with relief.

The part of the L closest to the road is actually the office, which, according to town building records, is part of a 992-square-foot apartment. Eventually Natalie, Elizabeth, and Larry let me inside the apartment, and several people told me that it was originally the house of a previous owner, although they and I could never verify which one. A portico extends from the office out into the parking lot, where it is secured by two poles sitting in large flower beds. These white wooden flower beds are stuck in a concrete median, along with a third flower bed that is not used for anything. Elizabeth made a habit of parking her car under the portico's 9-foot clearance. Between these supports hangs an American Express sign, although the motel no longer accepts credit cards. Hanging from the portico is a small, red, neon "no vacancy" sign. It always said "vacancy," even on occasions when I knew the motel was full. Above the portico, attached to the second floor, is a giant red sign with white lettering that vertically spells out "Motel," with bumblebee arrows pointing to the building. Sitting on the curb to the right of the office door is a regularly stocked local newspaper dispenser and the shell of a public telephone booth. On nice days I often saw Natalie, Elizabeth, and Larry sitting in chairs outside the office, with Mocha close by.

To enter the office one goes through two tan doors, both flanked by two levels of square windows with siding beneath them. These windows also display stickers for American Express, Visa, and MasterCard. Upon entering the office one is greeted by a small wooden table to the left, on which sits a small ash tray and sometimes coupons or menus. On the left wall is a large two-way mirror, and often whoever was working sat behind the mirror in a chair watching television in a separate room with a view of the office. Along the right wall of the office is a large gray hamper where residents place soiled towels and sheets. In the center is the counter where the transactions take place. The counter is dark wood, typically covered with local restaurant menus and HBO program guides, as well as a small woven basket where residents can pick up mail.[41]

Separating the clerk's portion of the counter and the main office is a large pane of glass that has a few inches of space at the bottom for money and other items to be passed through. Larger items such as new towels and toilet paper are given to residents through an often-locked door to the right of the glass. Behind this clerk's alcove and visible through the glass is another doorway with no door that reveals the living room of the apartment with its two couches and a table. Also visible through the glass is a green carpeted staircase to the right that leads up to the second floor.

The clerk's counter has a phone and usually a notebook and several pieces of paper. Elizabeth, Natalie, or Larry sat on a round stool, and when I came in to pay my rent they would swivel it to check the calendar behind them. From what I observed, they used the notebook to keep track of who had paid, what rooms social services was using, and which rooms housed sex offenders. Receipts were made on carbon paper from a generic receipt book and then stamped with an ink stamp that displayed the name of the motel, the address (with incorrect zip code), and the phone number.[42]

While no observer would mistake the Boardwalk for a luxury hotel, several items in the office make clear its true nature. The most deterring is the sex-offender occupancy license posted to the left of the clerk's window, almost as high as the ceiling. The motel is required to display this license by law, and it states the name and address of the motel, how many occupancy points it is allowed (in this case 6), when it was issued, and when it expires.[43] Hanging on the left side of the clerk's glass is a framed piece of paper with red and black type that states:

"No phone calls from the office, office use only!"
"No outgoing calls, incoming only!"
"No children allowed!"
"All weekly payments must be made in full, no partial payments allowed!"
"Not responsible for any items left in room for one night or one week! Take everything with you when you live!!! [*sic*]"

Also taped to the inside of the glass was a sheet of loose-leaf paper with the handwritten words "No phone calls!" although this disappeared midway during my fieldwork. Finally, there is another framed piece of paper with the black typed words, "No hanging out in or around the office!"

Outside the office, a sidewalk extends around the corner and down the length of the motel. Around the corner from the office is a black metal two-level stairwell that leads to the second floor. There are two other identical stairwells, one at the middle of the motel near room 30 and another at the end near room 38. Above each stairwell is a small fire exit sign. At the bottom of the first stairwell is a well-stocked soft-drink machine that residents of the motel and trailer park use. Underneath this stairwell is a hodgepodge of debris, such as two by fours, wood panels, small plastic trash cans, and the occasional bike. Sitting near this first stairwell is a large green trashcan. A similar black trashcan sits at the base of the second stairwell, along with a collection of a half dozen bikes that Reg accumulated over time and locked to the metal.

On the first floor of the motel are rooms 1 through 15. The exterior of these rooms is red brick, and each room has a large, rectangular window with smaller, thinner windows that open outward on each side. These windows are painted with a sea green trim that matches

the doors. First-floor rooms have a front living area and back bedroom area that are separated by a floor-to-ceiling wall that juts out
into the entire space, creating a C-shaped floor space. This wall has a
large, square window cut out of it that one could easily climb through
or pass large items through. The rooms feature dark aqua carpets and
light blue curtains. In the back left or right corner of each room is
the bathroom, which contains a toilet, shower stall, sink, and mirror.
The bathroom ceilings are square foam tiles, while the main room
has a solid stucco ceiling. In each bedroom area is an air conditioner/
heater unit—or, in some cases, an empty space where one would be.

Not all the first floor rooms were habitable. For the duration of
my stay at the motel, room 1 was never occupied. This was likely
due to its consistent state of neglect, evidenced by the dozens of
small, dead beetles smashed between the curtains and the window,
their brown skeletons crushed and falling apart. Room 6 at one time
belonged to Marc, and later Jake, who moved in with him to save
money. However, their stay ended in February 2013 when the ceiling
tiles of the bathroom caved in because of a leak. When my research
ended in June 2013, this room had still not been repaired to rent.
Room 5, which belonged to Jake, then me, was left uninhabitable
from December through the end of the study owing to a plumbing
problem, which I will describe later.

Room 8 is actually a storage room; at one time it was locked with
a padlock. Inside are boxes on boxes of soap made in Korea, sitting
unopened because they are not distributed to residents as intended.
Down a small set of stairs and sitting on a dirty floor in the back of
the room are a water heater and a set of breakers. Residents constantly blew fuses and needed to reset their breakers, which is why
the padlock was removed. Reg showed me this trick when I blew the
fuse after running my fridge, TV, microwave, and space heater all at
once. Rooms 11 and 12 are also used as storage and contain several
rolled rugs, broken air conditioning units, siding, chairs, and other
random items.

On the second floor are rooms 23 to 42 (rooms 16 to 22 were part
of a rear section of the motel that was demolished in 2011 because
of asbestos).[44] A landing with creaky wood paneling extends the
length of the motel from the first stairwell to the last. This landing is

covered with a very thin green carpet the shade of an unkempt min-
iature golf course and is torn in several places, exposing the wood
below. Lining the landing is a black metal railing about waist high.
Early on Natalie warned me not to lean on it as it did not seem safe.
The landing was often littered with chairs placed outside rooms, as
well as small tables, empty bottles and beer cars, and other debris
such as eggshells, TVs, and coffee cups.

Unlike the first floor, rooms on the second floor have three tall,
rectangular windows, the left and right of which open outward. The
doors, exterior lights, and window trim are the same as the first floor,
as is the brick exterior. These rooms are smaller than the first-floor
rooms, lacking the front and back sections. Each of these rooms has
at least one bed (several have two) and a bathroom in the back corner with a toilet and tub. The sink is outside of the bathroom with
a mirror above it. Mounted on the back wall between the bathroom
door and sink is an air conditioner/heater or the location where
one used to be. There are also air grates on the right or left walls
of the room. The carpet in most of these rooms is the same blue as
downstairs, although I saw several rooms with tan carpeting. Room
32 is used as storage and filled with shelves, toilets, a microwave,
and other materials. Despite the differences in appearance between
upstairs and downstairs rooms, the costs are exactly the same.[45]

LIVING CONDITIONS AT THE BOARDWALK MOTEL

The first room I moved into was room 34, on the second floor.
Even getting into my room was a chore because the old locks in the
rooms sometimes failed to work. I spent several minutes putting
the key in the lock, wrestling with it, and begging it to turn. There
was no obvious solution to this problem, so I would just remove
the key and wait a minute or two before trying again.[46] I saw other
residents struggle with this same problem, and early on I worried
that if I ever needed to quickly access my room as a safe haven, the
lock would be my undoing.

When I moved into room 34, the furniture included a bed, two
small wooden desks with one large drawer and a storage space
underneath, a wooden chair with worn red cushion, wooden table

with a phone book atop it, and a wooden dresser with four drawers and a bible and TV sitting on top. The windows featured a pair of blue/green/gray curtains with vertical tan lines that could have been ancient stains or part of the design. The top left portion of one curtain was not attached to the curtain rod so I had to keep the desk pushed up against the window to hold the curtain in place. The walls of the room were a fleshy white and featured a golf ball–sized hole and a large square of peeling paint. Above the bed was a framed painting of a lake surrounded by trees. (Just about every room in the motel had this same painting.) On either side of the painting were gold wall-mounted lamps with off-kilter and peeling shades. The dark blue carpet was so worn in places that there was tan thread exposure. Next to the dresser was a nonfunctioning lamp that was practically falling out of the wall, as well as a full-length mirror.

Above the sink was a harshly bright fluorescent light. A set of white towels sat on the counter. The basin of the sink was a sickly yellow, with rust near the drain and hair on the rim. The cold water came out with a bit of force, while the hot water was slower but got scalding almost immediately. Underneath the sink were exposed pipes and a hole that appeared to go down into the ceiling of the room below. A thin wooden panel was set against the counter to cover the hole (figure 4), but it could be easily moved, and I worried about rodents or insects crawling into the room. Next to the sink was a broken air conditioner, more of an exoskeleton really, as there were no knobs and the interior cover was missing, exposing a dusty interior with nothing inside that resembled anything in working order. The toilet was filled with blue cleaning liquid, and there was a plunger sitting next to it. A light switch turned on both the overhead light and the ceiling fan. The floor was white tile while the walls were white and tan. Several brown stains lined the tub, and several ceiling tiles were missing.

In some places the floor creaked uneasily when I walked; I worried that I might go crashing through it (which actually happened, later, to someone else). There was no fridge, microwave, phone, or trash can. None of these items was standard in any room, so residents had to obtain them on their own if they did not arrive at the motel with them. While other rooms had peepholes in their doors, mine did not. Fortunately, it did have a chain lock that appeared fairly sturdy. Unfortunately, the lock did not work properly. The bracket was damaged, and even when the lock did catch, the door itself could be pushed in several centimeters, so someone could generate enough force to break the chain lock with a kick or shoulder charge. On my first night I told Elizabeth and she called Randy from the Park Place, who appeared a few hours later and fixed it.

I ended up moving out at the end of June because the summer heat made the room unbearable without air conditioning. Other residents used fans and opened their windows during the evening, but I worried about someone entering my room through an open window when I was asleep. When Roy moved to room 14, I moved into his old room, which had a working air conditioner. Room 29 was similar to my original room, but the layout was flipped so the bed, sink, dresser, and bathroom were on the opposite side. Also flipped were the hot- and cold-water handles, so I kept turning on the hot water by accident and scalding my hands. The new room came equipped with a black refrigerator (the only time I ever observed this) and a TV, although the volume did not work so I switched it out with the one from room 34. I bought a remote controller from the department store and programmed it for the TV.[47] I learned that the light switches near the door also operated the outlet that many people plugged their refrigerators into, so I made a note to never flip it off.[48]

My stay in room 29 was incredibly comfortable in terms of temperature. I biked to and from the motel on nice days and was happy to enjoy a cool room. Unfortunately, there were other issues to contend with. One night in late July I was watching TV when I saw a small yellow spider about the size of an M&M on the bedspread. I brushed it off but soon saw another one, which I disposed of just as quickly. Wondering if perhaps they had hitched a ride from my old room, I shook out my bedspread. About ten minutes later I saw two more. I dealt with them and wondered where they were coming from. Then I made the awful mistake of looking up at the ceiling and, in a moment of traumatic comprehension like something out of a horror movie, saw that the spiders were crawling all over the ceiling and dropping onto the bed. This was too much for me to handle, so I retreated home for the night to choose my next course of action. Unlike true residents of the motel who were trapped in their suboptimal living conditions, my peripheral membership role and position of privilege allowed me this escape.

Luckily for me, Jake moved out of his room a few days later, so I took over his old space in room 5. Jake left me a blue couch, a fridge with some crumbs and dark brown liquid floating around inside it, and two wooden tables, one of which had a brown crust all over the top because he and Reg ate oysters off it one evening.[49] He also left me a power strip, because none of the outlets along the right wall actually worked, as well as a green trash can. The bathroom was absolutely disgusting, with mold, dirt, grime, and who knows what else on every surface, including the cracked tile floor of the shower. A gallery of dead bugs hung suspended from the cobwebs in the window. The toilet also required some DIY ethic from me when I noticed that it was improperly sealed to the floor. The water that was supposed to run into the tank ran onto the floor and puddled when the toilet was flushed. I fixed it with some caulk that I bought from Big Sales. The room lacked a working air conditioner, so I purchased a fan. I found out in the winter that the room also lacked heat, and I addressed this with a space heater.

My time in room 5 came to an end in the middle of December. I returned to the room after a few days away and when I opened the door my nose picked up the scent of decay, sending me scrambling to find whatever had died inside my room. The source of the smell was a pool of water an inch deep covering my bathroom floor. It had already soaked the carpet near the bathroom door, and the room was clearly uninhabitable. Larry attempted to fix the problem by running a vacuum through the shower drain, where he drew up sand and rocks. He also sucked up the water from the floor and dried it with towels. After an hour, water still rose through cracks in the floor and around the shower stall and seeped into the bedroom. Larry called the city water and sewer department, but when they arrived they could not access the pipes. The next day the motel owner brought in a plumber who told Larry that he needed to fix the toilet, which he did, but the water continued to pour in. At this point I asked for a different room and moved into room 27 upstairs, which had been inhabited by the tall and skinny Sam.[50] This game of musical rooms was fairly common due to the poor infrastructure of the motel. Dee and Toby moved from room 25 to room 10 after the ceiling tiles collapsed in their bathroom. They were afflicted by a water problem in room 10 that prevented them from using the shower for quite some time. Jake and Marc had to move from a room they shared after their bathroom ceiling tiles also collapsed.

I stayed uneventfully in room 27 until the end of my research in June 2013. I was fortunate to be able to disengage from the motel and resume my life of comfort. The other residents simply had to live with the deterioration on a daily basis. A common theme among residents was considerable frustration with the living conditions. Some even joked that getting locked up in jail would be a better experience than living at the motel. Residents felt demeaned by what they perceived as the owner's lack of care for them and the motel. Noonan said, "This guy gets away with murder. He's got three Home Cookings, he's a millionaire, drives around in his Escalade, and, you know what I mean? Talk about slumlords, wow. He's definitely a slumlord."

When Roy moved into a room that had just been vacated by long-term residents, he was forced to clean it himself and complained, "Some of the rooms, there are about three rooms that if OSHA [Occupational Safety and Health Administration] come up here, they would not pass." Later that day we sat in his room and he wondered aloud, "What's in my room that's missing? It's simple." I looked around and noticed a faint outline on the wall where a smoke detector should have been. Roy nodded and said, "Smoke detector! Word bond. That's the impression I get here, nobody gives a fuck."

In October 2012 Natalie gave Sam a smoke detector and told him he had to put it in his room because the inspector was coming back. Sam wondered why the rooms did not have carbon monoxide detectors as well, because so many residents used heaters. He was also concerned about fire hazards because he had seen melted and exposed wiring in the rooms. Sam told me, "Man, this place is just a goddamn, we sittin' on a keg a dynamite. Just a matter a time."

These conditions were the result of attitudes held by the owner and staff, in response to the type of residents who were given rooms by social services. Elizabeth stated as much when she complained about the amount of effort that Larry put into cleaning and maintaining the rooms:

> I told him, this ain't a suite, just fuckin' do the room, get it cleaned, paint it, patch up the holes and paint it. You know he does it, eh. Yeah, but it's not gonna stay that way. You're only getting guys from social services, they don't give a shit, just. The owner don't give a shit and he doesn't wanna spend a lot of money and here you wanna say, you need all these fuckin' tiles here and they cost money, they cost like $50. He says they're dirty or something, just paint over it, you know? I said look it, the owner ain't gonna go hire you to build a house for somebody, just fuckin' do the, do the, do it the best ya can. This ain't a . . . you been up in that fuckin' one room a week. But it doesn't matter, nobody gives a shit. All the owner wants you to do, patch up the holes and hurry up and paint it. I tried tellin' him that, I said you gonna learn. It ain't like the owner's gonna give you a cookie, he don't give a shit. You will learn! Do it the cheapest way you can.

Natalie echoed this when she said that the Boardwalk and the Park Place used to be nice and that the owner simply did not invest in them. According to her, the owner let the Boardwalk go when he started taking sex offenders because they guaranteed him money no matter what the conditions. Tat gave his own version of the fall from grace one night:

> I was here when this shit was like brand new. This shit was immaculate, this shit was immaculate, bro. Then once that new law for the sex offenders shit passed, you know that sex offenders could live anywhere but hotels are limited, to only have so many, that's when he started taking welfare recipients in. These nigga, they just started rippin' phones out the thing, takin' 'frigerators wid dem, know what I mean? Sellin' refrigerators for two hits, like, yo.

To be fair to Elizabeth and the owner, I did see similar behavior from residents during my stay. Biggie shamelessly scrapped a television and a refrigerator from an upstairs room when it was vacated, and when I moved out at the end of my study, Larry called me to make sure that the fridge and microwave I had taken from the room were indeed mine.

AN ERA OF HOSTILITY

The quotes from Elizabeth and Tat speak volumes about the tumultuous existence of the Boardwalk. The motel deteriorated because of a perpetuating and self-fulfilling prophecy. The owner took a position that the residents did not care about the condition of the motel, and residents took the position that because of the conditions, the owner and staff did not care about them. The result of this mutual hostility turned the Boardwalk Motel into an epicenter of cultural conflict: a dumping ground for those deemed socially unacceptable, and a lightning rod for criticism from the local middle-class community.

To the residents of Dutchland, the knee-jerk reaction was to stereotype the motel and its residents while calling for their removal from the area. The alternative would be to understand who the residents of the Boardwalk are, what the motel means to them, and how the state of the Boardwalk is symptomatic of societal problems much bigger and more complex than "sex offenders and all that." In the next several chapters I will use my observations and the words of the residents themselves to answer two important questions. Who are the residents of the Boardwalk Motel, and what role did the motel play in their lives?

2

Pathways to Motel Life

Nobody wanted us.
—*Dee*

To fully understand residents of the Boardwalk Motel, it is important to know how they arrived there in the first place. Residents of the motel can be conceptualized as "social refugees," persons who have been impelled to relocate within their own country of citizenship because of the influence of social context and/or social policy. While there are dramatic differences between refugees fleeing war-torn countries and those living in a motel, the literature on global refugees and internally displaced citizens provides an intriguing framework for understanding motel residents.

The refugee literature refers to two phases of movement and migration: that of "flight" and "settlement." Flight is the phase of voluntary or involuntary displacement that inspires a migrant to move. Settlement is the act that ends a migrant's flight.[1] Movement can also be viewed in terms of "push" and "pull" factors. The push factors provide migrants with causal motivations to leave their old home, while the pull factors of the new home give migrants a purpose and wish to migrate.[2] These migratory patterns and their relation to social refugees can be clearly seen in studies of migratory workers on the frontiers of America.[3]

The story of the Boardwalk begs the answers to two questions. Where did residents live prior to moving to the motel? What were the push and pull factors that brought them there? In this chapter

I will use this social refugee framework to describe the factors that influenced settlement at the Boardwalk.

PREVIOUS ENVIRONMENTS

On a simple level, this chapter is concerned with how residents got from their previous environments to the Boardwalk Motel. The motel was not universally experienced as a horrible place to live but rather was assessed in relation to where an individual came from and where he or she expected to go. Residents arrived at the motel via one of three trajectories dependent on their social position. Many sex offenders and other parolees came to the motel directly from prison, which made the motel a unique location for them because it lacked the institutional authority they had become accustomed to. Other residents viewed the motel as "stepping up" from their previous homes, while for others the motel was a "step down." By showing how residents viewed their move to the motel, we can get a sense of the meanings that these social refugees attributed to events in their lives.

Prison

For those returning to society directly from prison (which included Ryan, Slash, Noonan, Patch, Sonny, Cinque, Dale, Darryl, Price, Tat, Walt, Jasper, and Harry), the motel represented a completely different environment.[4] Sociologist Erving Goffman describes prison as a "total institution" that is both designed and administered to protect the public from those inside.[5] Prison is a unique housing environment because it is custodial, and inmates in prison have little to no control over their living situations. Because the immediate goal of prison is community protection, the welfare and care of inmates are not priorities for prison administrators.[6] Rather, according to sociologist Gresham Sykes, the prison experience deprives inmates of liberty, goods and services, heterosexual relationships, autonomy, and security.[7] The ex-prisoners who resided at the Boardwalk Motel recognized that prison was a fairly unique environment, as the dreadlocked Cinque told me, "It's its own world." However, some aspects of prison culture did seep into motel life. Darryl, a registered sex offender, brought his prison mindset to the motel, and when I asked how he adjusted to the motel, he said, "Just like prison. You scope out the place, pay attention to what's going on, then decide who you wanna talk to. The same thing, there's no difference whatsoever."

When inmates left prison they arrived at the Boardwalk in the context of reentry. Criminologist Joan Petersilia describes reentry as "all activities and programming conducted to prepare ex-convicts to return safely to the community and to live as law-abiding citizens."[8] Those who have not faced reentry themselves lack knowledge about the hardships it presents. While ex-prisoners face the challenge of finding jobs and establishing prosocial relationships, perhaps the biggest challenge for reentering ex-offenders is finding a viable housing option.[9] Therefore the primary role of the Boardwalk was to provide ex-offenders with a roof over their head.

When parolees are released from prison, they must provide their parole officer with a proposed residence. Often these proposed residences are not viable for a variety of reasons, such as a lack of stability or the presence of other residents with criminal histories. In such instances, the parolee would apply for emergency housing at the Riverfort DSS office. DSS then coordinated with onsite workers from the Homeless and Traveler's Aid Society (HATAS) to place them in emergency housing. HATAS is a DSS-funded service that is intended to centralize intake of all homeless individuals and coordinate housing placements for DSS. This housing included shelters such as the Riverfort city mission, or motels such as the Boardwalk that were designated as "emergency shelters." Those in need of housing after DSS had closed were immediately referred to HATAS and then approved through DSS the next business day.[10] Although homeless parolees and registered sex offenders were sent to locations other than the Boardwalk, the Boardwalk was particularly viable because it did not violate the New York State Sexual Assault Reform Act, which prohibited level 3 sex offenders or those with victims under the age of eighteen from knowingly going within 1,000 feet of any location that serves primarily children.

Cinque had fourteen months of parole left when he was released to the Boardwalk on what he claimed were gun charges. He thought the motel was "alright" and told me that DSS put him there because he "didn't have a place to go." Like other parolees who arrived directly from prison, Darryl was placed at the Boardwalk by social services. He told me about the day he was released:

> I didn't get to Riverfort until ten-thirty at night. They made me go to the city mission, to call HATAS, then HATAS had me to go the Boardwalk. And I asked, so how am I s'posed to get out there? That's not my problem, walk. Luckily the buses were running when I had to come up. HATAS will call the Board-walk and ask if they have a room and tell 'em they have some-one coming in. They got their own little thing mapped out.

While the Boardwalk provided housing for ex-offenders, it did not satisfy the important need for employment. Most residents were working to find stable employment and move out. Parolees were often required to find jobs and get off of DSS within a speci-fied time frame or they risked being sent back to prison. This added another element of pressure from the criminal justice system. In some ways, the location of the motel made it an ideal first step in reentry because the sustaining habitat was filled with places that, in theory, provided job opportunities. Unfortunately, the job prospects for those with criminal histories are quite bleak. A criminal history substantially reduces the likelihood of job callbacks. In an experi-ment conducted by sociologist Devah Pager, 17 percent of whites with criminal records received callbacks, compared to 34 percent without, while 5 percent of blacks with criminal records received callbacks, compared to 14 percent without. The striking finding from this research is that whites with criminal records receive a greater number of callbacks than blacks without.[11]

DSS and parole wanted residents to get legitimate jobs, and resi-dents wanted any sort of income to help them live day to day. A month after Darryl's release, Jake and I were hanging out on the stairs and Darryl mentioned that he had put in over forty appli-cations around the area and had not been offered a single job. He lamented, "Eighteen years in prison and I'm twisted. No one wants to hire me, fuck 'em."

Without legitimate employment, the pressure to find other sources of income grew. Parolees with criminal histories wrestled with whether to continue criminal careers at the motel. Many claimed to have been involved with crime from a young age, and the temptation of criminality was enduring. Cinque's justification for his early entrance into criminal behavior was, "I'm a product of my environment," and he spoke highly of the drug dealers that he saw in his neighborhood as a child. "I'm seeing new mitts, new sneakers, I'm seeing fresh stuff every day. So in the back of my mind already, that's what I wanna be. Bam! I was like eleven, ten. Wanted to be that right there." This criminal activity had a direct impact on his transience because he claimed he was released from prison for drugs and weapons charges. When he came to the motel, he returned to selling marijuana to earn more income (he did not get enough hours at his Waste Management job) and was eventually sent back to prison for this behavior.

Like Cinque, Tat had a history of selling drugs, and he reflected, "I kinda fucked up my whole entire life with that." When Tat got out of prison he knew that he could make easy money by going back to his old ways, but he was determined to move on. He told me, "But, right now, God is givin' me another chance. If I don't die by some miraculous lightning strike, you know what I mean? Um, then, uh, I will keep steppin' my right foot forward." He was still looking for legitimate work when he got kicked out of the motel a few weeks later for playing loud music.

Darryl also claimed to have been involved with crime from a young age: "I grew up in a very criminal environment. Eight years old I was moving drugs, nine years old I was given a .22, a girl, and a blunt for my birthday. Uh, by the time I was twelve, I was doin' robberies, burglaries, cons. I'm one of nine kids, the youngest of seven boys, every one of my brothers has been to prison. Family business."

He chuckled and said, "Boy, I really did a lotta foul things, didn't I?" These foul things included claims of being a drug mule in New York City when he was eleven, and later, laundering millions of dollars by having senior citizens go to Atlantic City and exchange $9,500 cash for chips and then cash the chips out in the form of a check. Darryl told me on several occasions that he should not have been sent to prison for the sex offense he was convicted of but could have served similar time for any number of other crimes. Upon release from prison, he told me he had old friends offering him drugs and guns to sell in order to get back on his feet. Darryl turned these opportunities down because he felt that the prison experience had changed his life goals:

> Don't need anything, I need a job, a place to live, that's it. I don't need money. I need, I need enough money to live on, I don't need to be rich. I don't need to own everything in sight. What I need is a nice little job, enough to pay my bills. And my bills are simple. Give me some place to live, and I pay the gas and lights, lemme pay for cable, have some food in the house, and pay for my phone and the bus. And then let me find a mate, a significant other. That's it.[12]

These experiences highlight how problematic it was to place ex-offenders at the Boardwalk. Much of the motel culture revolved around drug use, and because of this, when parolees had difficulty finding work, their parole-approved housing situation provided a tempting black market for those looking to become suppliers. This is just one way in which the parole experience at the Boardwalk left much to be desired.

The stigma attached to parolees was certainly a cause for the dearth of employment opportunities given to those at the Board-walk, but this was not the only stigma that hampered reentry. At the motel, all parolees were viewed as potential sexual offenders, which added another land mine that reentering ex-offenders had to navigate when dealing with other residents. In the juvenile justice system, youth released from placement contend with a "dual transi-tion" from placement to community and from youth to adulthood.[13] Parolees at the Boardwalk faced a dual stigma as parolees in society and parolees living at the motel.

Cinque, Dale, Darryl, Price, Tat, Walt, Jasper, and Harry were all registered sex offenders released to the motel on parole. Their con-victions ranged from adult rape to child sexual abuse, and they were all considered level 2 and 3 offenders, or at medium or high risk of reoffense, respectively. The NYS Sex Offender Registry did not list level 1 offenders (low risk of reoffense) on the public registry, and I did not encounter any parolees who admitted to being level 1 offenders (although Reg was a level 1 sex offender who was not on parole).

Cinque was convicted in 1997 of attempted sexual abuse against a thirteen-year-old girl. He was sentenced to a maximum of three years in prison and after that release was caught with weapons and drugs and sent back to prison for ten years. He and Darryl were required to wear GPS ankle bracelets at all times, although Darryl told me he did not mind because parole could never claim he was at a location the GPS did not register.

Like Cinque, Darryl was coming out of prison for a conviction other than his sexual offense. He was in prison from 1994 to 2011 for sexual abuse and sodomy with an eight-year-old boy, a crime that Darryl vehemently denied. After being released in April 2011, Darryl lived in a rooming house in Riverfort. He told me:

> Well, the first time around it was overwhelming, coming outta jail after seventeen years everything changed. Cell phones, listen, people walking around in flip flops. This is going to sound a little bit crazy, but I actually have problems adjusting back to society. It was great to have peace and quiet and not have to talk to people, but after three weeks the peace and quiet actually started to bother me. You have a lot of free time in prison, you hang out with people. Then you're out here, you're running around looking for a job, but you really don't sit down and just, talk. You just don't converse.

He was sent back to prison in August 2011 for violating his parole: "What happened was two friends came over, they missed the bus, ended up spending the night. Parole knew they were there. Next morning I left at eight o'clock, they left, nine o'clock they broke back into my room, they got into it with the day manager, the day manager called DSS. DSS sanctioned me for thirty days, parole violated me for thirteen months."

When I met Darryl upon his second release, his parole had been extended until 2019. I asked him after a month and a half if he expected to be where he was, and he said, "It's hard to say 'cause last time I was at this point, and I didn't get nowhere else."

The many challenges of reentry wore on Darryl as he attempted to navigate the world of work, housing, and parole. He claimed that DSS threatened him and told me, "My caseworker, she said if I don't find an apartment for $350 a month by next week she's gonna kick me off DSS for thirty days." Jake exclaimed, "Where the fuck is there an apartment for three fifty a month? Nowhere! If there was, I would be there." Darryl's and Jake's concerns were well founded. In 2013 the median monthly rent in the city of Riverfort was $904, and only 7.5 percent of rental units could be rented for less than $399 per month.[14]

Darryl worried about finding housing because if he lost his DSS benefits then parole would violate him and send him back to prison. DSS told him to go on Craigslist and look for housing, but Darryl was not allowed to use a computer and his parole officer would not let him live with another person, which made a rooming house or single-room occupancy the only affordable option. More important, his sex-offender status made many locations off-limits because his parole conditions prohibited him from being (and therefore living) within 300 yards of places where children congregated and 1,000 feet from schools.

I encountered several other parolees who agreed to participate in the study but offered no more insight into their lives other than telling me they were on parole. Darryl, Tat, and Cinque were the only ones who disclosed significant details and socialized with me on a regular basis. There is good reason for this: parolees put themselves at risk by being around drugs and alcohol or other activities prohibited by their conditions of parole. Therefore the safest course of action for many was to stay to themselves and try to move out as soon as possible. They recognized that the motel was not a step up or step down but rather a thin sheet of ice that had to be carefully navigated if they wanted to remain out of prison.

Stepping Up

The residents who viewed coming to the Boardwalk Motel as stepping up migrated from environments that were undesirable for a variety of reasons. These conditions acted to push residents out in search of settlement. Two qualities in particular attracted them to the Boardwalk: independence/autonomy and safety, which often went hand in hand.

Many residents stepped up to the Boardwalk from locations specifically designed to house the homeless. These locations included shelters and rooming houses, which typically provided little autonomy and safety. Burt, or "Mr. Clean," previously lived in such a rooming house in downtown Riverfort, where he shared a bedroom with eight other men. The Boardwalk afforded him more privacy and security than the boarding house, and he told me, "If I leave things here, it's still there when I come back." For Burt, the safety of his possessions was paramount, and the Boardwalk afforded him the peace of mind to leave belongings in his room.

Moving to the Boardwalk was considered a huge step up by Dee and Toby, recovering addicts who had previously lived apart in separate shelters for the homeless where they lacked safety and independence as a couple. When Toby had accrued the maximum allowed thirty days at his shelter, HATAS placed him at the Boardwalk. Because DSS was paying rent for Toby only, Dee had to sneak into the motel because she technically was not supposed to be staying with him. I sat with Dee and Toby one day in January and Dee recalled:

Um, our first night here was like sanctuary. Like, we were scared we were gonna get caught 'cause I wasn't supposed to be here. Yeah, so for the first two weeks, I would sneak in, um, yup, I would sneak in and it was like sanctuary, it was so important that we had a room to ourselves 'cause we had to live homeless separate. So to actually live together, it was, it was utterly phenomenal. Oh yeah, we were mixed with, with happiness and 'joyment, but yet we were scared. Scared that it's gonna be taken away from us, like how long are they gonna let us stay here and then what can we do to keep it?

And then our unemployment kicked in and we had decided, we had two ways to go. Go back to where we were, stay in, in homeless places, like I'd stay with Guy [her former john] and he'd be at the shelter, stay there, save our unemployment 'til we get an apartment. Or, stay here where we're together. Right now, we are together and that's where we feel safe and comfortable. Nobody wants us 'cause we're drug addicts, like, let's just face facts. Nobody wanted us.

Dee and Toby were pulled to the Boardwalk because it represented a safe place for them to live together. As a couple, they desired a location that felt like a home, instead of a warehouse full of the homeless. The psychological comfort that they gained from sharing a living space between only the two of them was so important that they risked DSS sanctions until they could pay for it on their own.

Many single men came to the motel from the city mission, which, like other shelters for the homeless, did not offer independence or safety. Darryl's romantic partner, Digital, found the mission intolerable because he did not enjoy being around large groups of people in a confined space. The Boardwalk allowed him to live in relative privacy and avoid conflict that he feared could land him in jail. After his first night in the motel, he smiled and said, "It was great, it was peaceful man, bed's comfy. It's better than the mission." Riley also came from the mission, and though he did not plan on staying for long, he said, "This is nice, I have independence, I can do what I want to do."[15]

Other residents faced a lack of autonomy and safety in environments not specifically sanctioned for the homeless. Biggie and Deirdre lived with a friend in downtown Riverfort and were looking for an alternative that they could afford on their disability and retirement benefits. The fact that they lived in a dangerous neighborhood with regular shootings served as a substantial push factor. After looking at alternatives, they decided to move to the motel because Biggie said, "It was peaceful and without drama."[16] They also desired independence that was missing in an apartment leased to someone else. Living in a shared apartment threatened Biggie's and Deirdre's identities, particularly Biggie's role as a successful provider for his partner. Biggie acknowledged the motel's pull: "I love this motel, best thing about it, it's not the best, but it helped me get my mind back together, all about taking care of me and my girl. I wanted to be finally independent and even though I'm doing it out of a hotel room I'm doing it now."

Larry, a veteran, moved to the motel in October in another considerable step up that was rooted in a desire for independence. He had been living out of his tan Chevy Lumina while waiting for his next unemployment check to be issued. Larry said that when it finally arrived, "I says, you know what, I wasn't brought up like this, you know, and uh, I'm not gonna, I'm not. Whatever it costs, to get a room, which is $200, out of my $400, and I says, I'm just doin' it. I'm just tired of it, you know? I mean, you gotta go ask people where you can shower and, you know. Anyway, this is how I ended up here." He looked at other motels but decided on the Boardwalk because it was the cheapest. There were rooms available closer to Riverfort, but they required sharing a bathroom, and Larry was "not big into that." While Larry could have stepped up from his car to a rooming house, he chose not to because it provided less independence than the motel. For Larry, the motel gave him the feelings of independence that allowed him to feel more in control of his day-to-day life because he did not share amenities with other people.

These examples of stepping up to the motel illustrate that transient living is subject to a large degree of relativity. The prior housing situations of many social refugees were often quite dire. Compared to the inside of a car or a shared room at a shelter, the Boardwalk Motel was tantamount to a safe haven. Outsiders' judgment of the Boardwalk as a terrible living space masks the fact that it was better than what some residents had experienced previously. Stepping up to the motel required a social refugee to live in an environment that he or she considered "worse" than the Boardwalk. For many in the middle class, living somewhere "worse" than the Boardwalk is almost incomprehensible, but the residents who stepped up realized that because some living situations instilled more desperation than others, a move to the motel was the best option.

Stepping Down

Other residents stepped down from housing that provided more autonomy, safety, and relative comfort. Residents who were pushed from these situations stepped down to the Boardwalk in order to regain footholds in lives that had become suddenly precarious. In this respect, the Boardwalk represented a middle ground on which social refugees settled before possibly stepping further down to starker forms of homelessness.

Sam, the tall and gregarious veteran who grew up in Chicago, and his partner, Justine, stepped down to the Boardwalk from an apartment in Riverfort when he lost his job and could not afford the rent (although Justine moved out shortly after because she could not stand the conditions). When we spoke about the move to the motel, Sam said:

Well, it served its purpose, we didn't have nowhere to stay and we found this place. So you know we found this and it offered us shelter for the time, mostly for me, not for her [Justine]. Mostly for me. I was grateful for it. They coulda said we ain't got no room. I could went to the shelter or whatever. God knows where I'd be right now. I'm glad I was here, it gave me a chance to get things together, so I ain't so mad, you know. And the owner ain't real funny. Sometimes we be late a couple times with the rent and he didn't make a big thing about it.

Sam appreciated the bigger picture and realized that while the Boardwalk was not as nice as where he came from, it was better than where he could be. Sam's move was out of desperation, and he acknowledged that when he said, "Hard times make a monkey eat hot peppers." Such hard times brought Sam and Justine to the motel despite its reputation.

One day, Sam explained the mindset that he brought to his search for housing and how he prepared himself to deal with certain situations:

Chris, when you're in the elements, you gotta think about survival. People don't think about that. Sam, I'm put you next door to this guy, he's a good guy but he hurts people. That's the only room I got available. Chris, the wind howlin', got snow on the ground, where am I gonna go, Chris? But I got enough money to pay for this month. I'll worry about next month when it comes. I can either go back out there in the snow and cold and keep trying to find a place or I can live next door to the murderer. I'll take my chances, I'm a military guy, I'll take my chances. He a murderer, he did his time, he's out. See what I'm sayin', I have to look at the whole picture. He ain't hurt nobody lately. He's got a swastika on his goddamn arm and chest, I don't think I wanna live right next door to him, but you know, to get out the cold so.

When he finally arrived at the Boardwalk, he was not placed next to a murderer but still had to reconcile with living near registered sex offenders:

We came here, you know, Miss Elizabeth told me we got a room. She told me you know, we got pedophiles here, can't have no kids, she explained some a da rules, I said okay. My girl's like, wow, Sam, says whatchu wanna do, honey? I say, baby, we can take it for now, hopefully we be outta here in a month or two.

Stepping down was a marker of residential instability because it was usually the result of being pushed from a previous environment rather than being allured by the motel. Ed and I sat outside drinking beers one day and I asked him what he thought of it. He touched his long hair and mused, "It's a dump, no room service or anything, no maids." Before Ed came to the motel, his caseworker placed him at a boarding house in Riverfort. When I asked why he left, he raised his beer and said, "This, they didn't allow drinking. But I drank anyway. They have rats, other people who live there, tell the manager what's going on." Ed did not plan on staying at the motel long and found its location somewhat inconvenient. "I've got a, all my business and stuff is in the city, you know. So I gotta walk half a fuckin' mile down there to get the bus stop and half an hour on the bus, you know, pain in the ass."

The young couple Elisha and Avery lived in an apartment rented by Avery's parents, but fights between them and Elisha made the situation untenable. The two moved out and decided on the Boardwalk at the recommendation of a friend. When asked what he thought of the move, Avery shrugged and said, "It's not what I'm used to. I stick to myself, make sure my room is clean so I got that." In a strange twist of circumstance, Elisha's parents and her brother, Clive, moved into the motel in the winter after Elisha and Avery had left. Clive told me that his father had lost his welding job, and he justified their presence at the motel by saying, "We're tight on money, that's the only reason we're living here." The need for Clive to provide a reason for living at the Boardwalk spoke to his view that the motel was a step down.

Many residents moved to the Boardwalk from other motels or hotels. Patch was staying at a motel used by DSS as an emergency shelter when he was kicked out for having a woman in his room. This violated his parole conditions as well as the emergency housing stipulations provided by DSS. HATAS then placed him at the Boardwalk, where Tat and I encountered him the night he arrived. Patch was on the phone with HATAS trying to get moved because he felt the Boardwalk was an obvious step down. He explained his situation to us:

> But they fuckin' kicked me, I was fuckin' right down there, man, in this nice ho-fuckin' hotel, man. Fuckin' kicked me out, man. I'm tryin' to call HATAS, man, so I can tell these motherfuckers, that I'm, that I'm here. That's there's mice and all this shit up in here so they can move me the fuck outta here. I had it good down in that hotel, man. I had it fucking good down there, man.

Roy and his girlfriend arrived at the Boardwalk from a motel on Main Street closer to Riverfort. They spent several days at that motel but ended up moving to the Boardwalk because Roy could not justify paying $250 a week. "It was too much, and it was too small. It was okay for a day or two, but not a week."

Many residents migrated from the Save More Inn, only a hundred yards away on Main Street. Jake lived at the Save More and met Reg and Sky through work at KFC. They talked Jake into moving to the Boardwalk to be closer to them and to save $20 a week in rent. While at the Save More, Jake had a brand new mattress, box spring, and air conditioner. He told me, "They actually keep the place up around there. It's nicer than it is here." Jake chose to move to the Boardwalk, but it was a step down because the Save More offered better living conditions.

Other residents viewed the Save More as more reputable because of its clientele. Reg said, "It's family oriented. They don't house no fricken pedophiles. . . . Yeah, they're decent down there, good people." He and Sky lived there for four months before moving to the Boardwalk. They were pushed out of the Save More because the owners found out about Reg's sex-offender status, which is somewhat ironic given Reg's earlier statement. As Sky told me, "Then they found out about Reg's thing. We don't house that type of people here." They were not able to get the money together for an apartment so they moved into the Boardwalk.[17]

Love and her son, Ben, arrived at the Boardwalk from the Save More in late May with their belongings piled in the back of a red pickup truck. When Love moved in she was immediately put off by the conditions, which she claimed were worse than the Save More. She complained to Larry, who then vented to Spike and me:

This room is clean, there's nothing wrong with it! Where the fuck am I gonna get curtains from? It is what it is, they're all nasty! Motherfucker, she says, it's worse. How could it be worse? I cleaned every fucking thing. I tried to be nice to her. I said, I'm sorry, I was, I got a little upset. Then I asked her, I said is this better than that other place? No, it's worse. Well then move the fuck back then!

Vito and Slash lived at the Save More Inn with Vito's sister. However, when unspecified consequences of the sister's drug addiction led to them losing their room, Vito and Slash moved into the Boardwalk.[18] Ramòn and his girlfriend lived at the Save More before coming to the Boardwalk, and he told me, "Honestly, we only left, whatever the case 'cause the room we were in at that time had an issue. They didn't have another room for us and they said you can come back in like a week. But we didn't have nowhere to go so we came here." Like Clive, Ramòn felt the need to justify why they came to the Boardwalk.

The concept of having "nowhere to go" requires some elaboration. Terri Lewinson, June Hopps, and Patricia Reeves call the similar emotional struggle among residents of a higher-tier extended-stay motel "liminal living."[19] While Boardwalk residents who stepped down sometimes did have other places to go, these options were viewed as so undesirable or unacceptable that, essentially, they felt they had no other option. Unmarried couples without children who went to DSS faced the prospect of being sent to separate shelters. The few residents with cars could have lived out of their vehicles, but that was hardly a stable situation. Those who stepped down viewed the Boardwalk as the one place to "flop" (or sleep) that was not on the streets.[20] Jake and Sky acknowledged this one day as we sat outside and Jake muttered, "This place sucks." Sky nodded solemnly and said, "But if you got no money and no place to go." Sam summed it up when he ranted, "This is like the last stop motel, it really is. This is one fucking stop from the hell hole. They either fight to get back up on your feet or you get sucked down here."

HISTORIES OF TRANSIENCE

The path to the motel for many refugees was not a simple A to B movement. Instead, residents arrived at the motel after pinballing around a variety of housing locations. The push factors that led residents to the Boardwalk from their previous environments were only the most recent destabilizing events in what were often long histories of transience. When I asked residents what brought them to the Boardwalk, some chose answers that masked previous bouts of residential instability. For example, Vito and Reg both told me that they used to live in apartments of their own. It was only after getting to know them that I learned that they came from the Save More Inn. These attempts to hide the past speak to the presentation of self. Living in one motel could be presented as the result of bad luck, but a history of living in motels was harder to publicly justify. Therefore to understand how living in the Boardwalk influenced resident behavior, it is important to dive deeper into their transient lives.

Some residents offered me detailed glimpses into the histories of homelessness that preceded their arrival at the Boardwalk. Trim, the tattooed construction worker, mentioned that he had lived in a tent in Las Vegas several years prior; Cinque alluded to living in a shelter and other motels during a prior release on parole. Burt had a history of living in shelters through DSS and bounced between them because he could stay in each for only thirty days. He eventually moved around to different motels, including one that cost $88 a week where he killed twelve to fifteen roaches a day and heard rats gnawing under the floorboards. He commented, "It was just, uh, it was the worst of the worst." Roy had experience living in shelters in Alabama and described them as very unpleasant:

> Down South it was hurrrrible. If you go to any other state but New York you will hate how they treat you. Breakfast at 4:45 AM, they said you eat breakfast and go find a job at 5:30 in the morning. What's open at 5:30 in the morning? I started watching to see where everyone was going, they were going to the beverage store, oh, I'm just trying to get some change for some beer. At 5:30 in the fucking morning?! Oh no.[21]

Sky's friend Fran had an incredibly traumatic experience in a motel. Her husband passed away from an illness while they were both staying in the room. Fran told me, "After my husband died, that killed me, 'cause he died in the motel room we were staying in. And I had to go back to the motel room and sleep in the same bed we slept in." She worked at Burger King at the time and her coworkers told her to take time off, but she did not want to sit in the room all day.[22]

Staying with friends was a common living situation in the histories of motel residents. Biggie and Deirdre lived in the Save More Inn and then the Boardwalk before moving out to a friend's place in a rough section of downtown Riverfort. One night Biggie took the time to reflect on their relationship while he watched Deirdre sleep and decided, "We goin' back to the hotel." Larry was staying with a friend who rented an apartment in Riverfort, but Larry got the feeling that the landlord did not want two people staying there or wanted more money. He then moved in with another friend and stayed for a couple months before it became stressful: "After that, you know, it was just kinda like, he really didn't want me there. He kept sayin', this is a temporary thing. I said, if you don't want me here just tell me, 'cause there's nothing worse than not being wanted someplace, you know. So eventually I just got so tired of it, I left." From there, Larry lived out of his car and then moved to the Boardwalk.

Other residents stayed at numerous hotels or motels before set-
tling at the Boardwalk. Roy and his girlfriend lived at the Park Place
because it charged only $150 a week (compared to $270 and $250
at other nearby motels). They stayed at the Park Place for three
months and the experience disgusted Roy:

> The Park Place would not pass inspection, someone needs to,
> you wanna tell somebody, tell 'em about the owner, man, he is
> an asshole. Go into the office, the blue thing, oh my god, the
> piss, the funk, the gnats. Elizabeth in the office, she had noth-
> ing to offer. I ask her, how is this a motel? She said, we don't
> care about this motel, this is a pedophile area. I'm a tell you
> something, Chris, the worst three, four months of my life were
> at the Park Place.

They moved out and lived at a similar motel several miles down the
road for several days before turning to the Boardwalk for a cheaper
room.

Jake had a particularly chaotic and extended history of transience
that involved motels and rooming houses. It began by moving into
his sister's house after his father passed away:

> Then time and time and time went on, I was stayin' there. And
> then okay fine, I went back to Lincolnburg, got in a roomin'
> house there. That's when I met Jelly, and we got an apartment
> together, and that was goin' good. But, not good but. Jelly
> moved out and I took the apartment over, then, I can't really
> fuckin' do this by myself, so I ended up in Westford. In a nice
> fuckin' roomin' house, fuckin' all brand new shit, you know,
> um. Ninety bucks a week for a fuckin' two-room deal. Had
> like a little room, my bedroom and shit. The thing is, it was
> like all past GE and shit and there's like no bus that runs out
> there so it's like a half hour bike ride to get down to the city
> and in the winter time I can't fucking do that so I had to move
> back in with Jelly after his friend Dave moved out. And then
> he fucking wasn't, you know, like payin' his part of the shit
> and whatever.

And uh, I went to sister's house for Thanksgiving, for like fuckin' three days and then I came back and he's like, well, I'm runnin' power offa the people upstairs off their fuckin' box down in the basement. And I'm like, and obviously of course the landlord had to come for something and fuckin' see that shit. And fuckin' I'm like, dude. And then we fuckin' stay at his sister's house, fuckin', um, Snyder's Lake, and then her daughters, his sister's daughters came home from college and shit.

I had to come back to my fuckin' sister's house. And then I ended up down there at Save More for a while after I stayed there for a while. And then I went back to their house. Then I came here [the Boardwalk] for a week. Then I left again and went back down there [his sister's]. Then I went to the guy that owns fuckin' Lucky Club [a strip club] up there, he got those fuckin' rooms and shit. And I was fuckin' up there for a while for a week. Then back down to their house [his sister's].

Jake moved back to the Save More and was living there when he met Reg and Sky.

Reg and his partner Sky had an equally intense transient history. As Reg put it, "Me and her have been through hell and back, six fuckin' years." Sky met Reg in September 2006 at a soup kitchen near the town of Derby, about an hour north of Riverfort. She was living in low-income housing with her brother and Fran. Reg had been living with his cousin and Sky was in an abusive relationship. Sky told me:

I met him [Reg] at a soup kitchen in Derby. He heard from, 'cause I was hangin' out with his cousin at the time and I didn't know it was his cousin. And he had told him that my ex-boyfriend was beatin' the shit outta me. And so he would go to the soup kitchen every day waiting for he and I to show up. He didn't know who it was, all he heard was a woman was being beaten. He beat the crap outta him.

Reg claimed that Sky was mad initially, but they got drunk together, hooked up the next day, and had been together ever since. Sky said:

First night we hung out we stayed up 'til like four or five in the morning just talking and watching cartoons. Then Fran and my brother got in a fight, she tried to kill herself, she slit her wrist with a, a broken liquor bottle. So I had to leave and DSS put me up in a motel for the weekend 'til Monday when I could go get DSS and find somewhere to go. But by then everything was all said and done at Fran's house and Reg ended up comin' stayin' with me in the motel room and I stayed another week in a room down the way where his cousin was stayin' with him.

Sky then got fired from her job at Giant Foods in Derby and she and Reg spent several months living out of a small red convertible, then a Ford Contour, and then a minivan with a mattress in the back.[23] A friend of theirs owned some property, so they drove the van onto the property and parked in an area with trees overnight. As Sky put it, "All we had to do was go outta there and two minutes down the road was Stewart's [a convenience store] so I could get up and go pee in the mornin."

When I asked where they ate she said, "We were goin' to like um, free places, free lunch places, he still had food stamps at that point. So we were able to eat, but, when it came to getting money for cigarettes or his alcohol, it was just nonexistent." They also perfected small scams to get free food from places like Taco Bell, and Sky proudly told me, "We'd tell 'em we came through, something was wrong and they'd replace the order. We got 10 soft-shell tacos outta Taco Bell one time."

After three years together, Sky and Reg moved to an apartment north of Pinewood. One night Sky and Reg were sitting in the living room and a woman drove a pickup truck through their wall. Given their proximity to the crash, they were lucky not to be injured. With the apartment uninhabitable, they moved in with Sky's mother. This situation turned sour when Reg accused her of stealing $1,500 from him. He told me, "I ended up going outside and broke the fuckin' windshield on the fuckin' car. You wanna cost me that money? Now take that money and spend it on a new windshield. At least I know where it's going now." Sky's mother then kicked them out of the house and they were forced to live on her porch. Reg recalled:

We weren't even stayin' in the house dude, we were sleeping on her porch. I'd sit in the kitchen to drink and eat and I'd use her bathroom to shower and shit. I stayed on. A. Porch. We lived. On. A. Porch. Not a room. And I'm still handing you a hundred a week, that's how we get done dirty and I loan you a shit ton of money and then you fuckin' play us again after you stole from me. That's why I had so much animosity towards her mom, me and her mom we do not see eye to man.

They then moved in with Reg's uncle, who Sky referred to as a "crackhead." Sky complained, "You know how many times people tried to break into my bedroom? With me in there?" Soon after moving in, Sky got transferred to the KFC on Main Street near the Boardwalk. Given the situation with Reg's uncle, they moved into the Save More, which allowed Sky to be closer to work.[24] After four months the owners of the Save More found out about Reg's sexual offense and told them to leave, at which point they moved to the Boardwalk.

BIOGRAPHICAL DETERMINANTS OF FRAGILITY

What can explain this glut of transient experiences among motel residents? In many cases, episodes of transience were influenced by cascading events that increased fragility. Fragility is the lack of material goods and social capital that left residents vulnerable to unexpected or self-inflicted disruptions to short- and long-term goals.[25] Residents faced a cacophony of self-inflicted and unexpected life experiences that disrupted their goals to the point where transience became almost inevitable. In this section I will explore the biographical factors that residents presented as context for their lives as social refugees.

Traumatic Experiences

Many residents were scarred by traumatic experiences that occurred in childhood and adulthood. In several instances the loss of family was a significant catalyst for residential displacement. Roy was living in Alabama when his father fell ill back in Riverfort: "My dad got sick in July, August of last year, they gave him twenty-four hours to live, man. He ended up dying six months later. But my dad got sick and I was like, I'm gonna go see my dad."

Roy's father lived with a female partner, and Roy and his girlfriend stayed with them when they moved back to Riverfort. When Roy's father passed, the woman kicked Roy and his girlfriend out of the house: "Auntie came and got me. I'm not going to no shelter, we was broke." That displacement began the Riverfort-based transient careers that eventually brought Roy and his girlfriend to the Boardwalk.

Jake's biological father died when Jake was four months old. The man who then took on the role of Jake's father was killed in a violent crime a few years before I met Jake. We were enjoying beers out in the parking lot one day in May when he explicitly stated that his homelessness began "when that dumb fuckin' nigger killed my father." I asked if he could elaborate on what happened and he said:

The old man, he was murdered by the fuckin' two-bit nigger next door. I was at work that night. The fuckin' cops came and got me, you gotta come wid us. I'm like, what? And then I go down there and oh yeah, he was killed and shit. And then fuckin', well, he walked away scot free. 'Cause they were sayin' that I let 'em in the fuckin' house and it's fuckin' three against one. And I'm like, fucking, well, well, what? I'm not goin' to fuckin' jail for fuckin' shit I didn't do. So I'm like fine! I assume if I go along with them, fine, he's gonna get his fucking ass locked up for the rest of his fuckin' life. So I did that. And then, I got dragged through the mud and he fuckin' walked away scot free. Oh yeah, we knew him. He lived right next door and we fuckin' hung out with him and shit. One I day I went to work, and that's what fuckin' happened. And fuckin'. And now I'm fuckin' not happy.

Jake threw his beer on the ground and stormed inside his room. Reg came out and asked, "What's Jake's deal?" Sky shrugged and said, "I dunno, he started, I guess he talked to Chris about the guy who killed his dad and now he's in a bad mood." Given Jake's and Sky's reactions, I was inclined to take Jake at his word.

Reg lost both his parents due to illness, and that experience along with other events turned his life upside down. Prior to the terrorist attacks of September 11, 2001, Reg and his parents spent three years working up and down the East Coast running a traveling carnival. According to Reg, his parents purchased several game booths and then took ownership over a carnival that was already in existence. Some of his duties included assembling booths and attractions, including the Ferris wheel. After the attacks, attendance at the carnival dipped to the point where his parents were forced to sell $500,000 worth of equipment for $150,000 to pay their crew of workers, draining their savings in the process. Shortly after, Reg's father died of cancer and his mother passed away after a stroke. Losing his parents had a profound effect on Reg, and he took the holidays particularly hard. He hated St. Patrick's Day because it was his mother's birthday, and he felt the same about Christmas and Thanksgiving "because it's all about family. What kind of family I got?" Reg kept several mementos in his motel room that reminded him of his mother, including a pumpkin craft that she made for him on Halloween when he was six, as well as a blue angel that he brought to her in the hospital before her death.

Biggie's parents were still alive, but for all intents and purposes he lost them during a tumultuous childhood filled with abuse. One summer day Biggie recalled details about his upbringing. Usually loud and animated, he got very quiet as he told me about these experiences. He grew up in the South, and when he was two years old his family moved to Riverfort because his father got a job at a meat plant. His mother moved out when Biggie was seven years old because of domestic violence. "My dad used to beat the crap out of my mom and he used to beat me too. His favorite thing was an extension cord."

There were also several instances of sexual abuse in Biggie's childhood. Shortly after his family moved to Riverfort, an uncle moved in with them and molested Biggie until he turned thirteen. At age eight he witnessed what he thought was a case of sexual abuse at the hands of his brother:

> Going back to my childhood though, I was more depressed
> than anything else. One day I'm out playing baseball, I'm eight,

my mom had just left. Out there playing baseball, uncle just beaten, molested me the weekend before. Best friend said, we need something to drink, we need some water. I go and go to get water and my brother's at home. Knock on the door, what's taking so long? A little girl come to the door, no older than four. What you doing? I'm playing house. You know how old she is? I put the little girl out, told her never come back. I never told her parents, I never told anyone though, just she was okay.

Biggie also claimed that he was molested by a female cousin at age fourteen.[26] He reflected that these early experiences were certainly not what he envisioned for himself when he was younger: "I used to have dreams, dreams of getting married, having kids going to college, a wife staying at home, a good job. I used to dream about bein' a bus driver." He claimed that the abuse he suffered in his childhood led to the development of multiple personalities. While I never saw evidence of this, I noticed that his moods often swung quite drastically, and he received disability payments for reasons that he did not share.

Darryl also endured traumatic abuse in his childhood. We were talking about his community involvement with Narcotics Anonymous (NA), and Darryl mentioned that he enjoyed speaking about his past in NA because, "By doing your story over and over again to different groups, it gives you a chance to . . . 'cause like sometimes, alright, like." He shifted in his seat and sat silent for several seconds before he continued:

All right. I got molested when I was eight years old. All right, and, it was kind of my fault, because I forced my parents into putting me into Cub Scouts because I was a sick kid alright [meaning he was put in Cub Scouts because of his misbehavior and was subsequently molested there]. I've gotten over that. That really doesn't affect me anymore. But what I haven't gotten over and what I still have an issue with, is that when I told my parents after three months, my parents said to me, see, that's what you get.[27]

These traumatic experiences increased residents' fragility in profound ways. In the case of Roy, Jake, and Reg, their experiences affected their transience because they lost their housing as well as emotional connections. These causal episodes speak to the precarious social situations of the residents; for individuals with established independent households, the loss of a parent does not cause a loss of housing. Biggie and Darryl experienced abuse in their adolescence at the hands of authority figures, which may have affected their ability to relate to authority figures (particularly in the social service and criminal justice systems) that they encountered later in life. Darryl even convinced himself that the abuse was his fault. Clearly the impacts of the abuse were long lasting. At the very least, the events damaged their relationships with their parents, who otherwise could have played nurturing and supportive roles during their upbringing.

Substance Abuse

Residents arrived with significant histories of substance abuse, and the use of alcohol, marijuana, and other drugs such as cocaine and opiates was rampant at the motel.[28] As Ed mentioned earlier, alcoholism led to his removal from his previous living situation, and he took Ambien and Xanax for years. He was often seen at the Boardwalk crushing and snorting these pills. Curtis, the skinny resident who others called "tweaker," had worked in construction for seven years before he started using LSD and told me, "My brain fizzled out, on acid. Too much acid." Elisha's brother Clive was on probation for four years because of drugs but still smoked marijuana with Reg and others. Biggie was also an avid user of marijuana and referred to it as his "medicine." His partner Deirdre did not allow him to use harder drugs because she had lost family members to overdoses of cocaine and heroin. Marc, Reg, and Jake had histories of using crack/cocaine and a variety of pills. Rob regularly inhaled the aerosol from whipped cream canisters and was yelled at many times by Larry and Elizabeth for filling his room with empty cans.

Some residents attributed their drug use to specific incidents. Roy linked the start of his drug use to his father's death: "I love my daddy so much, when he died, I did drugs, I kinda went into the

Devil's web. My dad died, it was um, I was sad for just weeks, sit at home and eat, do drugs, shit I normally wouldn't do." Dale, a registered sex offender who served as an army nurse for twelve years and was involved in the first Gulf War, claimed that his military experience led him to alcohol abuse: "I used to drink three liters of whiskey a day, was in a blackout twenty-four hours a day man. Drivin' around, so glad I didn't kill somebody. I came home from the service in October, at 200 pounds. That next February, I was admitted to the VA at 98 pounds. Just drinking, I went crazy, PTSD, I just wanted to die."[29] Being on parole meant that Dale could not drink alcohol, but after five DWIs and his VA experiences, he had no interest in drinking anyway and steadfastly turned down alcohol whenever it was offered.

Elizabeth's daughter, Natalie, fought a battle with pill addiction for more than twenty years. Before working at the motel, she was a nurse in a doctor's office and was fired for writing fake checks to fund her addiction. This prevented her from getting future employment in medical environments, so she moved into a room at the Boardwalk and began working at the desk and cleaning rooms. After getting caught stealing from the motel office in October, she found a job at Bruegger's Bagels as a cashier. I saw her in March 2013 after she had been working there for five months. She seemed determined to keep working and told me, "I can't afford to fuck up. 'Cause jobs are just too hard to come by and it took me a while to get that shit place!" When I asked about the temptation to steal, she said, "There are a thousand cameras and if you do anything there you are the most retarded person." She celebrated her job: "This is the longest I ever went, not pattin' myself on the back, but since I lost my other career, I've had these little bullshit jobs. Dude, I'd last maybe a month or two, you know? I haven't missed a day yet, and that's a record for me."

Unfortunately, she was fired in fall 2013 for stealing money from the register. This most recent relapse wore on Elizabeth, who vented her frustration to me one day:

You're better than this, you did have a good job, you are, you're not a dummy, you're smart, alright, now you got a job. It's beneath you, you're not makin' six hundred a week, you're makin' two. But they put your trust in you, but you're not gonna outsmart anybody. Come on, knock it off with that shit. So she had a job, and what did she do? Of all stupid places. You're not smarter, Natalie, they got all the fuckin' cameras. I don't know what to say, I can't say I know how it feels, I know you're in pain, but then. You can't do what you're doin'. She won't wanna go to rehab 'cause she's scared of the pain of withdrawal.

Unfortunately for Natalie, even though she realized that trying to steal from Bruegger's was a losing endeavor, she could not help herself.

Toby and Dee were recovering, respectively, from alcoholism and heroin/cocaine addiction. They drank copious amounts of coffee because, as Dee put it, "We're both ex-drinkers, ex-alcoholics. So we covered it up with coffee." When I spoke to Dee about her history, she painted a complex picture of drug addiction, prostitution, and transient life. In her eyes, drug addiction led directly to her work as a prostitute:

> It was always to get drugs. Because you knew it's only an hour of my time or whatever. Close my eyes and get it done and over with. I rarely fucked people though, I'd give a thousand blowjobs, but rarely fucked somebody. You know, I wasn't the hundred dollar whore. I did turn into one, you know, in a bind, like, when I was all cracked out and shit like, okay, let's go do this, just get it over with, 'cause I wanted my drugs and I wanted 'em now.

The need for a location to turn tricks and then subsequently use drugs led Dee to lodging locations that included the Boardwalk Motel:

> I had an apartment in Ash Lake, which is fuckin' like an hour from here. And I would get in my car and drive. My dealer was in downtown Pinewood, so I would drive like an hour, hour and twenty minutes, three times a day sometimes, to come and get my shit, yeah. Or I would, I would have my own apartment but I'd stay in the motel 'cause I knew I wouldn't have gas. Because

all my money needed to go on drugs. I would have the guy get the room, and then I'd be like, um, are you using this room? You don't need this room, do you? And then I'll keep it, I'll just stay here. Or, I'll just take a shower, you gotta go, don't you? You know, little tricks to keep the room wherever I was, you know.

But yeah, for actual sex, I kinda held onto that, thank God. Not to say it never happened. In the beginning it happened a lot. 'Cause I was, uh, supporting myself single, on crack. So, I was suckin' and fuckin' everything that came near me. But always for hundreds of dollars. You know? 'Cause I'd have to stay to smoke crack at the Hilton. I wasn't smoking crack here. You know? I wouldn't do a show here, which turned into, I would never party here, or I'll do a show here but I'll never party here. Which turned into, well, I'll party and do a show here but I'll never live here. Which turned into, this is home.

Because drug use was so rampant at the motel, some recovering residents were quite concerned about relapsing. Drug and alcohol use were a key part of the motel's culture. I forged inroads with residents early on by sharing beer, and I was told on several occasions that establishing relationships at the motel was always easier when alcohol was involved. For recovering addicts placed at the motel by social services, or those who migrated there with plans to improve their lives, the fact that substances were used as social currency proved problematic, and they had to remind themselves constantly of their long-term goals.

The tattooed Trim dealt drugs for five years in Las Vegas; Sam had used crack in the past and was trying to wean himself off a ten-year smoking habit at Justine's request. In September Sam and Trim sat outside and discussed the drug use of others in the motel:

SAM: I was peekin' in the room last night and they were sniffing stuff that the guy from 23 gave them.
TRIM: I told them I had pot for sale but they didn't want it. I'm so used to seein' that shit it doesn't even bother me anymore. That's how we used to be years ago.
SAM: That's how I used to be, I used to be just like that.

TRIM: I just look at them like their fuckin' . . . that was me about twenty years ago. Now I got too much goin' for myself I just can't put myself in that predicament. My girl's comin' up, my son's comin' up. They be here next, uh, Wednesday. Then I gotta move outta here.

SAM: We moving out too.

TRIM: Yeah, I gotta move on with my life.

SAM: That's what we doing too, it be too long.

TRIM: When they start fuckin' callin' ya by name and wantin' to hang out with ya, even though you don't do no shit, man, you know it's time to go.

SAM: Same thing with me, same thing with me. I don't carry all these keychains for nothing [meaning those from Narcotics Anonymous]. I don't knock my friends, that's what they do, but I chose another path I wanna be on, man. My girl the same way, we make a good combination 'cause for so many years, she tried to get me to stop, Chris, and I wouldn't. I had to smoke weed, I had to have cocaine, I had to have a beer. And I worked my ass off and she still didn't do nothing, didn't even smoke a cigarette. She watched me spiral out of control 'til I went to prison. And she still hung with me, she still stuck it out with me. Today we laugh, 'cause now I can see what she was tryin' to get. I wish I had been much smarter then, but as men we macho, we don't want to see that. Shut the fuck up, don't tell me I can't have another beer, then I go out and buy another twelve pack, just to make her mad.

TRIM: You can't have no more cocaine, I go out and buy another eight ball.

SAM: And all they tryin' to do is help us, trying to keep us alive.

Both Sam and Trim were over fifty, and their age helped them avoid relapses in that they viewed themselves as qualitatively different from the younger drug users at the motel. Sam's connection to his partner Justine and his desire to find employment in order to move on were strong motivators in overcoming the temptations of the motel. Similarly, Trim focused on the future with his partner and son to avoid relapsing. Criminologists Robert Sampson and John Laub argue that strong adult social bonds inhibit criminal behavior, and in the case of Trim and Sam their attachment to their partners and children played a strong role in their desistance from drug use.[30] What also separated Sam's and Trim's lives from those of other couples at the motel, such as Reg and Sky and Dee and Toby, was that their partners did not live at the motel with them. For Sam and Trim, their partners represented stability and escape from the motel that was within reach if they could stay clean, whereas couples at the motel were in many ways trapped there together.

The "anything goes" atmosphere of the motel made it very easy for residents to find and use substances. For residents like Sam, Dale, and Trim, their histories of drug abuse made the motel treacherous because they were surrounded by temptation. However, they learned from their pasts in order to plan for their futures and avoid relapse. Others, such as Dee, Reg, Jake, Natalie, Marc, and Ed, continued to let drugs reign over certain aspects of their lives, sapping their resources and increasing their fragility in the process.

Criminal Behavior

Part of the Boardwalk's unsavory reputation in the community came from the fact that the motel housed individuals returning from prison. However, these individuals were not the only residents with criminal histories. Early involvement in crime was a common theme at the motel. After his father pulled a gun on him at age fifteen, Biggie grabbed a shotgun and told him, "That's the last time you pull a switch on me, a gun on me, next time I'll shoot you." Already scarred by abuse, Biggie left his home and ventured to downtown Riverfort in search of his mother. He found her working as a housekeeper at a local hospital, but she wanted nothing to do with him. Biggie then found solace with other youth from broken homes. "I hung out with anyone who could get me beer, drugs, and cigs. Because we come from broken families, none of us had parents, more like showing the parents that kids coming from broken homes didn't need parents." Biggie referred to this group as a gang and claimed that together they stole, used and sold drugs, and slept in shelters and abandoned buildings. Biggie also alluded to serving time in jail because of this but would not elaborate.

Love's son, Ben, was involved with drug dealing that led directly to Ben's residence at the motel. He lived in an apartment that his girlfriend Lisa rented with DSS assistance, but then he was caught selling marijuana. Ben went to jail and Lisa was sanctioned by DSS for having drugs in the apartment. When Ben returned from jail, he and Lisa moved in with Love at the Boardwalk because they had no other options.

Dee's criminal history involved shoplifting and working as a prostitute. Her involvement with prostitution led to both unexpected benefits and strain with Toby when Dee formed a strong bond with a client named Guy:

> We went down to shelters, like he [Toby] lived in a shelter, I lived in a shelter, you know? I didn't stay, I didn't stay, 'cause I had Guy. I only did it 'cause Toby was like, well how I come gotta stay in a shelter and you get to stay with Guy? So I was like, it was, either break away from Guy and go live in a shelter. Or, fuckin' lose your relationship with Toby. Bottom line is he could not stand the fact that I had a place to go. Which pissed me off, because again, I'm a girl. Why do you want your woman in a fuckin' shelter? You fucking scumhole. Especially 'cause Guy was bringin' me downtown every day to see Toby. And I would see Toby between, like I dunno, 6 and 8, and then I'd have, and then Guy would come back down and pick me up. 'Cause Guy knew Toby was number one. And even with that, Toby was jealous.

Once Dee and Toby moved into the motel, Guy played an important role in their lives, as Dee told me, "Guy's paid our rent, maybe twelve times, twelve weeks. But that's a lot and especially when we need it, he has helped us." I asked if her continuing relationship with Guy at the motel was a problem with Toby and she replied:

> Toby just doesn't care, as with any of my mates, has ever cared, as long as them bills get paid. You know, once they see the

money, and what, they gotta deal with Guy for a couple minutes out of a day? They don't give a fuck, you know, what the
fuck you do. If you live with me and you get to know me, then
you know where my virtue is. One, I'm not gonna tell you,
I'm gonna convince you that I'm not fuckin' him. Or two, I'm
gonna tell you and you're gonna deal with it. It depends on
what kinda relationship, ya know?

However, prostitution did place Dee in a significant amount of
danger. In 2011 she was living in the Boardwalk and was called out
to do a show:

I was actually living here and I went out and I didn't wanna
do the show. A girl, like crackhead, woke me up early in the
morning and, like, I was quitting crack and I didn't wanna
do the show. So I went there and I was like tryin' to get the
show goin' so I could come fuckin' home and I'd have a couple
hundred bucks in my pocket, or at least a hundred. Ended up
turning into just a crack show, so he'd give me crack as my
payment, and then I was like, well, gimme my payment so I
can leave. Which turned into, I'll get more crack, so I stayed.
Every time I wanted to leave it was, I'll buy more crack. Which
turned into cocaine psychosis, after you smoke awhile the guy
thought I was fuckin' robbing him, and just beat me fucking
blind, but I kept fighting back.
      So he held me in there for like, five hours. I ended up scream-
ing at the top a my lungs, the police came, I was taken in an
ambulance. Then I remember the police officer at the scene
asking me, are you working? And I was like, yeah. And so, it's
not like they met me at the hospital. They just, brushed it off, or
I don't even know if the guy was charged. You know, and I was
bringing it up in groups and stuff, and it was like, they passed
that crack pipe by me once, no. This is a crack pipe we're talkin'
about, I'm a crack addict! Pass it around twice, no! And the
third time that sucker came around, I don't think it got all the
way to me and I had it in my mouth. I was like, fuck, yeah, let's
go! Um, but, therapy, they were like, Dee, do you really wanna

bring this up and try and find this guy and drag it out and ask for the officer and press charges, or do you just wanna let this go? You're safe, you're not injured.

And then, you see on TV, like *Law and Order*, half the rapes, I wasn't raped, thank God. Thank f-, he wanted to rape me, bad. I just fought, I fought and I kicked and I fought and I punched. And the heaters that were on the floor, he tried yankin' out the cord. He was gonna whip me with it, so I fuckin' attacked him. It's like, there's no way you're getting that motherfuckin' cord outta the wall. You know, and uh, I had to be careful of the telephone, he busted it up. Thank God he didn't think to choke me. You know, but uh, let's see. That was really hard for me to get over.[31]

Many residents claimed that their criminal behaviors were the result of early experiences. They used early involvement in crime both as a status symbol and as a foundation for future behavior and identity creation. In many cases, such behavior was the reason (directly or indirectly) that residents arrived at the motel, and it continued once they got there. Some, like Cinque, could not resist going back to the drug game, and others, such as Darryl and Tat, were determined not to fall back on criminal enterprises. Residents shared narratives of either overcoming the allure of crime or relying on it. What is clear is that the criminal careers of residents were complex and intertwined with other life events (early childhood experiences, substance abuse) and the potent ways in which the motel environment encouraged a variety of behavior. Unfortunately, by bringing vulnerable individuals together without offering them any necessary supports, criminal justice and social welfare policies designed to correct or support had a hand in creating a criminogenic environment at the Boardwalk Motel. Sociologist Joan McCord and her colleagues refer to this as an "iatrogenic effect," an illness or condition introduced by medical treatment.[32] They examined a series of interventions for delinquent youth and found that some actually reinforced criminal behavior during peer aggregation of high-risk populations, due in part to the desire to impress peers through deviance.[33]

Disabilities

Many Boardwalk residents had mental and physical disabilities.[34] Some residents who were clearly suffering from mental disabilities chose not to participate in the research, so regrettably their experiences are not included here. Darryl's partner Digital found the motel to be better than a shelter because he had his own room and did not have to be around other people. When I asked why this was such a problem, he explained:

My um, I got this thing where, I get, I kept getting arrested, getting inta fights and stuff. Um, one day the judge was like, you know, he's like, somethin's wrong. He sent me to a psych evaluation and they came back with a diagnosis for me. And um, you know, I tried it for like about a month, the medication and stuff that they was givin' me. I'm like, I couldn't live like this, I couldn't do it. So I said screw it, I'm not gonna do it. I got in trouble a couple years later and it was suggested that I strongly give the treatment a try for six months.

I agreed, and um, during that six months you know, I found out a lotta stuff, that, 'cause they was tellin' me, and my pride was like, there ain't nuttin' wrong with me, I'm fine. Blah, blah, blah, blah, blah! And it turns out that all the problems I've been having were because of this same shit so. And one day my doctor's like, look. I told him, I said I can't keep takin' these medications. I'm 330 pounds, this shit got me fat. Every fuckin' three months you're switchin' medications on me, I'm takin' like four to six pills a day, I'm like, I don't wanna be on medication anymore. He said okay, he sent [me] to this um, group therapy program to learn copin' skills. He said, I'll make it so you won't be on medication, he said, but I don't want you working. He didn't want me in a small environment where I would have to be with other people. Otherwise I'll end up in jail again or back there again.

It's psychotic disorder NOS [not otherwise specified], um, but it has a, it comes with a buncha symptoms, and one of 'em bein' mostly is, um, antisocialism. I mean, you put me in a room by myself and give me a task, I'm fine, I can work all day long. Put other people and other personalities in that small space with me and, I, just. I can't function.

This condition was so severe that Digital received SSI compensation for an inability to work. Fortunately, he realized the scope of his condition and actively avoided any contact with other residents whenever possible. Other residents, such as the knife-carrying Nolan and the zombie-like Curtis, did not exercise this discretion and found themselves testing the patience of other residents.

Many residents claimed to be affected by posttraumatic stress disorder (PTSD). Dee claimed that her PTSD began when she went through basic training with the army and suffered "culture shock" during the training.[35] Ed never elaborated on how he developed PTSD but alluded to a career of military service and received disability. Darryl was beaten up and raped in prison because of his status as a sex offender. He also claimed that he was diagnosed as antisocial and bipolar, and when he was released in September he saw a psychiatrist in Riverfort on a weekly basis. By November he had stopped visiting the psychiatrist and told me it was because he simply did not have the time. "Parole wants me to look for jobs thirty-five hours a week." When I asked him about the treatment, he told me, "I mean it helped to a limited degree, I don't think much is gonna help me to a great degree to tell you the truth." Dale also discussed having PTSD and linked it to his battle with alcoholism after the first Gulf War.

Depressive disorders affected Dee, who claimed to be bipolar, and Fran, who told me that she had attempted suicide in the past by slicing her wrists and mixing antidepressants and alcohol. Fran described her first attempt to kill herself:

I looked at my mom. I'm like, I'm going to kill myself. I was seventeen at the time. She was like, go ahead, 'cause if you die I'm going to leave you on the floor. Without thinking I grabbed the bottle of Advil. It wasn't even open yet. Opened it, swallowed the entire bottle of pills. My mom left. Twenty minutes later, she comes back and says, are you dead yet? I go, no. And she goes, damn.

Fran's depression was so severe that she received disability and did not work anymore.

Remember that Biggie claimed enduring a history of abuse caused him to develop multiple personalities. He also told me that he had mental health problems for his entire life and showed me the scars on his wrists from past suicide attempts. Because of these issues, Biggie was involved with a program whose mission statement read: "Working collaboratively with individuals, families and the community Programs empowers and enables children and adults with neurologically based learning disabilities, autism and other developmental disorders to live independent, productive and fulfilling lives." The program gave Biggie a caseworker who visited Biggie and Deirdre at the motel and took them to programming and on errands, such as grocery shopping. Sometimes the program would also bring him food or Giant Foods gift cards.[36] Biggie did not particularly like his caseworker because he was always late for their appointments.

Like many residents, Biggie suffered from physical health problems. He had a history of heart attacks and had a large surgical scar running down the front of his chest. He tried to lose weight to take the pressure off his heart and told me, "My heart can't take no more stress, my mom already passed away and my dad's in the nursing home." His daily regimen of medication consisted of Nexium, Diovan, Aspirin, Lipitor, and Seroquel. Deirdre was on medication of her own for high blood pressure and had to limit her exposure to the sun because of the side effects.

Darryl suffered from a bad esophagus and had had two major surgeries to treat it. Doctors put a tube down his throat every eight months to stretch it out because it closed to the point where nothing could get past, making it impossible to eat. To deal with acid reflux, Darryl took a double dose of Nexium and a quadruple dose of Zantac every day. I once heard him on the phone with his caseworker, claiming that he sometimes threw up five to six times a day and could get the urge to throw up out of nowhere. Darryl showed me a form that his doctor filled out for DSS, which listed Darryl's ailments as back and stomach issues, with a recommendation that he be considered "permanently disabled."

Reg was also bothered by indigestion and claimed that he had acid pockets in this throat that needed to be popped on an infrequent basis. One of his personal remedies that I observed was mixing seltzer water with copious amounts of salt. He also received disability because of a physical condition that he said rendered him unable to work: "I was thirteen, walking across a railroad trestle. Needless to say, rotten railroad timber. Whooosh! Fell twenty feet to the concrete." As a result, Reg underwent three surgeries and had two metal rods inserted in his right arm. Both Reg and Sky also had poor dental hygiene. Sky blamed her mother, who wore dentures and never taught Sky how to brush her teeth. Reg had his teeth removed in early October 2012, and Sky had hers removed in summer 2013. They intended to get dentures once they had the funds but had not as of this writing.

Mental and physical afflictions contributed to vulnerability and fragility among residents. Those battling mental disorders faced thoughts of suicide, abused prescription drugs, and found it difficult to interact with other residents. When physical or mental issues made it impossible for residents to work, this hampered their ability to gain enough financial traction to improve their living situations and move out of the motel. Not surprisingly, the Boardwalk housed many residents with these issues because they could not afford more stable and expensive housing.

One overarching consequence of childhood trauma, criminal behavior, drug abuse, and mental health disorders was the loss of family and friends. On several occasions, residents asked me for favors because they had "no one else left to ask." This loss of social capital was particularly punishing because residents lost access to networks that might have provided valuable financial and social resources. Some residents had family they could count on (Jake and Larry spent time with their sisters, Sam often went into Riverfort to see his daughter, and Darryl visited his mother on a weekly basis), but these relationships were the exception and not the norm. Once family was lost, residents had a hard time connecting with individuals who might have served as surrogate family members and provided access to stable housing. Roy did not get along with the partner of his deceased father, and Reg had an incredibly strained relationship with Sky's mother.

The residents of the Boardwalk Motel were displaced from their previous environments because of a combination of factors, some within their control and some not, that affected their social status. Many residents revealed complex histories of fragility and transience. They were social refugees long before they set foot inside the Boardwalk. In the next chapter, I will examine how motel residents drew on their histories to create identities that managed the stigma of motel life.

3

Managing Stigma and Identity

It'd be so easy for me to get out, but I choose not to.
—Reg

Sociologist Erving Goffman describes stigma as "an attribute that is deeply discrediting" and argues that "we tend to impute a wide range of imperfections on the basis of the original one." When an individual is associated with a stigmatized person, this relationship "leads the wider society to treat both individuals in some respects as one." Goffman refers to this as a "courtesy stigma" or a stigma acquired simply by being associated with a stigmatized person.[1] The Dutchland community viewed motel residents as belonging to one or several devalued groups, such as drug addicts, drug sellers, prostitutes, child molesters, and welfare "queens." By virtue of simply living at the Boardwalk Motel, residents were easily viewed as fitting numerous stereotypes. In this instance, the courtesy stigma extended from the marginalized populations that the Boardwalk was known to serve to anyone who happened to be associated with the motel itself. These courtesy stigmas extended to residents regardless of their actual legal status or behavior and were seen as significant threats to self and identity.

In his study of Harlem crack dealers, sociologist Philippe Bourgois asserts that street culture "offers an alternative forum for autonomous personal dignity."[2] Residents at the Boardwalk Motel also created such a forum. In their search for personal dignity, they created identities in an attempt to overcome stigma and protect themselves against the discrediting attributes associated with the motel. This identity creation can be viewed as an act of resistance, or "active behavior, whether verbal, cognitive, or physical" in opposition to someone or something.[3] Sociologist Victor Rios notes that resistance as a response has the power to "radically alter worldviews and trajectories."[4] Therefore identity resistance at the motel was a valuable life strategy that allowed residents to preserve their dignity as they attempted to stabilize their lives.

A key part of this resistance among motel residents was the creation of identities that were based on those less or more stigmatized than them.[5] As sociologist Michèle Lamont argues, "Groups that find themselves in relatively similar structural positions can draw very different lines," and this "boundary work" creates symbolic divides within a community that on the surface seems quite homogenous.[6] Sociologist Lois Presser writes that "the self cannot be known without reference to other people."[7] At the Boardwalk, residents alleviated the harms of stigma by creating boundaries that referred to motel residents based on particular traits.

This chapter is concerned with how those in the Boardwalk Motel community used personal (or self-) narratives to resist the stigmas attached to them. When people present personal narratives, "what they emphasize and omit, their stance as protagonists or victims, the relationship the story establishes between teller and audience—all shape what individuals can claim of their own lives."[8] In this respect, "narratives (self-narratives) have an evaluative point to make about the self," and, more important, narratives allow individuals to paint pictures of themselves that they prefer to both see and be seen.[9] By presenting narratives of preferred self, residents created boundaries between themselves and other residents and resisted particular stigmas. I will begin by describing how residents resisted the stigma of criminal identities (particularly that associated with sexual offending) by creating boundaries between themselves and sexual predators. Then I will show how residents with criminal pasts used what criminologist Shadd Maruna calls "redemption scripts" to redefine their trajectories into those of desistance.[10]

RESISTANCE AGAINST CRIMINAL IDENTITIES

As illustrated in chapter 2, criminal histories were common among residents of the Boardwalk. In fact, jail and prison time were often celebrated as status symbols, and, as is often seen in certain sub-cultures, motel residents turned the middle-class stigma associated with criminal behavior and criminal histories on its head.[11] Just as in prison subculture, however, the one criminal behavior that drew disdain was sexual offending against children. Because many residents at the motel did not distinguish between types of sex offenders, a sex-offense conviction was automatically equated with victimization of a child. (Current criminal justice policy treats a wide variety of behaviors as sexual offenses, such as visiting or promoting a prostitute, consensual sex between teenagers, and exposing oneself in public).[12] Therefore parolees and those with sexual offense histories took different steps to resist the stigma of their offenses and create boundaries between themselves and the pedophile label.

Many sex offenders at the motel tried to resist their stigmatized identities by hiding them from others. Price, Dale, Jasper, Cinque, Walt, and Harry disclosed their status as parolees but hid their sex offense convictions. This is an example of what Goffman calls a "technique of informational control" that an "individual with a secret defect employs in managing crucial information about himself."[13] Unfortunately, because they were level 2 and 3 offenders, they were listed on the public sex offender registry, and therefore their attempts to conceal their stigma were neutralized because their convictions were visible to me and anyone at the motel with Internet access.

After Cinque moved in, I encountered Mike and Natalie looking up the registry on their cell phones as they sat outside the office. Mike looked at me, shook his phone, and said about Cinque, "It will tell you what level it is right here. There he is right there, mugshot right there. She was thirteen years old. That tells you everything right there, buddy." Natalie claimed that Cinque told her he was in prison for drugs and weapons charges and mentioned nothing about his sex-offense conviction.

Similarly, Reg attempted to hide his sex-offense conviction from other residents. He claimed that when he was eighteen, he and his good friend had consensual sex with a girl who was fifteen.[14] According to public records, he was charged with felony statutory rape and endangering the welfare of a child. He pleaded guilty to statutory rape and spent a year in jail and had to register as a level 1 sex offender. The girl later had a child by him, and for a time he viewed her as his "wife." Reg's sex-offender status made finding a residence quite difficult, and it was the factor that forced him and Sky to leave the Save More Inn. The task of hiding his status from those at the Boardwalk was made somewhat easier because he was only a level 1 offender and therefore not listed on the public registry. When Reg disclosed his conviction to me, he claimed that no one else at the motel knew about it. This turned out not to be the case, because Dee told me that she was aware of his status and said, "He thought it was this big secret." Vito told me that Elizabeth had outed Reg as a sex offender, though he admitted it was hard to believe. Elizabeth mocked Reg about his attempts to mask his status after he had moved out: "He's a sex offender, he tries to say he's not, he is. Stupid, a make fun a other ones, you're one yourself! 'Cause the guy [meaning a detective] comes around, you know he has a list a all the guys that are sex offenders. I dunno if he's a level 1 or 2, but anyway he is one, he tries to say he's not."[15] In a way, Reg's attempts to hide his status ended up directing more attention toward it when others found out.

In addition to trying to hide his sexual conviction, Reg created other boundaries to distance himself from other sexual offenders. Because his offense involved a girl he claimed was his girlfriend, he did not view himself as predatory and insisted that because the girl was fifteen he was not attracted to young children. In fact, he went out of his way to show his contempt for those he considered pedophiles and told me that he had no problem being violent toward the "sons a bitches who touched kids." When he returned from jail in April 2013, he talked about his experience working as a runner (bringing food from the kitchen to the cell blocks) and claimed, "So fricken, every fuckin', pedophile scumbag up in there dude, spittin' in their fuckin' trays, havin' fun wid 'em." He also explicitly referred to Darryl as "that fucking pedophile" on several occasions. Social psychologists refer to this type of behavior as "reaction formation," which can be described as a way of fighting off threats to self-esteem "by exhibiting an exaggerated or extreme reaction in the opposite direction."[16] Reg exhibited distaste for sexual offenders in the same way that social psychologists find that "people respond to the implication that they have some unacceptable trait by behaving in a way that would show them to have the opposite trait."[17]

Tat was the Dominican tattoo artist who arrived after Reg went to jail, and he took a different approach by disclosing his status as a sex offender. Hours after we had first met, we stood talking in the parking lot of the motel. I mentioned that the Boardwalk used to be a very nice place, and Tat claimed that it was before the motel started renting to sex offenders. He then said:

> Me, I'm a keep it a hundred [percent honest], I put it on first street. Me, when I was twenty-five, in 2005, when I was twenty-five, I fucked up and got drunk and had sex with an underage female. No, she wasn't my daughter, nope, she wasn't nobody in my family, ya understand me? It happened to be the neighbor's daughter's friend. Then I got home around two o'clock in the morning, drunk, hammered. And they come over. They're like, yo, can we drink wid you? I'm like, yeah sure! I went and grabbed a root beer, I said here, one for you, one for you. And I kept on drinkin' my rum and coke. They was like, nah we want a drink! I was like, nah, you ain't drinkin' wid me, nah, nah, no. I got crazy drunk.
>
> The mother, uh, the daughter of the, the lady from next door wound up leavin'. And she [the friend] throws her hand over me, and I'm like yo, give me a massage? Boom, she starts givin' me a massage. I just start takin' shit off. All the sudden, she started givin' me head. And then, she got on top a me and started ridin' me man. You know, I, I'm ashamed, yes. But at the time, I was intoxicated, I didn't give a fuck about anything, you understand me? But however, it's not like I was uh, um. Not like, um, I'm a fiend for that. It's not like um, um, um, that's my fetish. It's not like I go out my way to look for shit like dat, know what I mean?
>
> And I never let that shit happen again, I don't give a fuck. I put it on front street. Like, yup, yup, this is what happened.

Yup, it was underage. Yup, I got the, got the paperwork and everything. Yup, you know I mean?

Tat admitted his indiscretion but highlighted some important caveats that created boundaries with other sex offenders. He made it clear that the victim was in no way related to him, so his crime was not one of incest. He claimed that he was under the influence of alcohol, thus underscoring that the behavior was out of character. He also claimed that underage girls were not a fetish of his. In other words, he made an effort to portray his crime as a single poor decision that occurred while he was drunk, thereby resisting the predatory stigma attached to most sexual offenders. He said as much when he told me:

My thing is, if you do it more than once, then there's a problem. Then, there's a problem. If you do it once, and you don't do it again, then you know you can actually show by action that you learned from your mistake. But if you do it once, and you do it again, and you do it again, know what I mean, it's a problem.

I witnessed Tat "keeping it one hundred" hours later when we met Patch, who was also on parole. The three of us stood outside Patch's room talking about parole officers, and Patch asked Tat, "You violent? You a violent felon?" Tat responded:

Alright, check this out, I'm a keep it a hundred, I gotta keep it a hundred with everybody. When I was twenty-five, back in 2005, I wound up havin' sex with an underage chick, know what I mean? I was drunk, yeah, you know I mean, that's beside the point, you know I mean. It happened. She got pregnant, her pops didn't like that I was black, he pressed charges.

This confession was interesting because Tat added details that he did not share with me. The pregnancy and the impact of Tat's race seemed to implicate the father's decision to press charges as the reason for the conviction, and not the fact that Tat had done something that many considered deviant and stigmatic.

I asked Tat to elaborate on how his sex-offender status affected him and he said:

> Well, it's kinda hard, but I learned to live with it. In, in, in a way, all I gotta do, is register where I live. And anybody that I move around, I tell 'em the truth. Look listen, this is what it is. Oh, you mothafucker! Okay, cool, fine. I won't talk to you again. Know what I mean? If it like dat, I just, I just keep it movin' but.
>
> Last year, when I came here, when I came back here, some, 'cause it was switched over, it wasn't all, all sex offenders. It was a little bit a regular people. Some people that I met, you know I mean, they uh, got told by Elizabeth, watch it, he's a sex offender, he's okay. He's a good people but he's a sex offender. And they's like, oh okay, he's one a those, he's one a those. Now, this is before they got to meet the attitude, you know, the character. You know I mean? So, they all the sudden, like, when I was comin' around, I would see them like sneak over, and start talkin' over here. And I'm like, whatever, you know me, I don't care. I, I would come out, try to get, uh, twenty or thirty pack, do my little chippas on their weed, even though I wasn't smoking, uh you know I mean, and do little cookouts. And eventually they started seein' me a lot and they started seein' my character, and they was like, you know what? I thought you was, you was an asshole, but you're pretty decent. I was like, yo look listen, it happens.

Tat tried to be proactive in presenting his stigma to other residents. However, his attempts to limit potential damage to his identity were not always successful. Tat did not disclose his sex-offender status to the physically imposing resident Spike until weeks after he told me. This information did not sit well with Spike, who was happy to see Tat get kicked out of the motel a few weeks later for playing his music too loud:

> Larry says, I don't understand why they send these fuckin' weirdos over here. 'Cause ya'll take 'em, that's why. You the only hotel that take the weirdos, and I don't really care [about]

them, but I don't wanna hurt nobody's feelings, you know, sex offenders. Like what's his name there? Tat? But when he, I tell you, he had balls tellin' me to my face he was a level 2. I'm like, you know what? We good with our conversation. You can walk away from me now. He had balls tellin' me that! I'm like, dog, you know, you tellin' me this, and you know, if we was in jail, you woulda got it. Straight up. I told him straight up, you woulda got it, dog.

But yeah he had balls, he was ballsy to tell me some shit like that. I'm like, you know what? I'm good talkin' to you, man. Don't bother me and I won't mess with you. Like he was proud of it. You supposed to keep that on the hush, know what I mean? You don't want anybody to rock yo shit. I got nieces and nephews. But, I cut it short afta that. Now what I mean? He was running around promoting it like, you wanna put that shit on a t-shirt? Everybody, I'm like, come on, you can't be promotin' that, baby.

Spike's reaction was noteworthy because he mentioned his own nieces and nephews, thereby viewing them as potential victims of Tat. Like Reg, one goal of Tat's boundary construction was to challenge the public's perception that he was predatory and dangerous. By portraying themselves as engaging in consensual, albeit illegal sexual behavior, Tat and Reg created narratives that were intended to allay fears that they would engage in similar future behavior.[18]

Darryl was also forthcoming about his conviction with other residents but created boundaries from other convicted sexual offenders by staunchly claiming innocence. He told me the night we first met how this wrongful conviction occurred:

In 1993, I was accused of molesting a young man, uh, by a lady who I was having an affair with for eight years. Uh, behind her husband's back, who was one of my best friends. Well, I was gonna testify at the divorce proceeding, then they reconciled, then next thing I know I'm being charged with a crime. I disproved the day that they said that this supposedly happened. The judge extended the time frame to three days before and four days after. I couldn't prove where I was for seven days.

I asked Darryl how the sex-offender label affected his life, and he dismissed the idea that it had any effect on his psychological well-being:

I don't care. You know what, I did seventeen years, eighteen now, I really don't care. Say whachu wanna say about me. See, see for me it's a little bit different because where I grew up. I grew up in the hood, I slapped people's mouths quick. You know and like I still go to the hood and people know me and you know, say whachu wanna say, but you ain't gonna say it to my face. I try not to be a violent person but, and so what a person has to say really doesn't matter to me.

Darryl's narrative absolved him of his crime and certainly portrayed him as having a history of deviance. But he also offered a history of prosocial accomplishments that included running his own legitimate business and traveling on a wagon train with juvenile delinquents from Maine to Florida with the Visionquest program. He told me, "I was a perfect chameleon. Listen, I always had a job, was in the reserves, I played politics. I was a respected member of the community, a well-known member of the community. I was on the student senate in college."

Darryl claimed that growing older in prison had changed him and that when he looked back on his criminal past, it did not make him happy: "I thought that I was happy. I thought that I was getting everything that I wanted. But in a way, yeah, but in all reality, when you step back and really look about at it, it was hollow and empty. I got nothing left from it. A few people that I still talk to, but I really have nothing left from it. It destroyed my whole life."

Because of these past actions, Darryl appeared determined to right his ways, which he did in part by volunteering with the local AIDS Council in Riverfort. I asked him if giving back was important and he replied:

It's part of my growth process. I was a weapon of mass destruction. You laugh, but think of all the people I was selling drugs to, all the people I helped commit crimes, all the people I helped go to jail, all the people I helped destroy their families. I did more damage in that than this crime that I got charged with, and I have more problems with this crime than any of the shit I ever did. If I sell you crack, it just doesn't hurt you, it hurts your parents, your wife, your kids, there's a whole progression of people. I did this in my own neighborhoods and we destroyed our own neighborhoods.

This realization gave him a new outlook on life, and after he fell in love with Digital, Darryl claimed that his priorities had shifted: "What's happening between me and Dig right now, can't do anything but cause me some pain in my heart, 'cause it's only positive. It isn't about drugs, it isn't about getting high, it isn't about using another person, it isn't about manipulating another person. It's about happiness and joy."

Criminologist Shadd Maruna examined desistance narrative and argues that it "frequently involves reworking a delinquent history into a source of wisdom to be drawn from while acting as a drug counselor, youth worker, community volunteer, or mutual-help group participant."[19] We can see this in Darryl's narrative. He claimed he was three hundred hours short of being a certified alcohol and substance abuse counselor and told me he wanted to be a counselor in a drug or alcohol program or a sex-offender treatment program. He dreamed of opening his own ranch-style treatment and counseling center. Darryl was attempting to become what Maruna refers to as a "wounded healer." Wounded healers replace deviant careers with prosocial efforts to counsel others and help them desist from problematic behavior. Darryl's goals were also a prime example of generative scripts that addressed a need for fulfillment, exoneration, legitimacy, and therapy.[20]

Some of Darryl's claims seemed too good to be true, such as having a Mensa-worthy IQ or running drug rings inside of prison. Regardless of the actual truth of his statements, they served to create a specific public identity. Darryl portrayed himself as a man trained to be a criminal at an early age, whose prosocial accomplishments hid the fact that he was a manipulative criminal mastermind. His crimes allowed him to live a decadent life until his lack of loyalties landed him in prison for a crime he did not commit. Now that he was out of prison, Darryl wanted to repent for his past behavior and lead a simple life. His new ambitions allowed him to distinguish himself from the other residents at the motel who still engaged in criminal activity. These scripts helped Darryl resist the idea that he was "doomed to deviance."[21] This narrative was a combination of what Maruna would call a "redemption script" and a well-rehearsed presentation.[22] Darryl had clearly performed this narrative many times, and as audiences continued to accept it, it became engrained into his identity and sense of self. He used his narrative to alter his future trajectory and improve his chances of successful reentry.

The issue of "truth" and narrative must again be considered in light of the aforementioned analysis. While I argue that Reg, Tat, and Darryl all employed narratives with the explicit purpose of creating boundaries with other convicted sexual offenders, the truth is that their alleged actions were very different from one another. This difficulty in separating boundary construction from the differences in sex-offense-eligible behavior is important to acknowledge, even if it cannot be definitively resolved. However, in consideration of Reg's reaction formation, Tat's concentrated effort to appear non-predatory, and Darryl's well-rehearsed redemption script, I believe these narratives serve a more strategic purpose than simply describing the particulars of how they acquired their master status as sexual offenders.

RESISTANCE AGAINST OTHER STIGMA

Criminal histories aside, all those living at the Boardwalk still had to contend with the stigma of relying on the motel for shelter. Residents made their lives meaningful by taking ownership of the ways in which their lives were portrayed. These contrasting portrayals were based on views concerning issues such as material comfort, the value of work, conceptions of partnership and masculinity, suggestion of failure, self-sufficiency, and goal setting. In this section I will explore how residents used these boundary narratives to combat the psychological threats posed by the stigma of living at the Boardwalk Motel.

For recovering addicts Dee and Toby, the physical environment was a constant reminder of the fragility they faced on a daily basis. Because of this, they established a narrative of comfort to combat the psychological stress of the motel's living conditions. I visited their room in early December 2012 and was amazed to see that they had decorated a large Christmas tree that Dee had gotten from an ex-partner. Dee offered me a glass of eggnog as we chatted, and she claimed that there were 172 decorations on the tree. They had also put up two stockings, and Dee said, "We live in a household that does not exchange gifts. We exchange love and the fact we've got a roof over our heads. 'Cause you know we live here weekly, you never know what's gonna come next week. Are we gonna have the money? Do we have to move out, are we gonna get evicted? We're always livin' like that."

Toby chimed in, "We don't choose to live here, this is where we have to live." Dee nodded and said, "I fuckin' hate it in here, but it's my home you know, I hate it, I love it."

Through these statements, Dee and Toby acknowledged that they treaded a fine line between shelter and homelessness. The roof over their head was guaranteed on only a week to week basis, and any number of chaotic events in and out of their control could threaten that security. I asked if they considered themselves homeless, and Toby shook his head and said, "We pay our own, so I don't. No, I mean, I consider what we pay for this we could have an apartment. Eight hundred dollars a month, there's no reason why, we're payin' our, we pay our rent. It's not DSS payin', so, it's like a studio apartment kinda. If DSS was payin', no I wouldn't, then I would think I was kinda still homeless. But since you're payin' for it yourself and you're not, ya know, it's not so much payin' for you."

The fact that Dee and Toby lived in the room unsupported by public assistance, however fragile their situation, allowed them to feel in control of their living situation and have a certain measure of success. Despite the fact that Toby felt they had no choice but to live at the motel, they had the money to pay for a studio apartment, which elevated their status above those placed at the motel by DSS. This created a distinct mental boundary between them and other residents, whom they viewed as less self-sufficient.

Dee then elaborated on how envisioning the room as a studio apartment protected their psychological well-being: "We think about this as a studio apartment. We have to, 'cause if we continue to realize where we're at in life, we would spiral into a massive depression. And the house cleaning that we do would not get done. You know, and uh, the job wouldn't be happening and we'd just go on full DSS and, uh, we would just die. I call it home and I cry on the thought of losing it 'cause this is all I have."

Viewing the motel room as a studio apartment was a form of resistance that required Dee to spend most of her free time trying to make their room feel like a home. This labor of love created a fantastical narrative that kept Dee and Toby psychologically buoyant by masking the miserable conditions that plagued many rooms in the motel. One day in February, I visited Dee and she gave me a tour of their room. Figure 5 represents the most complete view of the room, while figures 6–8 illustrate particular aspects of the room that she felt were meaningful and important.

These visuals show how Dee and Toby used material comforts to cope with the motel's stigma. By decorating their room like a small apartment, they changed how they viewed their lives and the way their identities were created. The appearance of their room also allowed them to distinguish themselves from other residents on a level of mainstream material comfort and cleanliness. It very much resembled a normal apartment, while others did not have the material goods to decorate with or were unable to maintain such a pristine environment. While Dee showed me around her room, she created substantial boundaries between her and other residents when she said, "Another pet peeve is looking at your food. Like Sky's got food all over her place, and um, it was a big thing for me not having my food going all the way across and stuck on here, you know." Dee again compared her room to Sky's: "Why would I wanna go in her dark, drabby house when it's beautiful out? At least open a fuckin' window, get the fuckin' comforter off the window. It's ridiculous, she wonders why she's depressed, she has no vitamin D. She's covering her windows, there's no sunlight, and you don't go outside, so. Why are you depressed again? You don't go tanning."

What makes Dee's comments interesting is that Reg and Sky were very similar to Toby and Dee. They had lived at the motel for a similar amount of time (almost two years) and enjoyed similar material comforts; in some ways they could be viewed as equals. When compared to many other residents of the motel (particularly those placed by DSS), Reg and Sky lived like royalty in terms of material possessions. Because they had "stepped down" from apartments and other more stable living situations, they brought many possessions with them and accumulated others during the course of their two-year tenure at the motel. As with Dee and Toby, these items allowed them to create a living space that resembled a home. Reg and Sky's room was decorated with a 60-inch television, a desk filled with books, two refrigerators, a toaster oven, a large electronic skillet, a tall glass case full of small crafts, and several posters and trinkets that honored Sky's love of *Family Guy* (figures 9–10). When Dee made explicit contrasts to Sky, she created boundaries between them in order to distinguish her and Toby's situation from one that could be considered very similar to, or perhaps more comfortable than, their own.

There did come a point when Dee's efforts to make their room feel homey created problems between her and Toby. Dee often spent what little money she and Toby had on decorations and fancy items that Toby considered unnecessary. One day I visited their room and Dee said, "We're having a awesome fight, this is awesome." I apologized for intruding and Toby said, "This dumbass spends her fuckin' whole food stamp check in one week. Then what do we got for the rest of the month? Nothing. It all goes fuckin' bad. Every time she does it no matter what I say. Fuckin' retard." He and I then stepped outside so he could smoke a cigarette and he continued, "I don't need body spray, I don't need this shit. I'm trying to save money, and making minimum wage. I don't need this." While Toby appreciated certain aspects of the studio apartment narrative, he felt that Dee's efforts to distinguish themselves in luxurious ways (in this instance, buying unnecessary bath items) threatened their very survival. Because their resistance depended on material goods, it became powerless once the money ran out.

Biggie crafted a particular identity around the role of work in order to counter stereotypes of motel residents as lazy individuals living off welfare. Instead of viewing the room that he and Deirdre shared as a motel room, he constructed an elaborate narrative of self-employment that he presented without reservation to other residents. The first day that I met Biggie, he told me that he was a "businessman" and looking to hire some employees for his operation that was "open from five in the morning to five in the afternoon." I asked him what the business was, and he said confidently, "We do everything," telling me that they could provide anyone in the motel with whatever they wanted.

It took me several days to realize that because Biggie took apart items for scrap metal inside the room, he envisioned himself as an entrepreneur running a business and referred to the room as his "shop." One afternoon I watched him sitting on his bed working on a crossword puzzle as he said, "Usually when I have off, my work's done in the workshop, I come to the office and I'll take an hour to do one of those, then I'll go right into my paperwork." Figure 11 shows a portion of Biggie's "shop."

This narrative of work helped Biggie present himself in stark contrast to other residents who did not put in the effort to support themselves. I knocked on his door on an August morning as he was throwing some circuit boards in the trash and we had the following exchange in which he sternly pointed out that he worked harder than I did:

> ME: You working?
> BIGGIE: No.
> ME: I don't want to bother you if you're working. How's the car?
> BIGGIE: Very good.
> ME: You guys get to the track yet?
> BIGGIE: I go to work, son.
> ME: I know.
> BIGGIE: Okay, so when do I have time to do anything but
> work? I get up a lot earlier than you do.

The businessman narrative helped shield Biggie's identity from stigma by giving his daily life a sense of purpose and accomplishment. It also allowed him to craft an identity for himself as an upstanding partner for Deirdre. He used his profits from scrapping to buy items for her and told me, "She gets whatever she wants." When I met Biggie, he had just bought a gas grill that he claimed was "for her" and told me he wanted to buy her a larger grill, as well as a new coffee maker, blender, and deep fryer. He was intently focused on "taking care of my girl" and contrasted his treatment of Deirdre with Reg and Sky's relationship. Biggie said of Reg, "You take your wife's money, spend all her money, beat the shit out of her, yell all the time. You a Nazi, you come from a family of hate." Biggie created a clear boundary between him and Reg by portraying Reg as a nonworking, abusive partner, living off his wife's efforts. This was the polar opposite of how Biggie conceived himself, and he even linked Reg's behavior to ideology and upbringing, which implied that Biggie had been raised differently.

Biggie bought a car in July, and when he brought it to the motel he told me, "It was worth it, 'cause now my girl's happy, now she had a ride. She lives like a queen." This accomplishment was a real source of pride to Biggie, and he spent a good fifteen minutes ranting excitedly to me about what it meant to them:

Now that I got the car I'll have money all the time. 'Cause now, my girl's all set. Now that's one less argument I ain't gotta worry about. Not only one less argument, but another thing 'cause she was upset, because I had lost $30. She can look at it, oh now my man's doing alright. Now he's moving back where he should be, I'm saying, you can see it ain't all about his medicine or his herb, it's all about me. It ain't he won't sacrifice for me, know what I'm sayin'? It's been two years since we haven't had a car. And, that, that, that's because I love family and I love my kids. Now it's all about me and my girl, man. And my business. Now I can go to the scrapyard, yo let's get a ride into the scrapyard.

He finished by saying, "My girl messin' up with a straight-up gangsta, my boy. Gangster, father, and worker. Oh, plus the businessman, don't let her forget that." Getting a car was a game changer that moved Biggie and Deirdre closer to leaving the motel. Biggie again contrasted his desire to leave with Reg by saying, "My plan is get the fuck outta here. Unless you content here, if you beat your wife or take advantage of people smaller than you, then you content here, you don't want to leave." In Biggie's mind, he was achieving the middle-class markers of success by working and providing, so he could not be content at the motel. By contrast, Biggie felt Reg was comfortable at the motel because it suited his achievements.

Many residents picked up on the complexity of Biggie's business narrative. Roy said, "He go to pick sheet metal and get twenty to forty dollars a day and that's his business in his mind. So if to him that's his business, that's cool with me." Sam laughed when he told me:

> When I first met him, he blew me away, Chris, let me tell you how he blew me away. 'Cause he said he had an office, was a businessman, he said I'm a businessman, I got an office, I run my business you know. But he picks up scrap metal. I put two and two together, 'cause he had me thinking he had a real office. And he did, like he said, in his mind his apartment is his office. So these are the little insights you gotta see, they not bad people, but they got problems man that you gotta process.

Biggie blended the fact that he lived in a motel with his scrapping efforts to create a narrative of work and provision. The facts were that Biggie lived in a motel, was officially unemployed, and was so conscious of money that he picked up every coin he saw on the ground. However, when compared to other residents, he saw a hard-working and successful provider for his partner. This boundary allowed him to live up to the middle-class measure of masculine success and gave Biggie a sense of pride in his day-to-day activities that would otherwise have been overshadowed by the stigma of the motel.

Sam was another resident who relied on a narrative of work and achievement. He often spoke of his desire to work in contrast with Reg and others, who he felt had given up the desire to work and move on from the motel:

> I wanna work 'cause I wanna start livin' again. This ain't livin', Chris, this is not livin'. This is not livin'. I don't knock Reg and

them, but they too young to not be livin' life. And I talks to him too, you know, but this is not living. I always said this was a stepping stone, this was a stepping stone on to something else. You know we all run into hardships, we all get problems. But you know, there's gotta be something way, way greater than this, Chris.

They just get so complacent. They think this is the end of the road and they can't do no better, so they just stay at the end of the road. I say brother, the road winds, and twists and turns, and curves, and you just gotta get on it and follow it to the end and I guarantee you you'll find life more adventurous. But if you stay at the dead-end street, well you know one of them days you gotta walk off the dead end 'cause that's as far as you go is the dead end. You got to take the road and see where it winds and curves and goes and 'fore you know it, you'll be glad you did 'cause it's a whole big world out there, man. They don't wanna get out there and live, man.

Sam held the view that residents sought to stay at the motel because their failure to achieve success made the motel appealing. He created boundaries between himself and residents who he felt had gotten too "comfortable" and "complacent." Sam often used these words when talking about Reg, Jake, Marc, and Ramòn, and he went on a long rant while we sat outside his room on a hot summer day:

I'm too old for some of these cats. They all alcoholics and they all think they still slick with dey mouth. They busted and done, all of them. They done, you can bake them mothafuckas off and set 'em on the side. They all done. But they still think they got it. They sit there and drink all day long. If you listen to 'em talk they swear they philosophers, scientists, engineers, like the greatest people in the world. All they do is sit there and one cheap ass beer after another.

That's the life they wanna live, they all complacent. This is the end of the road for dem. It is the end of the road, they ain't tryin' to go nowhere, ain't tryin' to get nowhere. I guess sometimes you give up on life, that's what happens when you give up. Guess they had a plan, didn't have a plan B and plan A collapsed. I ain't got no plan B, so I just sit here and drink.

It's that word "complacent," come on, Chris. Once you get to that point, there is nothing else. You don't have nothing else to motivate you. Only way they get outta there the motherfucker burn down and Red Cross come and move their ass somewhere. That's the only way that'll happen. Other than that they ain't goin' nowhere.

Sam's age contributed to his outlook, as he was fifty-four and Reg, Jake, Marc, and Ramòn were in their thirties. In Sam's eyes, those young residents used drugs because they had given up on the prospect of moving forward. When Sam moved out, Reg asked to see Sam's new apartment and Sam rebuffed him, citing Reg's behavior:

Reg wanted to come by one day, you know I had talked to him I guess, right before Thanksgiving, and you know, everywhere you go you bring misery, man. You a drug addict and you don't see that you have a problem, see, and you get $900 of money from the government, part of that is my tax payment, I dunno what percentage I give you, prolly three dollas, 'cause I only make $7.50 an hour. But still that disability money is taxpayers' money, that's how you get paid, sitting around drinkin' and druggin.' You know that bothers me too, 'cause you a young man, you can work, you can sling beer cans up and down your gut all day long and sniff dope up your nose and smoke crack, but you can't work. That's some bullshit too, but to each his own. I'm not mad at him, but like I told him, I don't think I'll ever have you to my house either.

This distance that Sam created reflected his concern that Reg was not living the fulfilling life that he could be.

Sam also resisted filing for unemployment because he believed that "checks make people complacent." When Justine pressed him to go to DSS, he said:

I said no, no, no, that's for motherfuckers that can't do no better. I kept tellin' her that. That's for people that really gave up. Now I can see if you got a mortgage that's due and, you know you ain't found a job right away, sometime you forced to go do it, Chris. But I said baby, you workin', we can, we can make it, it's gonna be a little hard but we can make it. I said but if I go down there and start getting checks, man, you start getting them checks, Chris, eventually you will not go to work, that's a fact.[23]

Sam felt that government benefits threatened his identity as a hardworking individual persevering in the face of adversity. Because his presentation of self involved resistance in the form of work, it was easy to see how people who Sam felt did not possess a similar drive aggravated him. Sam had internalized popular discourse about the poor in his disapproval and criticism of Reg and others. This created boundaries between him and their "complacency" and gave meaning to his efforts.

Other residents echoed the concerns about being identified as a welfare recipient. Reg and Mike had the following exchange one afternoon as they sat in the garden near the rear of the motel:

REG: Hey yo, I live off the system too but I make my money on the side.

MIKE: No, no, no, no. You get a check. You don't get welfare. You don't get welfare. They get welfare.

REG: I hate that shit, motherfuckers looking for a free ride. Then they try and live off of you while they're here.

MIKE: No matter how much I drink, I still go to work.

REG: I don't work but I have my hustles. My cigarettes, I sell what I can get. I do what I do, man, but I make a living. I have my extra money, my check is not my life. I could live without that check and still be happy.

Similarly, Biggie and Deirdre were adamant that they did not live off DSS. As Biggie continually told me, "We pay our own rent." The creation of boundaries between welfare recipients and others demonstrated the importance of the ability to "make a living." This identity of achievement was an active form of resistance against the welfare stigma attached to the Boardwalk.

Like Sam, other residents condemned the thought of getting too comfortable at the motel; living there was a necessity, but they did not want to become stuck there. This created clear boundaries between residents who felt they had more to achieve in life and the residents they viewed as having given up. The always friendly Roy voiced this concern at the Boardwalk when he said, "These people here, they forty, fifty, they old, they are satisfied, they content in this environment, it's not about getting ahead." Because Roy was forty-three and one could assume that he was similarly content, he made it clear that he was quite different from other residents and was only at the motel because of unfortunate circumstances:

> Most of the women here are on what? Drugs. Drugs, and most of the men are pedophiles. Why would a person in their right mind want to live here? You a druggie or you a pedophile. I went to business college and what fucked it up was I had a kid! I'm determined to make something happen. Once I get a job, I'm outta this place. I'm just a guy who just be trying to be, just trying to make it, man.

To Roy, others his age had given up "trying to make it," and it was important that people understood that, unlike others, he was working to step up from the motel.

In many ways, Larry's outlook was similar to Sam's. When Larry moved into the Boardwalk from his car in October, I asked him early on what he thought about the motel's reputation of housing sex offenders. He said:

> As long as, like I said, they don't bother me, I don't bother them. Like I said, a lot of times you don't know the whole story anyway. You know you hear it from one said, you know that guy's a fuckin' asshole, blah, blah, blah. Just like any situation, there's always two sides to a story. You can't judge somebody on one person's, uh . . . one person's accusations. I was brought

up the right way. I'm courteous to people. I'm respectable and I respect people, that's just the way I am. I guess I'm kinda soft in a way at some times, that's just me.

I was struck by this tolerance of sex offenders because it was often lacking at the motel. On several occasions Larry's efforts to assist residents he viewed as vulnerable proved that his point of view was not just lip service. However, as Larry became more involved with the motel's residents, his tolerance began to wither.

Within a few weeks of moving in, Larry was doing maintenance jobs around the motel, such as cleaning the office windows and sweeping around the parking lot.[24] By the end of October he had assumed a daytime manager position and rented out rooms in addition to doing maintenance. He received $10 a day for this work and admitted that it hurt his pride to make so little, but he could not turn down the opportunity to make money. With this new job came a new and free residence when Larry moved into the house next to the Park Place that Elizabeth and Natalie inhabited. Sam told me: "He moved over there, 'cause once you take the little job here they move you to the blue house. Then from the blue house, they move you out to the street again. Most people don't stay in that blue house long. I told him that, it's like a curse on that blue house. None of the maintenance people, in all the years I been comin' up here, they don't stay long."

Fortunately for Larry, he bucked this trend and was still living in the house when I concluded my fieldwork. This move from resident to employee did not sit well with others, and Reg complained, "Larry, he's been acting like a fuckin' douche, since he's become fuckin', whatever he is here." Reg's observation was fairly astute because as Larry's involvement in the managerial aspect of the motel increased, so did his social distance from other residents.[25] The physical distance created by Larry's move to the "blue house" amplified the boundaries between him and the residents of the Boardwalk.

Despite the fact that he used to reside at the Boardwalk, after starting his job as day manager Larry consistently created boundaries between himself and motel residents based on what he perceived were differences in intelligence and behavior. A month after moving out of the motel, Larry told me: "It's easy to get along with you because you have smarts. It's hard around here because there's people with such different personalities and some people don't have a lot goin' on upstairs. You're the only one that has common sense, the rest of these guys here. I mean, don't get me wrong, I don't dislike 'em, I just like talkin' intelligent to people, these guys, they're just not too bright."

My presence and friendship allowed Larry to share in my status prestige, and he took full advantage of it when discussing other residents. This statement was less of a compliment to me and more of an attempt by Larry to use my presence to create boundaries with residents who he felt lacked the capacity to carry on a conversation with someone who was atypical of the motel. One day Reg declined a ride that Larry offered and Larry complained to me:

> I don't even know why I offer people sumpin', 'cause there, they got nothin', nothing upstairs you know what I'm sayin'? I mean I'm not sayin' they're bad people, but they're headed down the wrong road, he's only thirty-seven years old, I went through that shit. It's a lot of fun when you're young, but when you get older it's a job, it's no fun after a while. I don't think you ever been through it, which is a good thing, Chris. I don't think you ever will, you don't seem that type of person.

By asserting that I was not the type of person to use drugs like Reg, Larry made a claim about Reg and placed Reg's social status below mine. He also distanced himself from Reg. Because he used to behave in a similar manner to Reg but had changed his ways, Larry was smarter than Reg and held a higher social position.

Another way that Larry created boundaries was by linking behavior to how people were raised. When we first met he spoke about his past drug use and told me: "Even if you do drugs, you'll start thinking, you know I wasn't brought up like this. When you're brought up properly it's instilled in your mind. I got a good family and I was brought up properly, it's just, things went sour only because of my doing you know, I'm not blaming anyone else but myself."

In Larry's mind, behavior was determined by upbringing. He presented himself as a man who overcame drug abuse because his family environment had given him that power. More to the point, the argument "I wasn't brought up that way" created boundaries and identity because it placed Larry in a completely different social class from those at the motel. It implied that motel residents came from families where that sort of behavior was tolerated or encouraged.

When I asked Larry one day in December how things were going, he responded:

> Well, I really wanna get outta here, it's just too much. Too much bullshit, you know? Too many people are just crazy. I wasn't brought up like that. I mean, believe me, I lived on the street too, but. Everybody's either drinking or they're doing drugs. I have some beers too, you know. I'm not really worried about getting caught up with it. It's just that the people are so phony, you know what I mean? You know it's always lies and gossip. I, I just don't like that shit. But, that's just the way life is I guess. In places like this, know what I mean.

By attributing motel culture to upbringing, Larry crafted an identity for himself that made him qualitatively different from other residents. It was not just that he acted differently, but because of his family background, he had been and would always be different. His comment about "places like this" made it clear that Larry linked the location with the behavior that he condemned. In Larry's presentation of self, his destiny and social standing were predetermined, as if he was programmed from an early age to behave better. His boundaries established that he was not cut from the same cloth as the residents of the Boardwalk and therefore could never be comfortable in that environment or viewed as the same.

Despite the fact that Larry felt he had created an upstanding identity for himself, others did not always see it that way. After Sam moved out, he and Larry kept in touch by phone, and, like Reg, Larry asked if he could come over to Sam's new place. When they both lived at the motel, Sam felt that he and Larry were kindred spirits because of their age. Sam reversed course after he left and told Larry that coming over to his apartment was not a good idea:

I dunno if he got offended by it or what, but you know uh, I mean what it is, is what it is. I said, Larry, you know, I know you, but we ain't, we ain't friendly like that, you know, 'cause you drink and all that. I mean, I don't or nothin', I don't want none of that shit around me, Chris.

Don't get me wrong, I like Larry, he's a nice guy. Like Justine say, you know he let me use the car a couple times, you know, and and, but you know, at the same token, we talkin' 'bout my home, you know. And some things we have to separate.

You know everybody you meet and you smile at they face, ain't a friend. You just can't be draggin' everybody to your house, you know that just something you just don't do. These guys you know, I told Larry, you a drifter Larry, you know, I know what you do, you a drifter. I don't know how long you'll be at the Boardwalk, once you get in your car and pack up and leave one day, we might not never see you again, you know. I mean you came here like a warm breeze, you fuckin' leave out the same way.

Me and you, we sat down, we talked when you was always drunk after about four beers you wanna sit down and talk with me, so I sat down and talked with you and you know that was basically it you know. And you know, you out buyin' prostitutes and shit, I mean, I, I, I ain't livin' like that, Larry. I mean, I understand, you a single man, that's your cup a tea, not mine. And I told you guys when I moved out, that, you know, I'll see you guys when I see you but, it wasn't gonna be that kinda party, you know.

Once Sam left the motel, he used physical distance to lay down more concrete boundaries with individuals still at the motel. His willingness to interact with Larry and Reg at the Boardwalk but then limit interaction when gone put him in the category of what Reg called a "motel friend" versus a "real friend." "Motel friends" are a prime example of what sociologist Matthew Desmond calls "disposable ties," or "relations between new acquaintances characterized by accelerated and simulated intimacy, a high amount of physical copresence, reciprocal or semireciprocal resource exchange, and (usually) a relatively short life span."[26] Because life at the Boardwalk was so transient, Reg realized that most social interaction was simply based on proximity and that these interactions were those of "motel friends." Once a person moved out, there was often little incentive to keep in contact. Those who established an emotional connection that lasted beyond life at the motel were considered "real friends."

Motel residents often compared themselves to Reg in their boundary construction because Reg put forth a unique narrative of his life at the motel. Reg's resistance against the stigma of living in the motel was summed up when he stated, "I like it here." When other residents complained about the living conditions and day-to-day existence at the motel, it solidified the concept of living at the Boardwalk as a negative. By framing his life in the motel as a preference, Reg negated any sign of failure. This created a clear boundary between himself and other residents. While they lived there because their lives had spiraled out of control, Reg *chose* to live there and was therefore still in control of his trajectory.

The importance of this narrative became clear when Reg took instant offense to any threats against his boundary work. One day Sky wanted to ask other residents for cigarettes and Reg screamed at her, "Acting like we're fucking poor, asking people for shit! Get the fuck over that!" When I told him that I viewed the motel as a place for people with nowhere else to go, he quickly corrected me: "I like it here. It'd be so easy for me to get out, but I choose not to." I mentioned that it would be nice to have a real kitchen, and Reg looked at me and said, "What can't I cook? I have everything, what can't I cook? You've had stuff baked in my toaster oven." Reg's boundary creation was a clear attempt to combat the stigma of failure, as he contrasted himself with other residents whom he saw as lacking the means to control their lives. If Reg was in full control of his destiny, then there was no reason to equate an outcome like living at the motel with failure to achieve a goal.

This identity of full situational control was also seen when Reg made substantial efforts to portray himself as a man who was not afraid of any challenge. He told Mike one day: "The first motherfucker that wants to question my manhood? Oh, I'm coming out, let's go. I don't care if I get my ass beat. Since you seen me here though, have you ever seen me back down from a motherfucker? Do you think I'm going to? It's not going to happen and I don't care if this motherfucker's three times my size."

This lack of fear was also evident when Trim and Sam discussed prison and Sam warned Reg that they would not be able to be friends in prison because of race relations. Reg brushed this idea aside and said, "No, I'd stick up for my friends." Sam and Trim claimed that they had the same idea, but it all changed when they entered prison. Reg refused to relent and said, "I'm not you," staking a claim that traditional rules of powerlessness did not apply to him. There were also several instances when he gave the impression that he did not hesitate to be aggressive with authority figures. When a building inspector came by one day looking to check out his room, Reg told me: "Said buddy you got a better chance a getting Bin Laden than getting through that fuckin' door. My wife's naked on the other side a that wall. I said, now have a good fucking day and slammed the door in his face. Even if the owner says you're comin' I'll tell you to go fuck yourself. He'd a went through me and he'd a ended up on his ass."

These narratives portrayed Reg as a man capable of extreme violence but always cool and dismissive about danger to himself. Sociologist Jack Katz describes being cool as "to view the immediate social situation as ontologically inferior, nontranscendent, and too mundane to compel one's complete attentions."[27] By appearing cool and controlled when faced with any situation, particularly one involving physical danger, Reg elevated his social status among those at the motel and fought off the stigma of weakness. This strutting also suggested that living in the motel was a threat to Reg's masculinity. Since he did not have a legitimate job and Sky did, his male identity as capable provider was threatened, and he reclaimed this masculine status by emphasizing his physical capabilities.[28]

This is not to say that Reg's narrative lacked justification. His "king of the hill" mentality was epitomized when he referred to himself as "the bull" of the motel. Certainly, his hulking size made him the biggest resident of the Boardwalk, and he was by far its most public figure. According to Reg's definition of masculinity, this made him the alpha male and created clear boundaries between him and other males at the motel simply based on size and aggression.

Reg's resistance narrative also included using copious amounts of alcohol on a regular basis. He referred to himself as an alcoholic and said things like "I got so fucked up last night, Jake and I killed two six packs and the leftover cider we had." However, Reg did not view himself as a "drunk" and admitted that he had a problem but knew when to stop. He also regularly used marijuana and occasionally abused other drugs and pills. This drug use was part of a narrative that celebrated deviance but, more important, served as a coping mechanism for motel life. Psychologist Jeffrey Schaler argues that drug addiction is used to cope with, or avoid coping with, reality.[29] In Reg's case, his reality was that he lived in a motel rife with stigma and devoid of many markers of middle-class success. Drug use was accepted and promoted at the motel, so using drugs changed his reality and created an identity of status because he could use many substances and remain none the worse for wear.

There were times when Reg's cool and controlled narrative broke down. As Thanksgiving approached he said to me, "Every time I think I like it here I think I wanna move. A yard would be nice, a backyard, a porch, a kitchen where you can actually cook a turkey." While this came mere days after he claimed that he could cook anything he wanted, Reg should not be viewed as dishonest. In many ways he enjoyed the motel because it gave him respect and a large degree of freedom that he might not have found in other locations. He reveled in his role of what Jack Katz describes as a "badass." According to Katz, a badass must be tough, project an alien and unnerving posture, and act with a measure of meanness.[30] Reg celebrated behavior that was symbolic of deviance and created boundaries between himself and other motel residents that gave him power and status. However, because his public identity was a form of resistance that limited the damage to his ego that came from living at the motel, it was impossible for him to forget where he once was. Therefore, while Reg distanced himself from other residents in ways that increased his social status, he was still reminded that there were those who possessed a higher social status at his own expense.

The social psychological strategy of creating boundaries and warding off stigma was an important part of everyday life at the Boardwalk Motel. It must be noted, however, that creating distinctions and boundaries is a feature of many social groups, not just those that are stigmatized. The process of "othering" has been well documented among what may be considered fairly mainstream social groups, such as nurses, radiologists, college athletes, religious groups, rural whites, sororities, and sports fans.[31]

The aforementioned coping strategies of creating comfort as well as resisting complacency echo previous work by social worker Terri Lewinson. Lewinson conducted interviews with residents of an extended-stay hotel that offered many more comforts than the Boardwalk (including a kitchenette with burners, a fridge, and microwave, and Internet access). Despite these amenities, residents were stressed by the confined space and felt that their inability to leave was a marker of personal failure. To cope with this stress, they engaged in behavior similar to that seen at the Boardwalk. Some personalized their rooms with decorations and, in particular, items that carried meaning, such as pictures of family. Others avoided decorating their rooms in order to reflect their goals of moving on, amid concerns of becoming too comfortable and not moving out.[32]

This chapter explored the ways in which residents resisted the stigma of motel life by creating and managing identities. A key part of these identities involved presentations of self that established boundaries with other residents. These boundaries served to inoculate residents against the psychological harm that occurred when residents considered their living situations in the context of middle-class success. Identity management met the very basic psychological need to cope with the courtesy stigma of the motel environment. However, the shared identity of the Boardwalk was not entirely destructive. Because they shared the same environment, motel residents encountered what Goffman refers to as "sympathetic others" in the form of other residents.[33] In many ways, encountering sympathetic others gave residents a common identity. One day Cinque complained that Elizabeth did not understand what he was going through and Sam called out to him, "Cinque, everybody is! Shit, everybody goin' through sumpin. Nigga, we all strugglin' out here. You think we all happy? We all struggling, alla us!" In the next chapter, I examine how residents worked together in their daily struggles to create a culture of community at the Boardwalk Motel.

Figure 1 The Boardwalk Motel
Photo courtesy of the author

Figure 2 Aerial photo of Boardwalk Motel property
Photo courtesy of the author

Figure 3 The shopping cart graveyard
Photo courtesy of the author

Figure 4 Unexplained hole in the floor
Photo courtesy of the author

Figure 5 Dee and Toby's room
"We think about this as a studio apartment."—Dee
Photo courtesy of the author

Figure 6 Dee and Toby's room
"Plants are key. It helps to have plants and lots
of candles because it is a small room and you
have two people smoking."—Dee
Photo courtesy of the author

Figure 7 Dee and Toby's room
"The entertainment center and the cat stand is what makes the room, I think. Makes the room look like a home."—Dee
Photo courtesy of the author

Figure 8 Dee and Toby's room
"I did this, up here, to make it look like it's a window, even though it's not. You know if you're in your kitchen, you usually have a kitchen window. Your space looks bigger if you just make it look like it's a kitchen fuckin' window."—Dee
Photo courtesy of the author

Figure 9 Reg and Sky's room
Photo courtesy of the author

Figure 10 Reg and Sky's room
Photo courtesy of the author

Figure 11 Biggie's "shop"
Photo courtesy of the author

Figure 12 Scene from a summer cookout
Photo courtesy of the author

Figure 13 Scene from a summer cookout
Photo courtesy of the author

Figure 14 A Thanksgiving cheese plate
Photo courtesy of the author

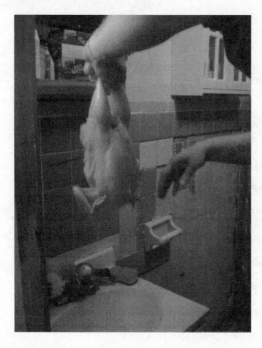

Figure 15 Reg prepping a Thanksgiving chicken in his bathroom sink
Photo courtesy of the author

Figure 16 The motel's living environment. Before Larry took it on himself to clean recently vacated rooms, residents found themselves moving into conditions like this.
Photo courtesy of the author

4

Community, Conflict, and Fragility

It's just people trying to get along.
—Burt

In the previous chapter I described the ways in which motel residents attempted to resist stigma from the outside world. One of the tools they used was narrative, or a story of the self. Narratives are important because they create a version of the truth. Dutchland residents also used narratives to create their own truths about the Boardwalk Motel. One online commenter wrote in response to a newspaper article about motels and the local economy: "The only economy it's helping is the slum lords [*sic*] pockets. Oh and maybe Giant Foods across the street where the tenants buy the beer for their cookouts during the day when the other Dutchland residents are working."[1] This narrative portrayed motel life as comfortable, as if motel residents basked in daily luxuries that hardworking residents of Dutchland could only dream of. As this chapter will show, residents of the Boardwalk lived lives of deprivation and insecurity, and living at the motel served only to exacerbate their vulnerabilities.

Boardwalk residents faced both material and social deprivations. These deprivations left residents with wants and needs that required attention, often on a daily basis. While some residents chose to address these needs in relative solitude, daily life at the motel was highly organized around calculated social interaction. Social interaction among these residents can be classified into two types of behavior: community and conflict. When motel residents attempted to alleviate their deprivations via one another, they engaged in community—the consensual transfer of resources between residents satisfying wants and needs. While these transfers proved mutually beneficial, they often led to conflict—perceived acts of disrespect created through social interaction. On many occasions the process of resolving conflict through violence, threats of violence, or blacklisting increased fragility among residents. As I explained earlier, fragility is the shortage of material goods and social capital that leaves one vulnerable to unexpected or self-inflicted disruptions to short- and long-term goals.

Community, conflict, and fragility are best viewed as a cycle. Residents of the Boardwalk Motel arrived in states of fragility and attempted to address their shortages of material goods and social capital by engaging in community. These community interactions often led to conflict when residents perceived that they had been disrespected. Conflict resolution then increased fragility, leading residents to engage in more community to address any deprivations that had increased as a result of conflict.

The cycle of community, conflict, and fragility is an extension of previous research into survival strategies of the urban poor. Carol Stack's insightful treatment of this issue in her book *All Our Kin* (1974) found that poor black residents in the Flats survived by engaging with a large network of family and friends, with whom they shared goods and services on a daily basis.[2] Expanding on Stack's work, sociologist Matthew Desmond explored how poor residents of the Green Street Mobile Home Park survived in the absence of family networks. Green Street residents relied on disposable ties, or "relations between new acquaintances characterized by accelerated and simulated intimacy, a high amount of physical copresence, reciprocal or semireciprocal resource exchange, and (usually) a relatively short life span."[3] In this chapter I show how the cycle of community, conflict, and fragility adds a new dynamic to understanding how the urban poor survive. Specifically, I will examine these themes by showing how they emerged through social interaction and describing how they affected the lives of motel residents for better, and often for the worse.

COMMUNITY

The Underground Economy

The most observable transfers of resources revolved around material goods in the motel's underground economy. Residents were acutely aware that although they all endured lives of relative deprivation, this did not translate into a complete lack of resources. Rather, each resident possessed varying amounts of material goods and social capital. Only though social interaction were residents able to "discover" the resources that others possessed and if these resources were available for transfer, borrowing, or exchange.[4]

Residents often discovered available resources simply by asking others for particular items. Sam told me about people knocking on his door asking, "You got a pack a hotdogs, you got a jar a peanut butter? It happens every day." When Tat returned to the motel from prison, he knocked on several doors looking for a pan, silverware, DVDs, and a hammer. Such inquiries also occurred in the public spaces outside rooms. Jake and I were walking through the parking lot one winter afternoon when a new resident asked if we had any empty cans. We said no, and Jake informed the man that everyone at the motel was on the lookout for empty cans. Late one April evening Tat and I were talking in the parking lot when Patch called out to us from his room several doors down, "Yo bro! You got a phone?" and later, "Yo bro, you got rollin' papers?" (Most residents at the motel had phones that were loaded with prepaid minutes. When those minutes ran out, often at the end of the month, the need for more minutes became pressing.)

Many residents spent warm and sunny days in the parking lot soaking up the sun and fresh air. On these desirable days, passing the time in this manner usually involved the consumption of beer, food, cigarettes, and marijuana. Those who chose to drink, smoke, and eat in full view opened themselves up to constant inquiries about their goods. Jake and I took advantage of an April day to drink cans of Coors Light in the parking lot, and a new resident sauntered up to ask, "Can I grab one of those cold ones offa you?" Jake asked if he had any money, and the man replied, "I got no food, no money."

Jake refused to give the man a beer, so we watched him walk down the street and he returned later with several cans of beer from the local drug store.

Vehicles were unique possessions at the motel. The few residents with cars (such as Biggie, Larry, and myself) became instant celebrities. Anytime residents arrived in a car or went out to their car, they opened themselves up to the question, "Is that your car?," which was inevitably followed by a request for a ride. Sam paid Biggie ten dollars for a ride to downtown Riverfort. Some residents, like Cinque, did not want to walk to locations in the sustaining habitat and would ask for rides to fast-food establishments. When Larry started working as the day manager he was unable to leave the premises; he asked me on a daily basis to drive to CVS for cans of Natural Ice beer, which he referred to as his "cornflakes" because he used them to start his morning. Other times, residents going on shopping trips did not want to carry purchases back to the motel or push them back in a cart. I was enlisted for rides when Reg and Jake accumulated huge bags of cans and bottles to be returned at Giant Foods to reclaim the deposit.[5] Then there were more demanding requests that involved a bigger investment of resources, such as when Dale asked if Biggie could drive him to his father's house an hour away to pick up some belongings.

Enterprising residents made an effort to advertise resources that were available for exchange. One of the more unique skills that residents advertised was the ability to draw tattoos. The Boardwalk was home to a few aspiring tattoo artists, which was not surprising given that many residents had spent time in prison. Tat, as his name suggests, envisioned tattooing as a way to earn money and legitimacy. One day he brought me into his room to show me his drawings. Some were hidden because they were sexual in nature, featuring anime-style depictions of women in various stages of undress; as a sex offender on parole, Tat was prohibited from having any sort of pornographic materials. Tat's relatives bought him a $300 tattoo kit. Tat showed me the kit, saying, "This is a career for me, I draw very good as you can see. And um, I'm thinking about maybe, um, filling out applications as a tattoo shop." He then offered to give me a tattoo for a very cheap price. I declined the offer but told Tat that others at the motel might be interested; later he offered tattoos to Jake and Spike.[6]

Residents advertised other resources in other ways. Ned loitered in the parking lot one day asking if anyone needed their bills paid by phone. Ned was unable to explain how this service would work, but Sam and I agreed to spread the word for him. Reg taped a hand-written sign in his window: "Cigarettes for sale. 50 cents a piece. No credit. 8AM to 8PM."[7] On a cold winter day, Eric, a Park Place resident, walked into the Boardwalk office with a black North Face jacket, which he tried to sell to me for fifty dollars. I suspected it was stolen so I declined and he then tried to sell it to Elizabeth, asking, "You got kids? How 'bout a husband?" She replied, "Oh, he's dead, I don't think he needs it." Eric then turned to me and said, "I'll take forty dollars, I just need the money."[8]

The motel's underground economy thrived on negotiation. Those who needed to offload items for cash were often at the mercy of those doing the purchasing. As Reg put it, "People need the money, they come here on their last dime." This made the Boardwalk a sell-er's market, as those who were approached for their goods and ser-vices had the upper hand and could refuse an exchange if they did not feel the price was right. Reg explained this to Curtis one day:

CURTIS: Can I have a cigarette?
REG: I sell them, I do not give them out.
CURTIS: Give you ten bucks later.
REG: Yeah, later I don't do. I don't mean that rudely, but I can't lose out.
CURTIS: For a quarter?
REG: I'll smoke it myself for that price. If you had forty or forty-five I might say okay, but not a quarter. I'm not that desperate.

Amid this chaos, the market did establish some going rates for goods and services. A cigarette ran between fifty cents and a dol-lar, and cans or bottles of beer, soda, or water were usually a dollar each. The ability to run errands on foot was also valuable. Residents were often interested in obtaining food, beer, or other items from the sustaining habitat but not interested in exerting the effort to pro-cure them. In these instances, those who obtained goods for others were paid with either some of the materials (such as a can of beer) or a negotiated sum of money.

Because cash was so scarce, it was not expected to be the primary method of payment for goods and services. Often the exchanges of goods and services occurred chaotically and haphazardly. Shawn, a male nurse in his late thirties, traded his green mountain bike to Reg for a nickel bag of marijuana; he told me that he parted with the bike because he got hit riding it and "it did enough to me." Later that evening, a new resident named Gene arrived on a gray bike and took a room on the second floor. Gene asked if anyone had a microwave he could use to cook some meat that he had just stolen from a local restaurant. He and Shawn entered into an agreement. According to Gene: "I traded my bike to the dude, I said take my bike, I don't fuckin' need it, here. I got a microwave now. He wanted ten bucks for it, I said you want a bicycle? He fuckin' rode it, said no problem."

A large part of the underground economy was devoted to drugs and medications. A variety of residents with mental health issues sold their prescriptions to others. Ed often sold his Xanax to Natalie and other residents.[9] However, the most popular drug at the Boardwalk was marijuana. Its availability fluctuated as dealers came and left. When I first arrived Roy was the only active drug seller at the motel. He sold marijuana and other drugs to residents of the Boardwalk, trailer park, and the Park Place, and several residents referred to him as "the weed man." Roy's connections to the drug world allowed him to control the market, and he charged upwards of fifty dollars for late-night runs into Riverfort. When Roy got evicted, the motel went without a source of marijuana for a week. Then Anthony, a tall and skinny Puerto Rican with dreadlocks, moved in next door to me at the end of June. He introduced himself by asking if I needed marijuana and told me, "Everybody smokes weed, like 80 percent of people." Anthony became the local dealer for residents in the area until he left without warning in the middle of July.

Cinque arrived in mid-August after being paroled on his weapons charge. He and Reg entered into an agreement to sell marijuana using Cinque's connections, despite the fact that Reg told me earlier, "It's not worth the hassle, it's not worth the money, it's not worth anything, it's really not." This attitude of wanting to deal drugs for the money but not wanting to face the potential risks was common among residents. Other residents, such as Natalie, Sam, Tat, and Darryl, told me that they thought of using their connections to sell drugs at the motel but could not risk getting in trouble because they all had criminal histories. Furthermore, Tat and Darryl were on parole and focused on going straight.

When Cinque was arrested on Halloween for failing a drug test, Reg continued using Cinque's supplier to sell marijuana at the motel. He told me, "I did not want to do it but I am. Entrepreneurial skills, brotha." Reg then urged me to see if I knew "any college kids who need a nic' [nickel bag]."[10] Despite the potential problems that drug dealing posed, these drug connections helped Reg satisfy his wants and needs as he often exchanged marijuana for goods and services. When Reg and Sky decided to move out of the motel, Reg used his profits to save for an apartment and provided marijuana as payment when he needed physical help moving.

Sharing Resources

The sharing of resources occurred when one resident transferred resources to another without any explicit expectation of immediate compensation—for example, Sam giving Cinque a microwaveable burger, or Biggie giving the vulnerable Steve a cigarette. In other instances, residents would borrow items for specific purposes and then return them. Ed borrowed a can opener from Toby to make a tuna sandwich, and Tat gave me a hooded sweatshirt to wear as the temperature started to drop one evening. This type of sharing occurred often, particularly among long-term residents who knew each other well.

Residents shared not only their material resources but their social capital as well. Jake and Sky were fairly unique in that they held jobs in the local community. At one point they worked together at KFC until Jake quit. Jake then got a job at McDonald's, which he held for a few months before quitting again and getting hired at the Indian restaurant next door to the motel. New residents of the Boardwalk who were on unemployment and parole were required to look for jobs. Jake and Sky were quick to tell them to stop by their places of work to fill out applications and use them as references. Sam did something similar when he encouraged Natalie to apply to the girl's detention facility where his wife worked. To my knowledge, no residents took jobs through these options, although, as I will explain later, Darryl did get a job offer with Sky's help, which led to conflict.

When Jake and Sky were employed at fast-food locations, they used their managerial positions to provide food for friends. One afternoon in June, Jake walked into the parking lot and announced that he was heading to KFC and asked the seven of us who were sitting there, "What do people want?" Several of us offered him money but he refused to take it. In October Reg, Jake, Cinque, Marc, and I grew hungry after an afternoon of drinking, so Reg invited us to go visit Sky at work at KFC for free dinner. We waltzed into KFC and Sky greeted us with, "The drunken parade's here!" In addition to giving us whatever we wanted off the menu, Sky gave us ice cream and soda.

Sharing also occurred when residents pooled their resources for mutual benefit. Steve took a roommate so that the two of them could save money on rent. The roommate worked the night shift at the twenty-four-hour Giant Foods; he got free food from work and brought it home around four or five in the morning. The two of them would eat together before the roommate went to bed. Pooling resources for mutual benefit occurred on an almost daily basis. Jake and Reg often woke up hungover, and their first act of the day was to combine whatever money they had in order to buy more beer. Cinque and Marc shared a love of pizza, and they pooled their money to order pizza and chicken wing dinners after long days of work. When Tat and Patch got to know each other, they spent the evening smoking loose cigarettes that they made by combining their change to buy rolling papers and tobacco. In these instances, residents realized that the only way they could satisfy their wants and needs was by working with one another.

Creating Care

When residents established close relationships with one another, they shared emotional resources as well as material ones; such actions can be viewed as acts of care. These emotional and material dimensions of community revolved around acts through which residents cared for, tended for, and cared about one another.[11] Care work theory is rooted in the examination of the hands-on work (predominantly by women) carried out by individuals in order to maintain and repair the world so it can be lived in as well as possible. According to care theorists Bernice Fisher and Joan Tronto, caregiving requires knowledge that is rooted in everyday understanding of those receiving the care.[12] At the motel, the intimacy of the living environment fostered the types of social interactions that led to everyday interactions and understanding between residents with varying vulnerabilities. Sam shared his insight into care at the motel when he told me:

But then overall, the picture up at the Boardwalk ain't a bad picture. People helpin' each other, they sharing stuff. Even though we all have our little moments, but I think we all, we basically like one big family. If I see Ed walkin' down the street and I see him trip and fall, I'ma help him up, just cause I know he lives at the Boardwalk, he live the same place I live. If I see somebody messin' with him by the CVS, I'll tell everybody, leave him alone that's my neighbor!

Residents often took steps to care for residents whom they viewed as more vulnerable or deprived than they were. Many residents who were placed at the motel by DSS or by concerned family members who could not care for them at home suffered from a combination of poverty, disability, and mental illness that made self-sufficiency almost impossible.

Those vulnerabilities did not go unnoticed by more functional residents. Reg commented to me, "There are a lot of mental patients here. They do not belong here." The belief among residents and even Elizabeth was that caseworkers simply placed their clients at the motel and forgot about them:

ELIZABETH: The caseworkers don't watch 'em.
SAM: Yeah, they don't never come check on 'em. I dunno why they got case managers for, they don't do nothin'. They just dump 'em up here. It's just a dumping ground for the

mentally ill. I don't know your job description, but I'm pretty sure it involves more than just leaving the mother-fuckers here.

Larry once told me that he was open to viewing each resident as a human being. Because of this, he was particularly haunted by the experiences of Curtis, whose mental health issues made him quite vulnerable. One day I walked into the office and encountered both of them inside. Curtis, who had rotting yellow teeth and a brown, shaggy beard, mumbled something about, "I'm in neverspace. My hands are not. My nose smells turkey. Do me a favor, reflect for me," and then walked out the door, holding his hands together like he was playing an invisible accordion. Larry sighed and said:

This isn't helpin' him. You got people you know, talkin' down to him. Makin' his self-esteem so fuckin' low, excuse my lan-guage, that he might not even wanna live, know what I mean? He's a good human being, he's got a good heart, but he needs attention, he's always lookin' for attention. He needs more than charity, he needs attention and people to talk to him and get him outta that state of mind that he's in. And I think it could work. I mean the little bit of time that I know him, he's listening to me. I mean, I give him attention you know what I mean? I don't say, Curtis get the fuck out. 'Cause I'm soft too, I don't like to be mean to people.

Larry finished by shaking his head, planting his hands on the desk, and saying, "I'm getting more worked up over it than his fam-ily probably does." Unable to disconnect emotionally, Larry became actively involved with caring for Curtis. I saw Larry try to socialize Curtis on many occasions by teaching him how to tie his shoes and instructing him to be respectful and not interrupt people when they were talking. Larry also gave Curtis a pair of sweatpants, several pairs of socks, and t-shirts, because Curtis walked around the park-ing lot barefoot in the same navy blue t-shirt and gray pants. He paid Curtis two cigarettes to shower and made sure he washed the bottoms of his feet. I also observed Larry knocking on Curtis's door on a regular basis; Larry explained that he was "checking to make sure he's still alive." Jake, who was sitting nearby, croaked, "Yeah, not like anyone else is going to."[13] Other residents took note of Larry's efforts, and one day Sam joked to Curtis, "You have two dads, 'cause he stay on you just like a son. Clean your room, change your sheets, vacuum it up!"

Curtis's father was a World War II veteran who lived in the Save More Inn and came to the Boardwalk via DSS to visit with Curtis every week or so. Before each visit, Dee and Natalie took Curtis into an empty room and showered him so he did not smell. When Curtis's father visited he gave Larry twenty dollars to hold for Curtis and ration out to him. Sam took it on himself to tell Curtis's father that Curtis was not eating and was not able to take care of himself. Sam was not sure if this resonated, so he gave Curtis some frozen hamburgers to eat and later made him macaroni and cheese and chicken tenders.

Other residents established similar caring relationships with vulnerable residents. Steve, for example, was obviously in need of care. For the week that I saw Steve, he always wore the same outfit: a tan button-up shirt covered in stains, black sweatpants, and shoes and socks so worn that his bare heels and gnarled toenails poked through. During one of our early conversations he simply leaned over in his chair and vomited into the parking lot, then continued talking. Biggie called down from his room, "You alright, Steve?" and Steve replied, "Yeah, I'm okay, B."

Early on in my fieldwork, I saw Biggie grilling pork ribs outside of his room. He gave several to Steve and told me, "I always cook outside, I give my leftovers to people who don't have." Another day, Steve had an encounter with Nolan, the perpetually drunk resident who carried a small pocketknife. Steve had returned from the store and sat down in a chair outside of his room to enjoy the day. Nolan stumbled over and yelled, "Get outta my chair!" and brandished his knife. Steve got up and walked over to where I was standing just as Biggie came out of his room and took notice. Biggie shielded Steve with his body and yelled at Nolan, "You better watch who the fuck you're talkin' to!" He then grabbed Steve's arm and brought him down to his room saying, "Steve, stand over here, man," while shooting a deep scowl at Nolan.

Reg cared for Steve as well. Similar to how Larry behaved with Curtis, Reg paid Steve in cigarettes to get him to shower. After returning from the food pantry one day, Reg dropped an unopened box of crackers at Steve's feet before heading into his room. Biggie observed this and called to Steve, "You say thank you?" Reg returned from his room with a pair of large, black boots and handed them to Steve, saying, "These are brand new fucking boots, here." He then looked at me and called out, "I couldn't stand seeing him in those shoes, you see them? They didn't have any soles!" A week later Reg called DSS and told them that Steve was unable to take care of himself, so Steve was moved to an assisted living facility. Reg said the last straw came when Steve lit his mattress on fire "during the day he was sleeping next to it and we saw the flames and were like, get out! And we got water and we put it out."

Besides caring for the explicitly vulnerable, residents created friendships as they grew to know one another. The sharing of resources over time or in response to a particular situation was a common act of care. Friendships emerged because residents valued relationships that helped them satisfy their human needs for social interaction. Sociologist Nels Anderson observes that homeless men look to break the monotony of life by interacting with companions.[14] Sam shed light on this when he told me, "Get lonely sittin' in that room by yourself all the time. That's a lonely ass feeling sometimes, man, man can only take so mucha that. Gotta interact with somebody, gotta talk with somebody you know."

These friendships were surprising not only to me as a researcher but to residents as well, because the stereotypes and stigma surrounding the motel painted a picture of a location devoid of any sort of community. When Avery and Elisha moved out of the motel into a trailer down the street, Avery invited Biggie, Deirdre, and me to visit, saying, "I didn't expect to meet anyone here, I figured we'd just come here and split."

Some of the most observable acts of care between friends emerged around food and cookouts. Biggie distinguished himself when he purchased a gas grill shortly after I moved into the motel.[15] When the weather was nice, he grilled burgers, ribs, and sausages, and he often invited me, Reg, and Sam to eat with him. Reg and Sam always refused, and I accepted selectively because Biggie's sanitary practices often left a lot to be desired.[16] Despite our misgivings about Biggie's methods of food preparation, his actions were genuine acts of care in which he wanted to share his material resources with us.

Reg and Sky used their relatively abundant resources to care for their friends by cooking for and feeding them. Although he lacked the luxury of a gas grill, Reg purchased a small charcoal grill from the local CVS for four dollars and used it whenever he could. His menus ranged in size and purpose. On some days he would make a large amount of food for himself, such as spaghetti, and then offer portions to his friends, such as Sam, me, Dee, and Toby. Other times he invited scores of residents to elaborate cookouts involving beer, wine coolers, chips, potatoes, steak, macaroni salad, and corn on the cob (figures 12–13). On Thanksgiving he prepared a cheese plate with crackers, cheese, pepperoni, and a homemade cheese log (figure 14). He also cooked baked beans, mashed potatoes, mixed vegetables, squash, and rolls. Instead of a turkey, Reg prepared a chicken in his toaster oven, washing it beforehand in his bathroom sink because he lacked a full kitchen (figure 15). He offered plates of food to me, Shawn, Biggie, Deirdre, Toby, Dee, and Elizabeth. Like Dee and Toby's apartment narrative from the previous chapter, Reg's elaborate cookouts and meals created a sense of material abundance that resembled mainstream notions of provision.

Cooking and care were also used to maintain friendships on special occasions. Sam was particularly excited one summer afternoon when he told me and Reg that he was close to getting a job at a local barbecue restaurant that had just opened up:

SAM: Hopefully I'll come back with some good, good, great news, I got a schedule hopefully.

REG: Well, when you do, man, I'll have to grill out, we'll have a little bbq for your congratulations.

SAM: It ain't written in stone yet 'til they tell me fill out that time card.

REG: Once it's written in stone we're gonna have pork chops, asparagus, baked potato, we'll do the full on, we'll do a nice little bbq for you, man. That's worth it.

Reg's proclamation that celebrating was "worth it" summed up the friendships between residents who cared for each other. Acts of care, especially cooking, used valuable material resources. When Reg cooked out he used his charcoal, food stamps, money, and food to create acts of care. In his mind that expenditure was "worth it" because it created and maintained the emotional connection between him and his friends. Therefore Boardwalk residents created friendships by demonstrating that they viewed the sharing of valuable resources as "worth it." This was echoed when Ramòn told me about the proper way to make friends at the motel, "You just gotta walk by, nod, and say hi. Then maybe a few days later walk by again, then another few days you bring some beers, you know that's always good, you know." Ramòn's words show that friendships were built on social interaction and the willingness to share personal resources to facilitate and maintain that interaction. Because residents were well aware that they lived in deprivation, sharing resources carried a strong emotional component that was interpreted as friendship and care.

CONFLICT

Today's Community to Tomorrow's Conflict

Conflict occurred when perceived acts of disrespect arose through social interaction. At the Boardwalk, conflict erupted early and often at all stages of resource exchange. One day Sam, Jake, Reg, and I sat outside smoking cigarettes and drinking beer. Ned cautiously approached and asked if anyone had a cigarette. Sam chastised him: "You could try to say hi to some of your brothas." Ned tried to defend himself: "I did say hi." Sam shook his head and said, "I ain't see you say shit." Sam viewed Ned as disrespectful for failing to acknowledge him as a potential friend and focusing only on his resources.[17]

Conflict also arose when residents refused to share their resources. Sam had family connections to the drug market, and some residents assumed that he would be willing to get them drugs. However, because Sam was a member of Narcotics and Alcoholics Anonymous and had been clean for several years, he found these requests disrespectful. One day Dee asked him to try to get her heroin, and he replied, "I don't do drugs. Don't ask me for that, don't ask me that again." When Nolan asked Sam to buy beer for him, Sam got similarly aggravated and yelled, "I'm not a hopper, I'm not going to the store for you 'cause I don't drink alcohol so I'm not gonna buy you something I don't drink."

Conflict also occurred among residents who were engaged in caring relationships. In these instances, disrespect was perceived when acts ignored or threatened the efforts to create friendships that revolved around acts of care.

The "can wars," as Sam called them, erupted in early June about a week into my fieldwork. Like many conflicts, they arose from an act of community. Reg supplemented his disability income by gathering empty bottles and cans from nearby locations, such as the trailer park, and returning them to Giant Foods for five cents each. Biggie also collected cans, so Reg showed him the places that he frequented with the understanding that Biggie could collect from them until Reg needed them back. When Reg told Biggie he needed the locations back, Biggie ignored him. As Reg complained to me and Sam:

REG: Dude, I'm the one that turned him onto the business because I didn't need the money. Then when I told him I needed to do it again, I needed my shit. All the sudden he wants to get up before me at like 3 AM in the morning to rob my ass? Knowing that I told him I needed my shit back, I'm broke! I let him take over 'cause he needed the money real bad you know? Don't do me grimy when you didn't have shit and I gave it to you. I need it back for a few weeks, then you wanna play me?

SAM: That's why I really like you, Reg, because you helped mostly everybody here, you ain't never turned nobody down. Somebody knock on your door say he hungry, I know you're gonna give him something to eat. They said they need a dollar, I know you a give it to him.

This all came to a head around ten o'clock one morning, when Reg and Biggie started fighting outside the motel. Reg yelled, "I will kick your fucking ass, run your fucking mouth! Wannabe gangster! I'm no pussy!" He tramped across the pavement to where Biggie was standing outside of his room. Biggie yelled back something about being a "gangster," and Reg shoved Biggie to the ground. Biggie got up screaming as Reg stomped back to his room, calling over his shoulder, "I am going to kick your ass! Run your fucking mouth, monkey!"

About ten minutes later, two police cars arrived, and officers went to both rooms to get statements. Biggie got very loud when he explained what happened, and at one point the police told him to calm down. Jake stepped in and told them, "That's just how he talks," not wanting the police to get the impression that Biggie was being aggressive. The police spoke to Reg and then left without taking any further action, telling Biggie, "Stay away from him, don't talk to him. It's over and done with when we drive away." When the police left, Reg called down to Biggie, "You fucking snitch, bitch! Go tell your buddies from the city how you called the cops on someone! Fucking snitch!" Reg spread the word about Biggie whenever his name came up. We were at the Park Place one day, and when one resident mentioned Biggie, Reg replied, "Fuck that bitch cop caller, man. Fuck that cop-calling faggot. Lucky I don't break his jaw, callin' the cops."

Reg shared other resources with Biggie, such as a wooden table and New York Giants locker that Biggie kept in his room. Biggie's actions with the cans were disrespectful because they increased Reg's fragility. Unable to collect cans, Reg lost access to income that could meet his needs. Biggie also disrespected Reg's attempts to create friendship. Giving Biggie furniture and access to can locations were acts that Reg considered "worth it." However, in Reg's eyes, Biggie did not hold up his end of the emotional bargain, and his disregard for Reg's acts of care created conflict between them. As Reg said during one of his rants, "This is grimy, two-faced, backstabbing shit, then you talk to me like a friend.[18] Biggie's reliance on outside authority to resolve conflict was viewed as a particular transgression because he violated an unspoken code among residents that conflict would be settled interpersonally between the parties involved.

Another instance of conflict occurred over social capital and employment. On Thanksgiving Day I was talking with Darryl in the parking lot as he headed to the bus to go to his mother's house. Reg and Sky were returning from the grocery store, clad in winter hats and hooded sweatshirts. Darryl extended them a simple "hi" as they passed. Instead of returning the salutation, Reg snarled, "You made my wife look bad. You put her name on that application, and she was giving you a job, you wouldn't leave it alone that you need forty hours. You made my wife look like a complete asshole, dude. That wasn't right, man, whatsoever." I was shocked by this exchange, and I watched Darryl continue silently on. Reg and Sky trudged back to their room, and Reg explained to me: "Douchebag. Guy says he needs a fucking job, my wife gets him in down there. And then the cocksucker fucking got hired, but he wouldn't leave fucking well enough alone. Oh well I need forty hours, I need forty hours. Well then I guess we don't need you, have a nice day. Make my wife look bad, dude. What the fuck's wrong with him?"

Because Sky had put her name on Darryl's application, her reputation was at stake. When I spoke to Darryl a few days later, he understood as much: "Twenty hours at $8.25 an hour. I couldn't take it, I can't live on that. But it's enough for me to lose my DSS. Even parole told me don't take a job like that. So Reg was mad at me 'cause he felt that I disrespected his wife for not taking the job 'cause she went out on a limb for me."

When Darryl refused the job, it had the potential to harm Sky's reputation, so Reg and Sky worried that she could lose her job.[19] A similar situation occurred when Jake tried to get one of Sky's friends a job at McDonald's, where he worked. He set up two interviews for her, and she failed to show for either. Jake told Sky afterward: "Fuckin' you're done, fucking I'm fucking new there, and you're getting me to fucking vouch for you and you're gonna fucking screw me like that, fuck you, that's not okay. I'm done fucking going out for people, fuck that shit, 'cause then I look like an asshole."

Jobs were precious to residents, and any acts that threatened their employment were seen as disrespectful. When assisting someone in getting a job suddenly became "not worth it" because it threatened a resident's own employment, community broke down into conflict. This reflects the reality that many residents could not completely disengage from community for fear of creating disrespect, but engaging in community inevitably resulted in them getting burned and resolving not to be taken again.

It was not surprising to see community lead to conflict when it involved residents with mental health issues. The motel brought together people with a variety of vulnerabilities who would not likely encounter one another in more stable settings. Therefore the conflict that arose between vulnerable residents was unique to the motel. As one example, Curtis experienced what he described as LSD-induced mental health problems and what others thought was schizophrenia. As I described earlier, many residents cared for Curtis and involved him in community activities because they recognized his vulnerabilities. However, Curtis's mental health issues often caused conflict.

Curtis was a chain smoker and inquired often about tobacco. He bought cigarettes from Reg and purchased loose tobacco from Dee and Toby, which he then rolled into cigarettes using newspaper and pages torn from a phonebook. Problems arose when Curtis would pace outside their rooms and stare into their windows, looking to buy more smokes. He also knocked on their doors in the early morning hours when they were asleep. When Sam instructed Curtis to stop his behavior, Curtis did not understand why and asked, "They don't have money?" Sam replied, "No, Curtis, people sleep that time of night." Curtis was also unable to register that his constant requests for free cigarettes were taxing on residents who had very little. An exasperated Sam vented to me one day, "And the irony of it all is, after I done gave him two, he bug me, I gave him another one, then he just come back again, like what the fuck?" Toby relayed a similar story: "I was rolling him some cigarettes after he asked and then he knocked on my door as I was rolling them and asked for even more."

Curtis found himself in the hottest water when he left lit cigarettes smoldering on the carpet of his room or the carpet on the second-floor landing. Reg was the first to chastise him for this: "Dude, you're gonna catch the place on fire, do not put cigarettes out like that or on your floor! You can't do that, dude! I live here!" Dee feared that Curtis's newspaper cigarettes posed an even greater threat of fire so she took them away and yelled, "Put the newspaper down or we're done rollin' you cigarettes. If I catch you smoking fuckin' newspaper again, we're done."

Many residents tried to tolerate Curtis's behavior, but at times they hit their breaking points and resorted to aggression. Cinque caught Curtis loitering outside his door and threatened to throw him over the railing, shoving him until Jake intervened and told Cinque to stop being a bully. When Curtis would not stop asking Reg for cigarettes after Reg repeatedly told him to leave, Reg reportedly pushed him into a mud puddle in the parking lot. Biggie was one of the few residents who loaned Curtis money, and when Curtis failed to repay him fifty dollars, Biggie called Curtis down to his room for a talk:

BIGGIE: I'm gonna give you this last chance. This time, when you get the money, you wait for me.

CURTIS: I what?

BIGGIE: You wait for me. Don't spend it and don't tell nobody you got it.

CURTIS: Yup.

BIGGIE: A'ight, young man. You heard? Do you hear me? You get that fifty dollars you save it 'til I get back. You hear me?

CURTIS: Yup.

BIGGIE: When you get that cash tomorrow, don't get all ah, bah, bah, bah. I'm talkin' to you!

CURTIS: Yeah, I already said yes, I said yes.

BIGGIE: I'm letting you know that now. You fuck up, I'll put you in the hospital. You hear what I'm sayin'?

CURTIS: Yeah.

BIGGIE: So you know the deal, right?

CURTIS: Yeah.

BIGGIE: So you think about that when you get your fifty bucks! You think about that ass whoppin'! You heard?

CURTIS: Why you hollerin' at me?

BIGGIE: 'Cause I know you. You get that fifty bucks, you spend it 'cause you got it. Don't do that tomorrow!

Rob was another resident with mental health issues who got involved in conflict. He liked to sniff the aerosol from cans of whipped cream, and it was rare to see him sober. When he got high, he would lock himself out of his room, which annoyed Larry to no end. On a nice day in May, Jake and I were drinking out in the parking lot when Jake ran out of beer. Rob lumbered downstairs looking for beer, so Jake gave him eight dollars to buy some with the promise that he would give him one upon his return. As Rob walked away Jake said, "I said if he robs me, I'll kill him." Thirty minutes passed and Jake grew impatient: "You wanna see what I do to someone who robs me? He lives here, so he's gonna be coming back. Obviously I can't kill him, but I'll beat the livin', fucking, I'll put him in an intensive care unit. I mean, what the fuck? What am I gonna do? Go to jail? It'd be no worse than livin' here."

After forty-five minutes, Jake hopped onto his mountain bike and rode down to the store in search of Rob. Jake rode back in after five minutes with a six pack of beer and said, "Stick around, Chris. You get to see me kill a guy. It's gonna happen. I tracked him down, he was there, bought a pack a something. I'm gonna kill him." It did not take long for Jake to finish off five of the beers, and we sat in the parking lot listening to the radio and waiting for Rob to return.

Rob eventually slinked back into the parking lot. Jake ran over to him, yelling, "Where's my fuckin' money? I went to the goddamn store down there! Who the fuck do you think you're fucking with?" In an attempt to avoid confrontation, Rob took off down the sidewalk, with Jake in pursuit. Jake caught up to him at the Park Place and tackled him into the grass, where they exchanged punches while Randy and other Park Place residents looked on. Rob disentangled himself and darted across four lanes of traffic to the parking lot of the Paulson Motel across the street. As Jake followed him across the street, Rob picked up a large rock and used it to keep Jake at a distance. With Jake at bay, Rob dropped the rock and ran back to the Boardwalk. At this point Reg and Sky bounded out of their room and stopped Jake in the parking lot as Rob ran up to his room. Jake struggled to get by Reg, who yelled, "Stop! Jake! Stop your fuckin' ass! Jake! Before the cops come!" Sky chimed in, "Elizabeth's gonna call the cops, you stupid fuck!" The threat of the police deterred Jake from further aggression. Whereas residents could employ physical violence as their most powerful tool, police could invoke official sanctions or arrests. Therefore the threat of calling the police was the ultimate trump card. Interestingly, when

Elizabeth threatened to call them, she was heeded; yet when other residents called the police to resolve their own conflicts, it was viewed as weakness.

Jake and Rob avoided each other for several days, until Rob approached Jake in the parking lot and told him he would give him his money back. Jake instructed him to simply apologize and return the money when Rob got the chance, not wanting any further problems. A few days later Slash and Vito confronted Rob as he walked by, yelling that Rob had robbed Jake and they were going to beat him up for it. Jake told them to stay out of his business and leave Rob alone because it was not worth the hassle. This shows that conflict was often impermanent, and residents of the Boardwalk were not always on the lookout to pick fights and hold grudges.[20]

In July Reg prepared an elaborate barbecue and invited several residents from the Boardwalk and the Park Place, as well as Sky's friends from work. Despite the fact that Reg spread the word, Sam, Trim, and I were the only ones from the Boardwalk to attend, and Neal was the only Park Place resident who showed up. This aggravated Reg, who ranted, "And those guys were just told down at the Park Place that I was doin' it. That's kinda fuckin' rude, if they didn't want to come they shoulda just fuckin' said so. I got a bunch of people to talk to over the next few days. Tell 'em exactly how the fuck I feel about 'em. They don't need to be coming back around anymore for a free fuckin' beer if they can't make it here."

He and Sky also cooked out for Spike and Mary Anne. The two couples became friendly because Sky and Mary Anne got along well and Spike had connections to marijuana. However, problems arose when Spike and Mary Anne failed to bring food for Reg to cook out with, despite their verbal promises to do so. Reg lamented to me:

Ever since they were supposed to do something with their stamps on the 1st with us they just fricken haven't even come down once. Fuck 'em. I can write people off like that real quick. If you say you're gonna do something then fuckin' do it. They were supposed to fricken buy food to come out and cook out with us. All the times I done it for them, you know? They were friggen sayin' they were gonna do it. Like, cool, shit whatever.

Hamburgers and hotdogs, cool. Just something. Then no, and excuses, this and that. It's like whatever. I don't wanna hear it.

Conflict was created because Reg had used his valuable resources to create acts of care for other residents, who then spurned his efforts. He had used his resources in an attempt to create friendships and social networks that never materialized. On these occasions, his actions were not "worth it," and hope of creating a friendship and care was lost.

These situations reveal another important aspect of social interaction at the Boardwalk: that of reciprocity. When residents requested resources, they had to make very clear what they were offering in return. If they did not offer resources in return, they could be viewed as a "moocher" or one who constantly took what others often paid for. By the same token, if one resident gave resources to another, the onus was on the giver to make clear what was expected in return. The potential for misunderstanding is illustrated by an exchange between Tat and Slash. Tat had just met Patch, who was looking for a cigarette. Tat spied Slash returning to his room from the soda machine with several cans of Pepsi. Tat introduced himself and asked, "You got a cigarette?" Slash nodded, took one out of his pocket, and gave it to Tat. Tat thanked him and walked away, calling out to Patch, "I finally got one, bro. I finally got one." Slash saw me a few days later and said, "Yo, that guy that asked me for that cigarette last night, I thought he was gonna pay me for it. That's why I gave it to him. He was like, yo, can I bother you for one of them cigarettes? I'm like, yeah sure, no problem. I thought he was gonna hand me like 50 cents." No confrontation came out of the situation, but it easily could have.

Although many residents engaged in acts of care, residents often assumed an implied reciprocity; there would be some sort of material or social payment later in exchange for resources now. French sociologist Marcel Mauss asserts that gifts are given to those who need or desire with the illusion that it is voluntary, when in fact it creates an obligation.[21] Cultural anthropologist Carol Stack expands on this finding: "An object given or traded represents a possession, a pledge, a loan, a trust, a bank account—given on the condition that something will be returned, that the giver can draw on the account, and that the initiator of the trade gains prerogatives in taking what he or she needs from the receiver."[22]

Reg commented on people not being welcome to come around for free beer and the fact that he had cooked out several times for Spike and Mary Anne. He was offended by their failure to acknowledge gifts of care in a meaningful way, such as by attending his elaborately orchestrated social gathering or reciprocating the offering of food. Sam commented on Reg's efforts when he and I observed that Reg was wearing a pair of jean shorts that Sam had given him:

> That was when I first met him, he was shocked that someone gave him something. Reg put 'em on and said, oh shit I like these, oh yeah. 'Cause he give so much nobody ever give him nothing. That's why I like him, even though his life is in a bottle, but he's still got a good heart. He still has a real, real good heart. He gives, he gives, he gives, and nobody ever gives him nothing. Nobody ever comes over and says, hey Reg, here cook these steaks, let's have a bbq, I'm buying the beers today.

Reg used cooking as a way to expand his social network and access to resources, as he admitted to me, "It's a way to meet people." These food illustrations show that Reg valued not just the material resources that other residents could provide but the emotional components as well. Like many Boardwalk residents, he wanted meaningful emotional relationships with people, and when they acted in ways that made him feel like he was not "worth it," it insulted his identity.

Transgressions over reciprocity also occurred with those who were more deprived than others and who received charitable donations from others. Cinque, for example, came to the motel on parole and had very little money until he started a job with a waste management company. He quickly alienated himself by asking constantly for resources without offering anything in return and by failing to provide resources for other residents when he got paid. Even worse, other residents viewed Cinque's job as a high-status position, and they resented how he failed to appreciate his good fortune. Sam complained one day:

He know he grimy, that's how he is. Just cut him off anyway 'cause Cinque is like that. That's how he do me. Oh Sam, you got no cheeseburgers? I said I done gave you two of my cheeseburgers, when you gonna bring some food up here, suppose I'm hungry one day, how am I gonna eat? And you workin'! And you got a job! And every Friday, I don't see you 'til Monday, and every Monday you always cryin' you broke.

Conflict arose when residents felt that they were being taken advantage of. Sam said:

He'll suggest, let's go to McDonald's, I'm hungry. And you jump in the car thinking he got money, you go to McDonald's, and he don't got a dime. He one a them type a guys. He asked me for a cheeseburger. Let me tell ya something, man, I'm not working. Wasn't for my girl, I probably be starving, to, death! And how am I gonna take what she buys for me to give to you? But I hate to turn a person down when they say they hungry, so don't try to play me.

Charitable acts of community often led to conflict because residents had to manage two instincts whose outcomes were often at odds. Acts of care showed that residents did not enjoy seeing people suffering and living in deprivation. Residents were more than willing to transfer resources to others simply to make the recipients better off. I asked Sam if felt obligated to help Curtis, and he replied, "Not obligated, my heart didn't want to give it to him, but it's the right thing to do so I gave him a burger. I don't want to see him hungry. I'm glad I was here to help out but cannot take on the sins of this world. I ain't no world saver."

This instinct to care competed directly with another instinct, "you gotta do you." "You gotta do you" is the equivalent of looking out for number one. It is an individual way of thinking in which a resident puts his or her priorities ahead of any others. Residents were aware that even if they wanted to help others, their ability was limited, and at some point the need to "do you" would win out. Conflict arose when residents on the receiving or asking end failed to appreciate that continued provision of resources challenged the giver's ability to look out for his or her own interests. By the same token, those asking for or receiving resources did so because they were looking out for themselves. Thus conflict emerged when residents with individual priorities collided in the community. This helps explain why some residents were caring one day and focused on their own needs the next. Because caring had its limitations, residents constantly had to weigh the costs and benefits of their communal actions. The motel brought together so many residents with different vulnerabilities that community transgressing into conflict was unavoidable. It was distressing that the failures of the mental health and social service systems meant that those taking up caring activities had so little to work with themselves. However, I often found it inspiring to see the residents of the Boardwalk caring for one another despite their own hardships.

Environmental Conflict

I use the term "environmental conflict" to describe behavior that threatened the privacy, reputation, and/or autonomy of residents. Environmental conflict often arose out of social interactions outside the underground economy and acts of care. Because so many social refugees lived in such close proximity at the motel, environmental conflict was the inevitable outcome. Steve got into trouble with Ramòn because Steve loitered outside Ramòn's door while his girlfriend was inside, making her uncomfortable. Sam and I listened to Ramòn explain how this situation led to violence when he finally confronted Steve in his doorway:

> I'm like this, you can't keep this and that right here. My wife is very uncomfortable, you gotta go about your business. I was right here, my little cousin came over, [makes a punching motion] paaap! All the sudden he [Steve] was like, he was on the stairs. He was like, ohhhh. Like he did this shit like a dog would yell, so I, I, got mad emotional. I almost felt like, whoa, are you alright? Cause he was ohhhrrr, roaarrrh. I was like [to my cousin], dude get in the fuckin' house you idiot, and I had to

have the girls hold him down. And I went over to him [Steve] on the stairs and I was like, are you alright?

Sam defended Ramòn's actions because they both believed that Boardwalk residents had a right to defend their property from one another.

Environmental conflict occurred on other occasions as well. Burt was the tall, bald resident who worked in his room on the phone. One day Reg was playing loud music outside and Burt complained to Elizabeth, who asked Reg to turn down his music. Reg muttered that "Mr. Clean" was annoying him, and he later called up toward Burt's room, "Yo Kojak!" One evening Darryl and I were talking outside Darryl's room and Burt came out of his room next door and said, "Excuse me, I'm sorry to say anything to you guys, I know it's a public place. I have to get up at four o'clock to go to work, so any help you can give me I sure appreciate it. Thanks a lot." In contrast to Reg's behavior, Darryl and I quieted our conversation.

Noonan relayed a story to me about environmental conflict that erupted between him and Eric at the Park Place:

So I'm cookin' food in the microwave, you can make a lotta food in the microwave, it's amazing what you can do with a microwave. So he's smellin' it and he's drunk, he's pissy pissy drunk. So, he's like, you gonna feed me? I said, no, you got your own money, you got your own food, you go to your room and cook your own food. And he says, okay, I'm gonna go in my own room and since you're using your microwave, I'm gonna use my microwave and it'll shut off the power. I said, don't do that, let my stuff finish first. He says fuck you and he leaves.

Sure enough, five minutes later, boof! The power goes out. I come out, I go to turn it on, he won't let me by. So now he doesn't wanna let me by. I try and push my way by him and he swings at me. I get him on the ground, I'm on top of him, I get up, I go to the basement to turn the power on. So now Elizabeth pulls over [after driving over from the Boardwalk where she was working for the night], 'cause earlier, prior to that, I went over here, I said Elizabeth, you gotta do something about him, he's really goin' crazy. She comes over, pulls to the parking lot, and he says, what the fuck you want, cunt? You bitch! And dives right in the window! I swear to God he dove right in the window and started swingin' at her. She's like, ah get him off me, get him off me! I went over, pulled him out of the window, next thing you know, cops come.

I spoke to Burt a few days later, and he spoke about the environmental conflict that arose among residents when they went against the norms of the environment, a behavior that he called the "community action program":

> Long-term residents, they essentially run the community action program and if you're an asshole they'll let you know. If you behave yourself and are proper and respective, you usually do okay. And if you're an asshole they'll sniff you out in thirty seconds and then you're gonna have trouble the whole time you're here. But it is their community if they lived there a while, and, and they get very, uh, they, people have a tendency to habituate to a place, they get territorial. And you are, even if you're paying, you're still in their neighborhood and you gotta treat it that way. You can't go in there and say, hey asshole do this, do that, because you're gonna have trouble the whole time you're there. It's like any other community, it's people just trying to get along.[23]

"It's just people trying to get along" was an astute description of life at the Boardwalk that worked on two levels. Residents attempted to "get along" with respect to surviving day to day and procuring rent money, food, and other resources. They also worked to "get along" with each other as they interacted at the motel. In a way, trying to get along epitomized the struggle that social refugees confronted between engaging in community and following the mantra of "you gotta do you."

Because most of the Boardwalk's residents lived on meager means, material resources were heavily valued. Shampoo might seem like a trivial thing to many of us, but one day I saw Natalie post on a door a note that read, "Could you please give the office my shampoo or replace it. Thank you." Similarly, I might not even consider picking up a nickel lying on the ground, but residents actively searched the ground for any loose change or salvageable cigarette butts. Remember that Jake yelled at Slash for throwing away a few empty Pepsi cans, not because Jake was an environmentalist, but he recognized that Slash was throwing away five cents.

Many residents also lacked the social status indicators that are valued in middle- or upper-class life. High school and college diplomas were scarce, as were cars. The fact that residents were living at the Boardwalk symbolized that they were unable to find a stable home. Even though some residents had jobs, they were often temporary and paid little. Therefore residents were often left with nothing but their reputations to speak to their worth.

The importance that motel residents placed on respect is not limited to the Boardwalk Motel and other social refugee populations. As sociologist Elijah Anderson writes, "In the inner-city environment respect on the street may be viewed as a form of social capital that is very valuable, especially when various other forms of capital have been denied or are unavailable." Thus respect is a key part of life in street worlds, and the premium placed on respect is indicative of the living conditions found in these environments. When individuals face "the lack of jobs that pay a living wage, limited basic public services, the stigma of race, the fallout from rampant drug use and drug trafficking, and the resulting alienation and absence of hope for the future," status on the spot matters most because there is so little else to draw on.[24]

This similarity to the street sheds light on another aspect of the unspoken norms surrounding exchange at the Boardwalk. Following such norms (such as acknowledging someone before requesting resources, and showing up to community events when invited) created a sense of community. This community allowed residents to transcend the motel and, in those moments, experience a normalcy of life that was so often fleetingly found in street worlds. When residents broke these norms through acts of disrespect, it exposed the grim reality of their living situations, and the act of shattering the illusion of stability was damaging for residents' conceptions of self.

Therefore resolving conflict that arose through disrespect was a key part of life in the streets and at the Boardwalk Motel.

Conflict Resolution

Because motel residents lived with meager material, social, and emotional resources, conflict emerged when those resources were threatened. Residents defended their resources with threats of violence or actual violence. There are several reasons why residents relied on violence and aggression to resolve conflict.

Although Elizabeth was the manager, her powers were somewhat limited to managing the books. Residents respected her because she could supply them with resources such as clean towels and toilet paper, and ultimately she could call the police or throw residents out of the motel.[25] However, as she was pushing seventy and stood just over five feet in height, her ability to resolve interpersonal conflict between residents was limited. Another factor was that Elizabeth had worked at the Boardwalk and the Park Place for over twenty years. Being exposed to motel life for so long caused her to adopt a quite cynical and laissez-faire attitude toward the residents, as evidenced when she talked about a stabbing that occurred at the Park Place and muttered, "If you're gonna' kill someone, kill 'em, it's one less person to deal with."

Elizabeth knew about most of the illegal activities and conflict that occurred at the motel, but she ignored these situations until they got "annoying." Residents appreciated her turning a blind eye, and as one resident put it, "Her job is to take my money and keep her mouth shut." However, this left a void of authority that Reg summed up by saying, "This ain't high school, you can't go to the principal, gotta take care a shit yourself." Without any sort of formal authority figure to step in when conflict arose, residents were left to their own devices.

Darryl and I spoke one day about Elizabeth's role. He said, "I mean, if you really have a problem you just dial 911." While some residents called the police when conflict arose, it was seen as a last resort. Residents (especially those with criminal records) had extremely negative views of local police and referred to them as lazy and overweight "pricks" or "assholes." Because the Boardwalk was home to parolees, probationers, and many individuals with criminal histories, having police at the Boardwalk was asking for trouble. Residents avoided using the police to settle disputes because they worried about getting involved with the criminal justice system. The roots of a conflict also determined whether the police were called. Several instances of conflict arose over the illegal drug trade, and residents could not call the police to report that someone had yet to pay a drug debt or that they were being harassed at two in the morning to go make a drug run.

What deterred most residents from calling the police was the classic fear of being labeled a "snitch." Summoning the police indicated that a resident was unable take care of himself or herself, and snitches were viewed as those who went "to the cops to do their own retaliatory dirty work."[26] One day Reg passed the word to Mike that Park Place residents were calling Mike a "cop caller." Mike immediately defended himself, puffing out his chest and asking, "Why, 'cause I called the cops on them guys down there to get them off the property?" Not wanting to be accused of anything, Reg put his hands up and said, "Dude, I'm telling you what the fuck I'm hearing. Nothing to do with me, man." At a barbecue, Reg and Neal talked about Biggie calling the police, and Neal said, "I don't play that game." Reg nodded, "Take care of your own business, that's it. I might get mine, you might get yours, either way."

Residents also resorted to violence and aggressive posturing because they did not want to appear vulnerable or easily victimized. In his study of prison environments, sociologist Gresham Sykes finds that inmates are eventually tested for their resources, and how they defend themselves determines their social status in prison.[27] The same can be said of the Boardwalk Motel and the Park Place, where Eric fought when he first moved in because "I was new there and I didn't want to seem like a pussy." When residents were disrespected—especially if the slight became public knowledge—their reputation was on the line. Sam talked about how Jake made racist comments around him: "You know, you hear it but you kinda gotta let it go, but everyone in the crowd hears it. And I don't like that, 'cause it makes everyone think that, oh this motherfucker talkin' about Sam right in his face. So I said, yo Reg, get your boy before I break his neck."

Similar to prison, the motel's environment placed a premium on projecting toughness and physical prowess because residents had little else that gave them status.[28] Because of this, residents not only used violence to settle matters but often recounted acts of violence to each other in order to enhance their reputations. Biggie did this on several occasions when he spoke of his "original gangsta" past:

> I was really close with my brother Ron. We fought together, we shot together, son we kill people together, we kills families together man. Cs all day son. Blue, blood, yellow, and gold. I do everything, any flag in this motherfuckin' hood.
>
> Anywhere I go down to L.A. and we don't play down there. We kill niggas for real, son. There ain't no arguments. It's bang, bang, bang, shut the fuck up nigga, then we off. And snitches get two stitches down there, my nigga. And families don't live down there, my nigga. When we kill you, we killin' your family too. And whoever else you was with, son.

Most residents did not believe Biggie's stories, but the fact that Biggie told them is evidence that he thought it was prudent to do so. Residents also discussed what they would do in certain situations if they were disrespected. Sam talked hypothetically about Reg disrespecting Sam's wife, Justine:

> I would hate for you to scare her or her to come tell me you did something or said something out the way. That would make me be real smart, but you would never see another sunrise, you wouldn't see another sunrise. I would have to do something real, real nasty to you, I wouldn't want to. But I grew up in the ghettos of life, I would have to do something real nasty to you, bro. I can envision you callin' me a nigger and then I'd have to break your larynx so you can't talk.

Female residents also projected toughness. Spike's girlfriend Mary Anne recounted a verbal encounter with the resident living next to her and said, "Well if she comes runnin' her mouth, I can't guarantee what's gonna happen. I'm just warning you right now about it, so. 'Cause I have a bad temper." All this behavior served a purpose as it allowed residents to demonstrate that they were more than willing and able to defend their resources and reputations through violence.[29]

Finally, because many residents experienced mental illness or drug addiction, formal conflict resolution strategies were simply out of the question. Curtis, Steve, and Rob were often unaware as to how their actions created conflict. Elizabeth told vulnerable residents to stay to themselves and instructed Rob, "You gotta go up to your room and stay up there. Don't come down here." Elizabeth also warned residents not to interact with those with mental health issues and told Jake, "You don't give people who aren't right in the head money. You're just askin' for trouble." When Biggie complained about loaning Curtis money, Reg told Biggie, "I told you not to. No matter how much you want to, you can't do it." However, those with mental health issues were often the most deprived of material and social resources. This meant that they often attempted to satisfy their wants and needs through interaction, something that did not go unnoticed by more functional residents. Despite the recognition that these vulnerable residents should be left alone, that adage was rarely heeded.

FRAGILITY

Often, conflict increased the fragility of the residents of the Board-walk Motel. This loss of social capital and material goods left residents more vulnerable and deprived than before. With dwindling resources, residents were driven back into social interactions in order to meet their needs. It was not surprising to see residents engage in community one day, butt heads the next, and then repair their relationship a week or so later to transfer resources once again. Community and conflict were both rooted in and caused by fragility. Fragility created the need for community, community led to conflict, and conflict increased fragility.

Reg and Sky and Dee and Toby had been living at the motel for almost two years. During that time they entered into a friendship that satisfied many of their needs. They socialized (including going into downtown Riverfort on the 4th of July to watch fireworks), and Reg and Dee procured and used drugs together. Soon after I met them, the two began a sexual relationship that was born out of Toby's refusal to be intimate with Dee (which he admitted) and what Reg claimed was Sky's decreasing interest in sex. When Sky found out, she and Reg had a verbal confrontation and Reg contemplated leaving the motel with Dee but ended up maintaining his relationship with Sky. Conflict arose in mid-July when Dee slept with Marc for drug money, which set Reg off because he claimed, "She did it to piss me off because she knows I hate Mexicans."[30] A physical confrontation in the parking lot between Dee and Reg ended with the police being called to resolve the conflict, which they did without resorting to arrest.

This violence did not end the relationship between Reg and Dee, largely because the emotional and social benefits of keeping their friendship outweighed the costs of losing it in a transient setting where friendship was hard to come by. Weeks after the fight, Dee confessed to Reg and me that she was unhappy with Toby, saying, "I'll give him his money and he can go. How you gonna afford to live here, blah, blah, blah. Plain and simple, I'll suck cock for a living." Reg looked at her and said, "Sky and I will gladly pay your rent. We clearly stated that." Later Reg told me, "No matter with all the shit with me and Dee, man, I made a good friend outta her, no matter how you look at it."

In early December 2012 Reg and Sky celebrated their birthdays. Marc allowed them to use his room for the party, and Reg and Sky provided food and drinks, which included a keg of beer, birthday cake, Jell-O shots, cookies, deviled eggs, various chips, shrimp, pickles, cheese, and submarine sandwiches. Over twenty guests showed up, including several from the Park Place. As guests imbibed copious amounts of alcohol, a rumor spread that Jake and Dee were having sex in the bathroom while people sang happy birthday (which both of them denied), and this got back to Reg, who was offended. When Reg cut the cake, he yelled, "Hands off the cake! Back up!" Dee muttered, "Wow, what a dick," and Reg whirled around and called out, "Who wants to say what a dick?" Dee raised her hand, and Reg snarled, "Get out, you're done, goodbye." Dee was incredulous, and Reg conveyed his seriousness by yelling, "Fuck you, cunt! Fuck you, bitch, 'cause there are about five people here who will beat your fucking ass! Anyone here Dee's friend? Go with your skank. Go with your skank!" and ushered Dee's friend Guy out the door.

Moments later Toby arrived at the door, and Reg confronted him: "Do you wanna say something? Do you?" They exchanged shoves, which turned to grappling when Toby punched Reg in the face and Reg yelled to the crowd, "Beat this nigger's ass! Beat his ass! Beat this fucking punk!" Their battle carried them into the birthday cake and onto the floor. Dee and Sky intervened when Toby screamed as Reg attempted to stick his fingers in his eyes. Dee said later, "That scream was bloodcurdling. It was like a child screaming, that sound comes out of a grown man, you get fuckin' scared."

The couples were separated, and guests began a mass exodus from the room. Noonan looked at me and asked, "Do I really wanna come back here? Park Place, or here?" Reg continued to trade verbal barbs with Toby, yelling, "Get out, we're having you arrested right now, police are coming for you right now." Police and EMTs arrived, and Toby was placed on a stretcher, calling Reg a "pedophile" before being loaded into the ambulance. Dee stood outside her room singing, "It's my party, I can cry if I want to!" The police left without pressing charges, although they instructed Reg to call the police if Dee bothered them again. Reg took advantage of this later while several of us sat in his room, when he instructed Sky to call the police and tell them that Dee was outside the room screaming. This was fascinating because I had heard Reg claim, "I would not call the cops on my worst enemy." I left with several others before the police arrived; again, they left without taking any official action.

Conflict surfaced again on Christmas morning 2012 when Reg consumed a substantial amount of vodka and walked down to Dee and Toby's room, where they were spending the day with Petey. Reg slashed the tires of Petey's bike with a large knife, and when Dee came out to confront him, he snarled, "You want some? You wanna fuckin' die?" This was the last straw for Dee and Toby and they called the police, who arrested Reg. When I asked Reg about this, he claimed that he slashed Petey's tires because Petey held him back during the birthday fight, which led to him getting punched in the face.

Reg was held in jail for six months, and the psychological impact on Sky was profound. She fought back tears as she told me, "I haven't been sleeping, I've been living off my couch. I haven't slept in the bed, I let her [Fran] sleep in the bed, I'm not sleeping in the bed. 'Cause ya sleep on the couch, ya roll over, ya know nobody's gonna be there. Ya sleep in the bed, roll over, you expect somebody to be there. I can't do that. I'm depressed, horribly. I'm leavin' my Christmas tree up, I'm leaving all my fuckin' presents sittin' there."

While Sky blamed Dee for Reg's arrest, she still spent time with Dee while Reg was in jail, and Dee gave her money and cigarettes "because she was a girl." In fact, when Reg got arrested, Sky immediately went to Dee for solace and assistance in contacting people about bail money. This was a clear example of how Sky looked past previous conflict when her needs became the priority, and also an example of Dee acting in solidarity with one of the few female friends in her social network.

Even in her damaged state, Sky engaged in care by giving Jake several of their couch cushions to take to a boarding house in Pinewood that he was moving into. Jake's move lasted only a week before he moved back to the Boardwalk and into a room with Marc. Problems arose when Jake returned to the boarding house to retrieve items he had left there (including clothes, DVDs, and Sky's couch cushions) and found his room completely empty. Jake's fragility increased again when the ceiling in Marc's bathroom collapsed, prompting him to move in with Sky.

With Reg in jail, his disability payments were put on hold, and without this income, Sky's ability to meet her needs was threatened. This fragility was exacerbated when Sky was fired from her job at KFC after her boss accused her of neglecting her duties. Without income, Sky was hard pressed to pay rent. Her economic fragility intensified because she needed to put money on a phone card to call Reg in jail and provide him with $75 a week in commissary money.

Sky grew angry with Reg because she felt he did not understand her situation:

You got it easy, you don't have to worry about payin' for shit. I'm out here, worried 'bout making sure that I paid my rent! I didn't send him no money, 'cause I had to give Elizabeth something! I don't want her to serve me papers, I only gave her $45, that's all I had. I owe $470 right now.

Like he doesn't understand that I'm fucking going without shit. I have two stamps left, for letters, that's it. And then waiting for the fuckin' unemployment with no job. Yah, that's a lotta fuckin' money that I've gone without for three months. He doesn't understand that.

In the face of this fragility, Sky turned to her friend Fran, who, along with Jake, moved into the room to help Sky pay the rent. Fortunately her tax refund arrived, which allowed her to make rent payments. Sky eventually won her unemployment case against her boss, but without Jake's and Fran's financial support, it is likely she would have been evicted. As a token of her gratitude, she cooked us all a taco dinner one evening.

Reg's arrest and the events leading to it also caused both couples to seek a move away from the Boardwalk. In mid-January 2013 Dee told me excitedly, "We're moving!" and made it clear that the conflict of the motel had gotten to her and Toby:

We've lost sooo many friends that took advantage of us, we had a guy here with one leg, he was supposed to be a friend, I ended up, just anyway, long story short, we lost so many cigarettes, money, trust, everything, just lost. And I mean, even now like, with the whole Reg thing, that was just ongoing, that was just the first generation of people that lived here, like, we're the last two couples left, everybody else is gone.

Her words reflected the reality that community often led to conflict, which broke down social ties and relationships to the point where maintaining those relationships was impossible. When this happened, residents often distanced themselves from tense situations by moving. By the time Reg returned from jail in April, Dee and Toby had moved, and Sky said, "Second he, we're straight and he's home, we're outta here." Reg lamented, "I don't think anybody from the original crew is here anymore, I really don't." In Reg's eyes, Dee and Toby represented the last semblance of community that he had at the motel. When they left, the motel failed to meet Reg and Sky's needs, and they began to search for a more hospitable environment.

THE CYCLE OF COMMUNITY, CONFLICT, AND FRAGILITY

This chapter explored the subculture that resulted from social interactions at the Boardwalk Motel. Like the inner city, the Boardwalk was characterized by impoverished residents looking to improve their circumstances by engaging in social interaction, such as that found in the underground economy.[31] Residents engaged their social networks and formed networks of exchange in ways similar to Stack's findings in the Flats and Desmond's research in Green Street Mobile Home Park.[32] Social interaction was also dictated by the "code of the street," and respect was earned by engaging in self-defense when required.[33] Implicit in this code was a ban on snitching, which was manifested at the motel by reporting incidents to the manager or, in the worst-case scenario, the police.[34]

Despite these striking similarities to the inner city, the motel atmosphere differed from urban neighborhoods in several ways. Because of the policy that placed registered sex offenders at the motel, no one under the age of eighteen was allowed to live there. This created an absence of youth at the Boardwalk, and also a complete lack of a gang presence. Finally, the motel environment was male-dominated, since single women on DSS were placed at other motels. That meant most of the women living at the Boardwalk were living there with their partners.

The Boardwalk population was forced there by economic forces as well as the criminal justice and social welfare systems. Because of this, residents were a unique population living in a unique social setting. While conventional measures of social disorganization, such as poverty, residential mobility, and racial heterogeneity, were clearly present at the motel, the daily interactions of residents were in fact highly organized around the cycle of community, conflict, and fragility.[35]

Regardless of their previous environment, residents arrived at the Boardwalk suffering from fragility. Fragility led residents to engage in "community" in order to meet the material and social requirements of daily life. "Conflict" emerged when communal interactions created feelings of disrespect among parties, often because fragility had increased because of someone's actions. Conflict resolution was achieved through violence and, in some cases, police authority. Conflict resolution itself increased fragility because social networks and community resources broke down. In extreme cases, police intervention led to fragility when sanctions were placed on individuals that further depleted their resources. "Fragility" then sent residents scrambling back into the community to address their new lack of resources, and the transgression from community to conflict was primed to resume. Over time, the cycle of community and conflict increased fragility to a breaking point when there were no more social networks to be tapped. "Displacement" occurred when the well of community dried up, and residents were pushed from the motel in search of another settlement.

This cycle gives insight into why so many residents had stark histories of transience. The motel, like other locations used to house the marginalized, forced residents to live in close proximity to other problematic individuals. Therefore the culture of the Boardwalk was one where vulnerable individuals attempted to address their needs with anyone they encountered, and these individuals were included in the interaction only because they shared a common residence. The only way to avoid the cycle was to not interact with anyone, but that required self-sufficiency that residents rarely possessed. Even if they spurned the requests of others, this created conflict because residents did not like to be ignored. Ultimately, residing at the motel was a lose-lose situation for many residents because it increased their fragility and left them vulnerable to displacement to a similar location.

These environmental symbolic interactions tell an important story that is ignored by stereotypes and likely to be missed by more generalizable theoretical labels. Records from the Dutchland police department (retrieved through the Freedom of Information Act) concerning police responses to the motel that occurred during my fieldwork show that most were not from calls to respond to crimes, and rarely did calls result in arrest. Surprisingly, instead of creating a haven for predatory crime, the motel environment saw residents organize around meeting the needs of daily life in pursuit of survival.

Residents shared the expectation that those with would help those without, and this collective mindset led to the cycle of community, conflict, and fragility. This analysis demonstrates the importance of approaching social settings without preconceptions of social disorganization. Rather, the goal of scientific inquiry in any community is to examine the ways in which it is highly organized and to understand why that organization occurs. As sociologist William Whyte demonstrated in his study of Cornerville, telling a community's story through its organization shows how the community "appears to the people who live and act there" and how they "symbolically represent the world to themselves."[36] The social organization of residents at the Boardwalk hinged on the social interactions between stigmatized groups, such as sex offenders, the poor, and the mentally ill. It is a story of resident behavior that can be understood only in the context of which it was formed. In the next chapter I will explore the story of resident behavior in the context of interactions with the Dutchland community.

5

Interactions with the Community

All they know is this is a pedophile hotel.
—*Sam*

One of the most intriguing aspects of life at the Boardwalk, to me, was the way that residents interacted with one another to create a self-contained community. Residents helped fulfill the material and emotional needs of themselves and others via an underground economy and caring relationships. However, the Boardwalk Motel did not exist in a vacuum. Motel residents interacted with the local community of Dutchland and extended communities of Riverfort and Pinewood on a daily basis. These interactions were memorable because Dutchland residents made it clear that they were none too pleased with the presence of the motel. In the introduction I used sociologist Harvey Siegal's framework of the motel as "an outpost of the poor located in a comfortable middle and upper-class area which is actively hostile to its presence."[1] These attitudes can be thought of as efforts to "sanitize" the social space of Dutchland.[2]

"Sanitization" is the action or desired goal to remove an unwanted socio-spatial presence, and as sociologist Jeff Ferrell argues, it is supported by rhetoric about "quality of life," "civility," and "order," that ultimately serves to police and control public space in a way that benefits groups with the political upper hand. Citizens rally behind sanitization because they fear the potential fallout for their communities based on their proximity to what they perceive as harmful, and because the spatial presence of particular populations threatens the "Disneyfication" of their social worlds.[3]

This chapter sets out to answer two questions. First, what harms were Dutchland citizens concerned about when they advocated sanitization? Second, how did the behavior of motel residents reflect these concerns? I first examine how the citizens of Dutchland viewed the Boardwalk in the context of sanitization and the battle over social space. Then I explore how motel residents used this shared social space as a source of food, work, and other social nutrients. These findings serve to paint a more accurate picture of the Boardwalk Motel as a counterforce to sanitization.

SANITIZATION

Sex Offenders in Shared Social Space

The concerns of Dutchland residents revolved first and foremost around the presence of registered sex offenders, as evidenced by anonymous online comments from the local newspaper's website:

America needs an island prison-colony like Devil's Island. The rate of recidivism among sex-offenders is far too high to try to rehabilitate them around decent citizens. Sex offenders gave up their right to live among us when they committed their crimes. Frankly, I'd vote for execution.[4]

The writer of this article is very sympathetic towards the "working poor" but what he does not tell you (but definitely should have) is that these motels also house a very high concentration of the areas registered sex offenders. I do not have any sympathy for these people and I recommend that you not let your children anywhere near these motels.[5]

Take a look at the sex offender registry and the number of occupants of these hotels who are on it. I just received a notice today that two moved into one of the hotels mentioned in that article this week. You know how far these establishments are from schools, day cares and churches? I am sorry . . . I don't care, stay away from my home, my children.[6]

Dutchland residents were concerned about sex offender recidivism in their community, and it is hard to blame them for this reaction to what they perceived as a threat to child safety.[7] There is no denying that some residents of the Boardwalk had sexual-offense convictions, but to my knowledge no resident was involved with any law enforcement action because of a recidivistic sexual offense during my fieldwork. Despite this, the mere presence of sex offenders at the motel was enough to encourage some community members to take action against what they saw as a threat. In these instances, Dutchland residents, who were unable to eradicate the motel from the area, engaged in symbolic acts to exert power over the motel residents they so despised.

While I never observed or heard of any vigilante violence directed from the Dutchland community toward motel residents, it was not uncommon to hear motorists call out insults from cars as they drove by the motel's parking lot. I distinctly remember standing in the parking lot when someone yelled, "Fucking pedophile!" from a vehicle. On another day a passenger yelled out, "Fuck you, man!" Reg and Sky were standing with me at the time, and Sky exclaimed, "I told you, the other day somebody drove by and yelled 'nigger' out the window!" Jake told me about an incident that occurred as he was walking back to the motel in early January: "These fuckin' two assholes in a fuckin' car ride by, call me a fuckin' pedophile. I started fuckin' screamin' at 'em, like who the fuck do you? They fuckin' start slowin' the car, like go ahead, get outta the fuckin' car, asshole. You're the one ridin' by screaming shit, bein' a fuckin' punk."

Sam commented on this verbal abuse when we spoke about the Dutchland community:

All they know is this is a pedophile hotel, everyone sitting out here is a pedophile. That's all they know. Everyone knew about the Boardwalk. They knew because they had to find somewhere to put these pedophiles, that's news to Ms. Johnson. She's sitting at home watching TV, she don't want these motherfuckers close to her kids. They ship them way out here. Then the people in Dutchland, there was a big protest about this 'cause they didn't want them up here neither, 'cause Dutchland was an old prestigious ass neighborhood for years.

These insights illustrate the fact that members of the public have a tendency to incorrectly equate all sexual offenders with pedophiles.[8] Jake acknowledged this when he told me, "That's one thing you gotta realize in your book too, just 'cause somebody's a sex offender don't make 'em a fuckin' child molester. That just means they fuckin' committed a sex crime." Many types of sex crimes require registration, including, in some jurisdictions, patronizing a prostitute, promoting prostitution, public urination, consensual sex between teenagers, and exposing genitals in public.[9]

Criminals in Shared Social Space

Dutchland residents also supported sanitization because they feared that motel residents taxed the resources of local law enforcement. In an editorial in the local paper, a legislator cited the fact that in a little over a year, there were six hundred police calls to four different motels in Dutchland.[10] During my fieldwork I observed police responding to the motel on eleven occasions and was informed of thirteen other incidents by residents. Official records from the Dutchland police show forty-nine police responses to the motel during my fieldwork. Because the parking lot of the Boardwalk was in full view of Main Street, it is understandable that Dutchland residents saw police cars at the motel and assumed that a crime had occurred. However, this was not always the reason for police presence.

While community concerns about crime by motel residents were understandable, the data show them to be somewhat of an overreaction. The attorney for the town of Dutchland himself admitted that most of the police calls to the Boardwalk were minor. When crimes did occur, most of the interactions with police that I observed did not result in formal sanctions. Official data show that only four calls resulted in arrest and that police did not record many calls as responses to crime. It is also important to highlight the fact that "jack-rolling," or the outright robbing of residents by other residents, was very rare.[11]

Even when conflict erupted into violence, police officers took on the role of mediators or peacekeepers and used the threat of arrest to quell disputes. These actions were a form of "order maintenance" policing, in which officers used their discretion to employ the least amount of force necessary to maintain public order and respect of authority.[12] This example of police discretion can be seen in the following police narrative of the birthday fight involving Reg, Dee, Toby, and Sky described in the previous chapter:

> PR [Dee] called police regarding fight between husband (PI1/ Toby) and PI2 [Reg]. PI2 says he was having birthday party in room and he and P1 were arguing and P1 punched him and knocked him down. P2 says he had to put his finger in his eye to get him off. P2 had a bloody nose but refused treatment. P1 says that P2 grabbed and shoved him first and that P2 gouged his eye as they were on the ground. P1 says he only punched P2 when P2 went to grab his girlfriend [Dee]. Left eye was red and swollen and transported to EMS for treatment. Claims she was hit during scuffle. Both parties determined to be mutual combatants and advised to stay away from each other.

Another prime example of "order maintenance" policing occurred in July. Jake was in the process of moving to the Save More and borrowed his sister's car for the move. He, Reg, and I drank beer outside his room as the car sat in the parking lot with the stereo blasting. At one point, Jake and Reg decided to smoke marijuana out of a pipe. They had just set the pipe on the ground when a Dutchland police car pulled into the parking lot. The officer informed us that there had been a noise complaint due to the music and that we were not allowed to drink outside. Reg replied that we had done it before and asked why it was not allowed. According to the officer, because those driving by could see us, we were drinking in public and violating the law.[13] As the officer requested everyone's identification, he noticed the pipe on the ground and a small bag of marijuana sitting on a table between Jake and Reg. Another officer arrived on a motorcycle and asked, "Whose weed is it?" No one said a word until the officer asked again, at which point Jake responded, "It's mine." When the officer asked if Jake had any more on him, Jake began to reach into his pocket, which caused the officer to exclaim, "Don't do that! I asked you a simple yes or no question. If you do that again I will put you on your ass." Walking over to the table, the officer from the car picked up the bag of weed, stared at the burnt offerings, and asked incredulously, "You guys were really smoking this?" The bike cop flashed a toothy smile and remarked, "Times are tough." His partner then dumped the contents onto the ground and the two smothered the marijuana in gravel using their black leather boots. As the bike cop left the scene, the first officer warned us that we were all very lucky and could have been ticketed for drinking outside and smoking marijuana.

The local legislator who cited the number of police responses to area motels added that the calls "don't even account for off-site crimes committed by motel residents."[14] I was aware of only a handful of nonviolent property crimes that motel residents committed off-site. Several were shoplifting offenses committed by Dee, who had a history of stealing and referred to herself as a "klepto." She stole small amounts of shampoo, other toiletries, and jewelry from Giant Foods, the dollar store, and several drugstores. This led to several arrests and an ongoing court case in Dutchland Town court. In consideration of her boundary work described earlier, her shoplifting was likely an attempt to maintain the "homey" feel of her motel room. Fran also shoplifted from CVS and was caught when she tried to steal sleeping pills, gummy bears, and a thirty-pack of beer. She was given a court date but moved out of the motel before I could learn of her disposition.[15] Roy told me about another female resident who stole clothes from the Meijer discount department store and cut her foot in the Burger King bathroom when she changed into the new clothes. He claimed the police followed the blood trail to the Boardwalk and arrested her as she attempted to hide in the bathroom with her boyfriend.

The other class of "off-site" crime that motel residents engaged in was selling drugs, mainly marijuana. Motel residents sold marijuana to residents of the trailer park, residents of the Park Place, workers at the Giant Foods grocery store, and Sky and Jake's coworkers at KFC and McDonald's. Unlike the verbal assaults on motel residents and shoplifting crimes from local stores, drug sales were mutual exchanges. Therefore, while some Dutchland residents viewed drug sales and drug use as problematic, such activities were certainly not limited to residents of the Boardwalk. However, the feeling still persisted that, "as these motels continue to decline, they are bringing our neighborhoods down with them."[16]

Community reactions to the Boardwalk and the behavior and social status of motel residents created what I call "stigmatic interactions." The social status of the motel and its residents drew hostility from Dutchland residents. Mass media coverage quickly moved the private lives of motel residents into the spotlight of public scrutiny.[17] Deviant behavior by motel residents did nothing to quell calls for sanitization. What is important to note, and what was largely missing from the public's perception of the motel, was that deviance was the exception to daily life, not the rule.

As social refugees, the residents of the Boardwalk were placed by social services or pushed and pulled toward the motel because of their social situations. These residents migrated to the Boardwalk because its location allowed them to meet many of their daily needs, a fact that Dutchland residents seemed unaware of. In the next section I will describe how motel residents used aspects of the sustaining habitat to address their deprivations.

MOTEL RESIDENTS AND THE SUSTAINING HABITAT

Most of the activity by motel residents in the sustaining habitat was geared toward surviving on a day-to-day basis. As I described in the introduction, for many residents, a substantial pull factor of the Boardwalk Motel was its location. Nestled within walking distance of bus stops and businesses, the motel gave residents the opportunity to engage in the same type of consumer relations that characterized the lives of their Dutchland detractors. Some residents washed their clothes at the laundromat for as little as $1.75 (depending on the size), and dryers cost $.25 cents for seven minutes of drying time.[18] Both Giant Foods and the CVS had DVD rental units, which residents used because watching movies was a popular way to pass the time.

Many residents had positive interactions when they went out into the sustaining habitat. Roy and I went to McDonald's one summer day with his friendly personality on full display. He called the man behind the register by name and joked with a little kid, saying that he was well behaved and that he did not like to see kids misbehaving at fast-food restaurants. The kid gave me several high fives, and Roy told me, "It means you have a good heart if kids like you. They're innocent, so if they come over and aren't scared, you're good." We then headed over to the gas station, where Roy greeted the blonde woman who was working there with, "Hey Miss Lady."[19] He paid for a 24-ounce beer and was given two cigarettes for free. Reg had a similar personality and constantly made small talk and laughed with workers at the places he frequented.

Searching for Food

Residents obtained food in various forms from several locations in the sustaining habitat, and this was the most important aspect of daily life for motel residents. Where residents shopped depended on their monetary resources, as well as their ability to cook or prepare food in their rooms. There was no guarantee that a room at the Boardwalk came equipped with a refrigerator or microwave. If residents did not bring these items with them to the motel, they obtained them by luck of the draw, and many attempted to move to better-equipped rooms as they became vacant.

Residents who lacked the means to cook visited local fast-food establishments on a daily basis. Because of dollar menus and two-for-one coupons found on the back of Giant Foods receipts, fast-food restaurants provided residents with cheap and filling meals within walking distance. It was common to see new residents who lacked refrigerators or microwaves walk back to their rooms with bags from these establishments around mealtimes. Residents visited other restaurants, such as the Home Cooking buffet and the local diner, but these visits were infrequent because meals there were significantly more expensive (Home Cooking's lunch and dinner prices were $9 and $13, respectively, while the diner had entrees that ranged from $6 to $16).[20] The Giant Foods was also a convenient and twenty-four-hour source of prepared food because it had a salad and hot food bar, and residents could buy items such as sandwiches and fried chicken that were ready to eat. In the same plaza was a Chinese restaurant and a pizzeria. When I asked Roy what he usually ate, he told me, "Chinese, KFC, Giant Foods, and pizza."

Having a refrigerator and microwave greatly increased the types of food that residents could buy. Instead of throwing away leftovers, residents could save them for several days. With a fridge and freezer, residents could also store milk, leftovers, cheese, meat, and frozen items. A microwave allowed residents to cook a wide variety of meals and reheat leftovers. Sam told me:

> I buy everything you can microwave, everything you can think of. I buy pancakes, sausage, hot dogs, um, I buy all kind of TV dinners that be on sale. Mostly stuff so I can live. I make sure I try to get vegetables, stuff that I can just put in the microwave. They got a lot of frozen vegetables and I buy a lot of those bags. Sometimes you get four bags for five dollars. I throw 'em in the microwave, boom, eat 'em just like that. Throw me a hotdog in there I'm good.

Darryl used his microwave to make meals out of precooked packaged rice and various frozen meats such as chicken tenders. He also reheated meals that he brought from his mother's house. Roy loved his microwave because he could cook "real food" such as steak and chicken. Meat was a high-value food source and considered a key part of the diet among motel residents. Sam spoke about Curtis eating only cereal and soda when he asked, "Where is the meat, mothafucka?" Dee told me, "There's a constant need for food. Meat is our biggest issue." One reliable source of meat was the food pantry in the church up Main Street, which gave out donations every other week. The donation bags almost always included hot dogs, in addition to bread, peanut butter, crackers, cheese, and canned items such as vegetables and hash.[21]

Reg and Sky were unique in that they had many different ways of cooking in their room. Not only did they have two refrigerators and a microwave, they also had toaster oven and electric skillet. They rarely ate fast food (save for free meals at KFC when Sky was working) and did most of their food shopping at Giant Foods because they received $200 in food stamps each month, which Reg claimed got them several weeks of food.[22] They brought me to Giant Foods in October to watch them shop, and Sky referred to it as showing me "how to live poor."

They began by scanning their discount card at a machine that printed out a page of relevant coupons. Their target was the dairy aisle, where they scoured the shelves for any items marked with square orange stickers. These stickers indicated items that were close to expiring and therefore marked down in price. On this particular day there were small fruit and yogurt smoothies on sale for a quarter each. Reg retrieved a bottle from the giant glass case and popped the top off in the middle of the aisle. He and Sky took turns tasting the bottle and he told me, "If we like 'em, we'll buy 'em all." They both approved of the taste, so Sky grabbed a basket, which they filled with a dozen bottles. No other items were on sale, so they decided to check out. As they arrived at the cashier, Reg stopped to look at a selection of discounted bakery items and bought a coffee cake for a dollar. Elizabeth happened to be checking out and we said hello to her as she scratched off several instant lottery tickets. As the cashier bagged Reg and Sky's discounted items, I picked up a copy of the *New York Times* and could not help but note the irony as I read an article in the dining section about $200 twelve-course tasting menus.

There is a common misperception that those on food stamps buy lavish food or purchase alcohol. In fact, food stamp cards could not be used for any alcohol or prepared food, so residents did not use them at McDonald's and could not use them to buy premade food or alcohol at Giant Foods.[23] Many of the residents on food stamps shopped the same way as other budget conscious consumers do in a frail economy.[24] Residents of the motel did not eat gourmet meals. Instead, I saw them often eating ramen (Reg garnished his with crushed Doritos and other chips), jalapeno peppers stuffed with cheese, simple sandwiches of many varieties (cheese, ham and cheese, peanut butter), frozen pizzas, and frozen entrees. When Reg cooked out using his food stamps, his burgers were bought frozen in twenty-four packs, and other meat was always bought on sale.

Searching for Work

One of the reasons the Dutchland community harbored ill will toward Boardwalk residents was the assumption that motel residents lived off of government benefits and did nothing to improve their life situations. This was summed up by one online commenter who wrote in response to a news article about the motel, "I work hard, so should they."[25] Counter to this belief, many Boardwalk residents pursued work within the sustaining habitat. Larry put out twenty-five resumes into the community, but he felt that he was not getting calls back because he was fifty-five and employers would rather hire someone half his age. Darryl and Spike made similar efforts to get hired at establishments nearby but to no avail, aside from Darryl's conflict with Reg and Sky over KFC.

Despite some setbacks, many motel residents were involved in the workforce, and several locations in the sustaining habitat provided employment for them. Sam and Reg worked at the Home Cooking buffet before I began my fieldwork, preparing food and washing dishes, respectively. When Ramòn lived at the motel, he worked at KFC while his girlfriend worked at the Big Sales discount store. Marc had a job washing cars at a dealership that was a short bus ride away. Jake and Sky worked at fast-food restaurants within walking distance. This proximity to their jobs made them valuable employees because they could work closing shifts well past when the buses stopped running and could come in on a moment's notice if someone failed to show. Jake later got a job washing dishes at the Indian restaurant next door to the Boardwalk and worked until 2 am because he could walk home.

Besides providing an income, jobs gave Jake and Sky beneficial social connections. Sky invited one of her managers and several coworkers to her birthday party. One of them gave Sky a large garbage bag full of clothes that the woman originally was going to take to the Salvation Army, but as Sky told me, "She doesn't want people payin' for them." Jake had a good relationship with a manager at McDonald's, and the two played Monopoly together in the dining room during their late shifts. These games got so intense that Jake went in on his days off to play.[26] In fact, the friendship between Sky, Reg, and Jake began when Jake and Sky met as coworkers at KFC. Sky told me:

> Um, Jake actually started working with me. And then, Reg was walking to meet me one day, saw Jake, and had seen him previously before that when I was talkin' about him and Reg would come see me at work. And then [Reg] invited him over for fish, so they had a fish dinner. Jake brought beer, brought me a little box a chocolates, they sat there goin' through VHS tapes and they been attached at the hip ever since. At that time, Jake was staying at the Save More Inn and then he got him to come down to the Boardwalk.

Sam was a cook whose job search took him to several locations in Riverfort and other nearby cities. He went to look for a job at a local college, could not find the right person to speak with, and left discouraged, "So I said, fuck it, I'm gonna catch the bus." He rode the bus into downtown Riverfort with the intention of applying at Waste Management where Cinque worked. Opportunity knocked while he was waiting for the bus outside the downtown Marriott: "I said yeah, let me go up here in this damn hotel and see if they hirin'. 'Cause that Waste Management bus be like twenty-two minutes, I said oh I got time to write a few application right quick. So I goes in there, they hired me on the spot. Hired me on the spot. I was so happy."

Sam was hired on an on-call basis at $11.79 an hour, which meant that his hours were varied because the hotel called him in only for special events. Despite the uneven work hours, this job meant a great deal to Sam: "Chris, I can say this one more time. You don't know how happy I am. Chris, part time, this sound like heavens opened up. I can't wait. Man, I told ya, Chris, I was gonna stay on, I was gonna get something. It's just it's funny 'cause, Chris, I was not thinking about no hotel, hotels are slow this time of the year, they not hirin.'"

Sam was so excited that he wanted me to come to the hotel when he had to fill out paperwork: "I'd like you to go meet Mr. Richards, the guy who hired me. He told me I had a dynamic personality. That'd be nice for you to get a chance to meet him." When I picked Sam up at the motel, I found him sitting outside the office with Natalie and Mike. As I walked up, Natalie looked at me and said, "He just feels better than thou 'cause he got himself a little j-o-b." Sam replied, "Yes, I do. I feel great about that, 'cause I been hitting these sidewalks. Every chance I get a few dollars, I run out, run out, run out. My feet got so sore one day from just fuckin' walkin.'"

When we arrived at the Marriott, Sam and I made our way into the human resources office in the basement, where he introduced me to a large black man wearing a shirt and tie. I told Sam's boss about my project and Sam jumped in, "Been monitoring my progress, finding jobs, going from destitute and dire straits. And I thought it was a wonderful thing."[27] Sam and I then sat outside the office while a woman instructed him politely about which pieces of paperwork he needed to sign. As we sat in plush, red leather chairs and Sam filled out his forms, he said to me, "You know, Chris, I was just thinkin' today. I'm kinda happy, I'd like to see all our people at the Boardwalk move to these levels. 'Cause most of 'em look at me, they say, they know I'm kinda smart, but they don't know everything I'm capable of doin.' So if they see me they be like, damn Sam. 'Cause I wanna give 'em inspiration and hope too."[28]

Other residents found employment in the extended community but sometimes at great cost. Toby's unemployment benefits lapsed in January so he looked for work but was unable to find anything within walking distance. He eventually found a job with a temp agency working an overnight shift Monday through Friday out past Pinewood: "We punch in at four-thirty. You never know what time you're gonna get out. Could be five the next morning, could be eleven that night, you don't know, it sucks. Generally, it's right after the buses fuckin' stop running, and I have to fuckin' take a cab home so I make minimum wage, and it fuckin' costs me ten dollars to get home, so it costs, it's like I'm not making too much, to be honest with you."

Dee commented on his hours: "He could be home at six or nine 'cause we don't want him home that early. He came home that early yesterday, that was not good. That meant he only got four hours worth of work. But sometimes he doesn't come home 'til, you know, after one o'clock in the morning."

To get to work, Toby took a bus into Pinewood and then caught a ride with a coworker to the job site. At the end of his shift he got dropped off again in Pinewood and had to find his own way back to the motel. He had been walking home recently, and it took him an hour and a half to get back to the motel. Toby told me, "This was to save a couple bucks, then it got too cold, then the next night it snowed, and then after that it got fucking cold as hell, and uh, so we kinda take cabs and shit." The job involved moving produce in a refrigerated area, and the layers Toby had to wear got constantly sweaty and dirty. He and Dee complained about having to spend money on laundry once a week just to keep his work clothes clean. Despite the trials and tribulations he went through to maintain the job, Toby kept it at least until he and Dee moved out of the motel in March.

If gaining employment increased residents' feelings of self-worth, losing employment quashed it. Roy was fired from a job at a local restaurant in the sustaining habitat by his supervisor, who was then fired by the manager for stealing liquor shipments.[29] Roy claimed that the manager had called him recently, not to rehire him but to ask for drugs. When Roy got fired, he spoke with the Boardwalk's owner about getting work at Home Cooking: "He said he could help me out and said to come by Home Cooking Monday and talk to the manager, but I go there Monday and the manager isn't even working that day."

Roy put in applications at local businesses such as Giant Foods and McDonald's but failed to get any interviews. He did get a job interview for a cook's position at a local college, but it never panned out. One of the most depressing moments came when Roy checked his phone messages and found one from his old boss, telling me, "It's a job, my old manager said he be trying to hire me." Roy was visibly excited by this, muttering in disbelief, "Oh fuck," as he returned the call. His manager answered and Roy asked eagerly, "You called me?" The reply came back cold and confused, "No, maybe the other day." Disappointed, Roy hung up and sighed, "Old message." I felt genuinely bad for Roy because I liked him and hated to see him lose hope. When he was evicted a few weeks later for not paying his rent, Roy was still unemployed.

Searching for Treasure

There is a cliché that one person's trash is another person's treasure. For some residents of the Boardwalk, salvaging what others chose to discard was a daily ritual. Although no residents referred to the practice as "dumpster diving," examining trash in the local community often reaped substantial rewards. One day Sam asked me to drive him over to the furniture store up Main Street because they threw out old mattresses behind the building, which he took for himself. On this occasion the workers informed us that they no longer disposed of mattresses in this manner, and Sam was disappointed because he hoped to get a mattress for his daughter, who lived in Riverfort. When Sky and Reg packed for their move, they raided dumpsters at the local dollar store for cardboard boxes. Sociologist Jeff Ferrell calls this world "the empire of scrounge" and said in reference to those who populate it, "Their role within the larger social ecology is to sort among the daily accumulations of trash, to imagine ways in which objects discarded as valueless might gain some new value."[30]

According to Ferrell, "scrounging remains an integral component of the economy's lower realms, perhaps even an increasingly necessary option for many of its occupants," and this certainly was the case at the Boardwalk.[31] The sustaining habitat provided not only items that could be reused but also ones that could be turned into currency. Reg frequently relied on the sustaining habitat to gather scrap metal and cans.[32] While his can collections netted him around ten dollars for a large bag, the scrap metal garnered significantly more income. One day I picked up Reg at the motel to drive him to a scrap yard in a suburb of Riverfort because he needed rent money. He had filled a plastic garbage bag, black plastic crate, small black canvas bag, and monstrous tan canvas bag with wire, batteries, piping, and other scrap metal. I attempted to lift each bag into my trunk but loaded the crate instead because I was afraid of throwing out my back. At the scrap yard, the aluminum copper radiators, electric motors, compressor motors, yellow brass, and batteries netted him $92. As we drove back to the motel and Reg counted the money, Sky exclaimed from the backseat, "Woohoo! We're rich!"

I asked Reg about gathering metal, and he told me that he just walked around finding it. Reg considered himself an expert on scrapping and had previously scrapped on a regular basis before moving to the Boardwalk:

> It's not the issue to know where it's at, it's just the issue to get your ass out there and look for it. Ride around, look for construction dumpsters, look for cleanouts. Look for any job you could do with a truck. Oh, you guys are trying to empty this house? Once I get some money flowing in, I'm gonna throw an ad in the paper, for house cleanouts and everything. Get insured all through Jake, if we wanna make it legal. If not we can just do it all tax free. Cash money. I'm telling you, scrapping is a fucking art, but it can be done easily. It's a fricken game, man, you go out, you ask around, you throw out business cards. Fricken see shit in people's yards, ask 'em about it. Putting yourself out there, seven days a week.

Reg claimed that he could make a hundred dollars with a truck "in a tenth of a morning. I salvage that shit from fricken dumpsters, people throw out a lotta shit that's worth a lotta money." In fact, purchasing a truck to haul scrap was a goal that Reg consistently talked about because it offered a quick source of off-the-books income. "I'm talkin' hundreds a dollars a day, tax free in my pocket. And doin' it on my own time, my own way." When Reg returned from jail he told Jake:

> Here's the deal, when I get my social security check, I'm getting a fuckin' pickup truck. So if you're down with me, we split insurance, we split the fuel, any repairs we split the cost a the repairs, truck will be half yours, half mine, pay you back for the half. And then, we'll split any money that comes in from it. We'll

scrap seven days a week if you want. Fuckin', we could make
some bookoo fuckin' bucks, dude. Five, six hundred bucks a
week, tax free.

Like many plans made at the motel, this one failed to materialize
because Jake quit his job and Reg began to save money in order
to move.

Scrounging also provided a benefit to the town of Dutchland
itself. When talking about his daily treks through the local streets,
Reg observed, "We're a very wasteful nation." The work done by
Boardwalk residents improved the physical landscape of Dutchland and reduced visual disorder, becoming what Ferrell called an
"essential counterforce to the ecological overload offered up by consumer society."[33] Motel residents took items that those wealthier
than them considered devoid of meaning and used them to improve
their lives. As a comic and music aficionado, Jake was happy to find
a toy Batcave and Batmobile in a recycling bin, as well as Mötley
Crüe and Bon Jovi CDs in a dumpster. Dee furnished her room with
a wooden entertainment center that Toby and Reg found by the side
of the road. Reg found two light-up Christmas trees made out of
white wiring and set them up during the winter. As he put it, "I find
things everywhere I go, man. Never fails."

The modern-day alchemy of scrapping was not the only way
in which residents turned items into cash. Situated in a plaza off
of Main Street was an electronics and media store that accepted
trade-ins for store credit or cash. It was within walking/biking distance of the motel, and because of this, Jake frequented it when he
needed money. Sometimes Jake used the proceeds from his sales
for rent, but more often than not he immediately spent the cash
on beer. This was the double-edge sword of the sustaining habitat.
Because so many locations sold binge-ready resources such as beer
and tobacco, residents often spent money on these fleeting items
instead of saving for other purposes. As sociologist Nels Anderson
notes: "The homeless man on a spree usually drinks as long as his
money lasts, and then he usually employs all the devices at his command to get money to prolong the debauch."[34]

There was a sentimental aspect to Jake's relationship with the trade-in store that was sad to observe. Jake was a huge movie/comic buff with aspirations of being a movie director or writing movie reviews in the vein of Leonard Maltin. When I first met him, he had a sizable DVD collection, as well as a PlayStation 2 and several video games. These items were meaningful to Jake, and he talked me through his collections on several occasions. When Jake got intoxicated and ran out of beer, his first instinct was to take these items to the trade-in store and purchase more alcohol. The one item that he did not sell was the complete series of *The Twilight Zone* on DVD, which he proudly showed off after his sister gave it to him for Christmas. However, it was not for lack of trying. Jake vocalized his intentions to sell it one drunken night, so Reg and Sky hid it from him because they knew he would regret it later. Reg shook his head and told me, "He's gonna get like six bucks for it and it's an eighty dollar DVD set."[35]

Death in Shared Social Space

For all the concerns about the Boardwalk Motel, there was a dangerous side to the interactions of motel residents with the Dutchland community, but not in the way that one might expect. From 2001 to 2013, six of sixteen fatalities on the five-lane, 40-mile-per-hour Main Street occurred in the area of the Boardwalk, where the gaps between crosswalks were almost half a mile.[36] When I asked Reg about not using crosswalks, he said, "When you have to walk everywhere you want to get from Point A to Point B as quickly as possible, especially when it's hot." Main Street became even more dangerous during the winter because the sidewalks remained mostly unplowed. Pedestrians had to walk in the road, and I saw several people in wheelchairs using a car lane because the sidewalks were impassable. I even noticed that during my year at the Boardwalk I became reluctant to walk to the crosswalk and found myself running across the highway.

In May 2013 a "use crosswalk" sign appeared at the bus stop outside the motel, although the closest crosswalk remained almost a half-mile away. Even when residents used the crosswalk they often disregarded the pedestrian signals and crossed before the lights had changed. For the most part, when residents found themselves on the opposite side of Main Street, they enacted a real-world version of Frogger and dashed across the lanes to the safety of the sidewalk. The most frequent culprits were Jerry and Vito, who drove their electric wheelchairs between groups of cars to cross the street. I never witnessed any pedestrians being struck, but Steve told me he was clipped while crossing near the gas station, and many residents worried about Ed being hit because he was usually under the influence of drugs or alcohol. These accidents epitomized the irony of the relationship between the Boardwalk and the Dutchland community. While motel residents were vilified for their presence, they were often content to go about their daily lives without doing harm to the local sustaining habitat. In some ways, the greatest dangers faced by any players in this game fell on motel residents when they attempted to cross the busy lanes of Main Street.

Sanitization is a powerful social force. At its root, it is fueled by a fear of the unknown. Residents of Dutchland called for the eradication of the motel because public discourse failed to address the realities of who motel residents were and how they behaved in the context of their social positions. Because these realities of motel life were hidden from the public, this study has attempted to paint a more comprehensive and accurate portrait of the Boardwalk Motel and the social refugees who settled there. When I began my research, it was my hope that this insight into the Boardwalk and its residents could be used to address their vulnerabilities and improve their lives. However, as the final chapter of this book will show, hope sometimes goes only so far.

Conclusion

POLICY FAILURE IN THE AGE
OF SOCIAL SANITIZATION

People can't live like this, they shouldn't have to live like this.
—*Larry*

THE BEGINNING OF THE END

My final day at the motel was a sunny June day with an amazing temperature of 64 degrees. Much had changed since my arrival, especially in terms of the true residents of the motel, who (unlike me) did not have an alternative living situation to retreat to. Of the participants who resided in the motel when I arrived, only Sky, Reg, Jake, Nolan, Rudy, and Kelly remained when I left. As for me, I was no longer trying to get my footing in a new environment. Rather, as residents let me into their daily lives, I had observed and partaken in enough activities to be viewed as somewhat of an "old head."[1] Through this experience, many participants viewed me as a motel friend and a real friend, whose acts of care viewed residents as human beings and not just research participants.

Sky, Reg, and Jake gave me a sendoff. I packed up my car and defrosted my refrigerator as they prepared a delicious meal of baked beans, deviled eggs, macaroni salad, grilled chicken, and hot dogs. We spent the afternoon in traditional motel fashion by stuffing our faces and drinking beer. As the sun set in the evening, I said goodbye to those I had met and headed home with a mixture of emotions. I was grateful to the residents who allowed me into their lives, and I was hopeful that I could stay in touch with them. There was also a sense of finality, in that the motel had played such a large role in my life for the past year. The most pressing emotion, however, was that of apprehension because I wondered what would ultimately happen to the motel and those who relied on it.

It turned out that my fear was not misplaced. A month after I finished my fieldwork, the Dutchland Town Board voted 6–0 to pass a set of regulations discouraging the construction of new motels on the Main Street corridor. During an open town hearing, which I attended, the board passed regulations that required prospective motel owners not only to get a building permit but also to prove that a motel was needed, have a plan for reducing pedestrian accidents, and show how single-family residences would be minimally impacted. The board passed these new laws with the explicit goal of shuttering the motels for good, as the town attorney stated: "What's going to happen economically is it's going to be in these operators' best interests to get out of the business. Is it going to solve the problem overnight? No."[2] While he was correct that the Boardwalk did not close overnight, a series of events occurred months later that made many residents feel as if it had.

In early December 2013 a resident was injured when he fell through a floor in the Boardwalk; the Town of Dutchland responded by obtaining a search warrant and sending in building inspectors to inspect every room of the motel. The violations observed by the town attorney during this inspection were enough to move him to file a case with the state Supreme Court to shut the Boardwalk down.[3] This was reported by the local news, and when I asked Elizabeth about it, she waved her hand and said, "No, he's just gotta, don't read the paper. They exaggerate, they lie a lotta times, the paper. The news people, they make it sound worse than what it was. Just he had to fix up some rooms that, like put heaters in 'em, that were old. The owner is gonna talk to people who will talk to people to make sure, ya know. He ain't gonna get shut down."

I asked Natalie what she thought, and, like Elizabeth, she dismissed the story: "It sounds worse than it is." Larry was working on cleaning out an incredibly messy room but spared a minute when I asked him what he would do if the motel was shut down. He laughed and said, "Drop back and punt. I dunno, they have to, I don't think they will."

While I was surprised by the lack of concern among Larry, Natalie, and Elizabeth, it made sense because they were used to inspections and threats against the motel. It was simply another day in the life of the Boardwalk. Circumstances changed quickly on January 14, 2014, when it was reported that inspectors had found over 250 code violations at the Boardwalk and that the owner would be fined as much as $750,000. Dutchland officials issued an ultimatum and gave residents until January 23 at 4:00 PM to find another residence, as at that time the Boardwalk would be rendered unlivable.[4]

I again sought out Elizabeth and Natalie in the motel office and enquired as to what was going to happen. Natalie replied, "We don't know yet. I hate to say it, but he [the motel owner] waited 'til the last minute." Natalie and Elizabeth were sorting through guest registration cards and, at the owner's behest, writing a petition for the twelve remaining residents to sign stating that they still wanted to live at the Boardwalk. Mike walked in and offered to help the owner with any repairs, to which Natalie sighed and said, "Mikey. It's beyond that, Mikey, come on. Let's just—." I asked if they had told residents about the closing, and Elizabeth said the owner instructed her to do nothing but create this petition and wait to hear from his attorney.

As the date of closing drew near, several developments occurred that epitomized the unfolding chaos. Larry claimed that on January 19 Elizabeth and Natalie fled the area with all the money that was stored at the motel, leaving him in charge. When I saw him on the 22nd, he pointed out that contractors had begun work on the motel and admitted that he did not know whether it would actually be closed the next day. Many rooms were in the process of being repaired; the sole available room had a frozen sink and a broken window, which was covered by plywood. A large green industrial dumpster sat outside the second stairwell, and two contractors tossed the remains of rooms into it all day long.

The morning of January 23 brought an unpleasant surprise for the remaining nine residents, as the wind chill hovered around −5 degrees that day and gusts were recorded as high as 30 mph. This was ironic given that when the closing was announced the week before, the town attorney said residents were being given time to find other housing because "we just didn't want to evict them in this kind of weather."[5] News trucks arrived from local stations, accompanied by local law enforcement officers who knocked on every inhabited room and informed residents that the motel was scheduled to be shut down at four o'clock that afternoon. This caught residents off guard because management had not informed them that the motel was set to close. (The town had posted signs on the motel several days earlier declaring that the motel was to be rendered uninhabitable, but no residents saw them because the rumor was that Elizabeth and Natalie were instructed to tear them down.)

Thomas was one resident who would not accept the possibility of having to move. He told me, "If you can't move on, you can't move on, they're not gonna throw us out on the street." He defended the owner and said the contractors had been working hard, and because he had heat and hot water he was satisfied to stay. Thomas told me that he had nowhere else to go, and when I asked him what was going to happen at 4:00, he said, "Nothing, they can come here and they can just tell ya look, you're s'posed to be out. You know if you can't get out, you can't get out." He claimed that his wife had diabetes and they could not find another place to live on such short notice.

The shock of the morning sent many residents into the office in search of heat and solace. Sarah lamented that if the closing could be postponed by three weeks, the apartment that she was eyeing would be ready to move into. Unfortunately, her husband was forced to get an advance on his work paycheck in order to rent a moving van so they could move into another motel on Main Street that afternoon. She told me, "Fuck it, if all else fails, I'll just sleep right in the van." Dusty complained that it was too cold to move people out and the town should have closed the motel the week prior when it was warm enough to survive outside in the elements. When I asked Dusty where he planned to go, he told me that God would take care of him, and he spent the afternoon drinking tall cans of Natural Ice. Larry tried to calm people down by saying, "We've all been in worse situations before, maybe when we were younger." Sarah shook her head and said, "I haven't had a few hours to move out before."

Residents were angry that they had paid the owner as recently as the day before and were told nothing about having to leave. Lenny was one such victim, and he stood in the office and railed against the absent owner, demanding that someone get in touch with him to fix the situation: "How are they gonna do that when I just paid him the money?" He kept staring intensely at me, and it became clear as to why when he asked, "That's [the owner] your father, right?" Dusty gave Lenny the number for a Dutchland detective who had visited the motel earlier to facilitate the closure and who told residents to call him if they were facing troubles moving out. In fact, Dusty had an idea of his own to pack up his things and ask the detective for money. Lenny then walked up Main Street with his dog to drop it off at a shelter because he was sure that wherever he was headed would not allow dogs.

The exodus started to pick up around 2:00 PM as reporters returned to prepare stories for the evening news, and town representatives, including attorneys and law enforcement, arrived to knock on residents' doors and instruct them to leave. Sarah's husband returned to the motel with a moving van, and they packed up their belongings in short order and left for another motel. Dusty was fairly intoxicated at this point and could not even form a coherent sentence. He slung his backpack over his shoulder and trudged down Main Street toward Riverfort in jeans and a red and blue winter jacket, without telling anyone where he was headed. Harry was the last registered sex offender at the Boardwalk, and his parole officer made arrangements to send him to another motel.

By 4:00 the only people remaining in rooms at the Boardwalk were Thomas and his wife, Lenny and his girlfriend, and two contractors who were working on the motel. Everyone else was barred from setting foot on the property. To their credit, town officials allowed the remaining four residents to stay until January 27 because they lacked the money to move that day. Lenny and his girlfriend planned to move to another motel as soon as they could, and one of the contactors actually gave Lenny over a hundred dollars to help pay for it. I felt a true sense of sadness as Larry packed up his belongings and moved into a room at the Park Place. We told each other that we would keep in touch, but my phone calls to him went to voicemail, and I did not hear from him for over a year. My inability to stay in contact with the majority of the Boardwalk's ex-residents is evidence itself of the problems they faced maintaining stability and social capital.

As of January 27 the motel was emptied of all residents, and yellow signs were posted on all the rooms stating that it was uninhabitable. It was reported that Elizabeth's dog, Mocha, had been locked in the office unattended, and Animal Control took her to a shelter.[6] The Town of Dutchland considered filing criminal charges against the owner because he had started unauthorized repairs in a frenetic attempt to keep the motel open.[7] An investigation into the Park Place began at the end of January, and on February 18 it too was shut down. At last count, the owner had pleaded not guilty to over 290 code violations at the Boardwalk and 418 violations at the Park Place.[8]

After the Town of Dutchland leveled $750,000 in fines and over 600 code violations against the motel's owner, the town made an offer to drop all charges and fines if the owner demolished both motels. The owner countered with his own offer to destroy the Park Place in exchange for being allowed to renovate the Boardwalk.[9] When this offer was rejected, he proposed to demolish the Park Place and convert the Boardwalk into office space.[10] Finally, in March 2015 the owner agreed to demolish both motels in order to avoid the fines and any possible jail time.[11] Around the same time, the Dutchland Town Board passed a new law regulating the use of motels with sixty rooms or less. The new law forces individuals in motels without kitchenettes or dining facilities to leave after four weeks unless they can prove they have another permanent residence or obtain a humanitarian exemption.[12] With the Boardwalk and Park Place motels erased from the Dutchland landscape, the new law ensured that other struggling motels in the area would not take their place.

I was surprised that the Boardwalk stayed open as long as it did, given the conditions I observed during my fieldwork. Residents were equally perplexed, and several assumed that the only reason it did was because the owner paid off inspectors. When Natalie told Roy that the rooms had passed inspection several times, he shook his head and muttered, "They pass? Then someone giving someone some money. It's a hustle." Reg was also convinced that the owner bribed inspectors to stay afloat and claimed, "He has someone in his pocket." After the Boardwalk was shut down, it was revealed that inspectors were not paid off, but rather sometimes they did not conduct inspections at all. A Riverfort County DSS inspector faked an August 2013 inspection of the Boardwalk, and DSS claimed that although it conducted inspections of rooms, "We do not have authority to do code enforcement at any of these motels that we have people in."[13]

These complaints ran counter to Elizabeth's view that residents did not care about their living environment. Elizabeth equated living at the motel with condoning the conditions. When residents complained, her response was, "Just leave!" or, "You want your room fixed? Go buy something, fix it." She failed to realize that residents simply wanted the motel to provide a safe and secure place to live. Larry genuinely felt for the residents and complained, "People can't live like this, they shouldn't have to live like this, this isn't right." Larry made an effort to improve the living conditions but was stymied by Elizabeth and the owner. He complained, "No one gives a fuck, the owner should fix the driveway but he won't, 'cause no one cares. When I try and do stuff, they say, oh let it go, let it go, let it go."

In an expression of their powerlessness over the motel's conditions, many residents fantasized about bringing the owner to his knees. Before Reg and Sky moved out, Sky claimed she was going to call the health department when they left, and Reg wondered how DSS could place disabled people in a motel with no air conditioning. He told me: "I know once I do move, I'm letting fucking everybody in this fucking room, I'm gonna pull that fuckin' ceiling down in that bathroom, show everybody the black mold. Show 'em plumbing, electrical problems that I know are throughout this whole building, and let 'em go from there."

Roy told me, "This is not a safe place to live, I don't think it passes inspection, no way it passes inspection. I'm gonna call the, the Betta, the Betta, Better Business Bureau and ask what is the policy for living in a motel."

Despite these fantasies, those who wanted the motel shut down acknowledged that closing it would create a logistical problem for those in need of housing, themselves included. In one of our discussions, Darryl told me: "When I first moved into the Boardwalk it was bad, with the bedbugs and everything and I was like, you know I had spoken to parole about it and I had spoken to DSS. And they said, you know you can file a complaint if you want and get 'em shut down and you're goin' back to jail."

Jake expressed his desire to report the conditions but said, "I can't just like fucking call the goddamn powers that be 'cause then fuckin' everybody here'd probably be homeless and I'd feel like a dirtbag." Digital was equally prophetic: "If someone got hurt and they had reported code violations there would be a problem. It's gonna take somebody getting seriously hurt or injured, then everyone's gonna be on the bandwagon." His voice got quiet and he said, "It's just really sad."

The saga of the Boardwalk Motel and its closing epitomizes society's attitudes toward marginalized populations. When Elizabeth and the owner neglected the living conditions at the motel, not only did they put the safety of residents at risk, they sent strong statements to the residents themselves. Elizabeth felt that residents did not care about the living conditions and justified the minimal effort that went into rooms with, "You're only getting guys from social services, they don't give a shit." She was wrong on both counts, and her statement showed a lack of awareness of who residents were and what the motel meant to them. This statement also claimed that those from a certain class were willing to accept any living situation. The fact is that many residents would have left for better quarters if they had the means.

Another truth is that Elizabeth did not authorize or fund repairs; ultimately, care of the motel was in the hands of the owner. It was obvious that he did not want to exert the effort or money to make the motel a suitable living environment. This made residents feel unworthy, and this negatively affected their conceptions of self. Local media portrayed the owner as a slumlord profiting by housing the poor, and during a town meeting about the motels the town attorney claimed that the owner made only the minimal repairs required by inspection.[14] Since the owner's prerogative was to make as much money from the motel as possible, it was almost understandable that he avoided pouring money into substantial repairs if the town did not require him to.

The Town of Dutchland used the closing of the Boardwalk as a chance to highlight its commitment to cleaning up problem motels. The town supervisor claimed that the town's action would send a message to other motel owners that "we can't have people living in these conditions."[15] This naïve pat on the back epitomized the saga of the Boardwalk Motel. Closing the Boardwalk was not a victory for anyone involved. If anything, it was the result of the dangerously potent combination of government ineptitude and community efforts to sanitize social space.

In a town meeting held on July 25, 2013, the town attorney stated that building inspections took place at the Boardwalk every two weeks. Given that the conditions of the motel were no worse when it closed than when I moved in, this claim is hard to believe. A local legislator then wrote a letter to the local paper stating that she received documents through the Freedom of Information Act that showed that such inspections were not occurring.[16] Considering the revelation that Riverfort County DSS faked building inspections of the Boardwalk, the government's dedication to providing livable conditions for marginalized populations must be called into question.

It was painfully obvious that nobody in any position of authority took responsibility for the well-being of the Boardwalk's residents. Riverfort County DSS claimed that it was unable to enforce any code violations found at the Boardwalk, despite the fact that as an agency, it conducted inspections, placed individuals at the motel, and paid the owner to house clients. According to DSS, Dutchland was responsible for enforcing municipal codes at the motel.[17] When the town inspected the motel in December 2013, the town attorney reacted as if the conditions of the motel were a complete surprise. If inspections were being conducted and reported to the town, this would not have been the case. Both Riverfort County and the Town of Dutchland exhibited extreme negligence in monitoring a location that housed the area's most vulnerable individuals. Why did these governments turn blind eyes as the Boardwalk Motel languished on life support and its living conditions endangered residents' lives?

The answer lies in the concerns about social space that plagued the Boardwalk for years. It was no secret that Dutchland residents and government officials actively sought to remove the motel from the area through political action. This was a difficult process because the motel's contract was with Riverfort County and not the Town of Dutchland. In a way, the perceived powerlessness on part of the Dutchland Town Board may have contributed to the accumulation of code violations that were eventually found at the motel. If Dutchland officials feared that the motel owner would address minor violations only enough to meet code and remain in business, then allowing violations to reach a crescendo of no return would place the blame squarely on the owner's shoulders. This would then give the town cause to shut the motel down for good.

When the town moved to make it harder to build new motels in Dutchland, the town attorney set the stage for the blame game when he said, "We have operators willing to take these people."[18] A legislator complained, "We are not addressing the root of the problem" and called for Dutchland to enforce the town's definition of the motel as a location that provided "transient overnight accommodations from persons away from their place of residence."[19] She was indeed correct that making it harder to build motels did not address the root of the problem, but her definition of the problem was limited to the concerns about social space that permeated relations between the Boardwalk Motel and the Dutchland community. The "problem" that plagued the town of Dutchland could not be fixed by regulating how many sex offenders could live at the Boardwalk, nor could it be addressed by making it harder to build motels. It would persist without the presence of the Boardwalk Motel. In 1923 sociologist Nels Anderson came to a similar conclusion when he wrote about his study of hobo culture in Hobohemia (a section of Chicago populated largely by homeless single men), "Some have proposed abolishing Hobohemia as a slum, but the many roads that lead to such a place as Hobohemia would still have to terminate at a common point."[20] The problem posed by the Boardwalk Motel was not the fact that it existed but the fact that it was needed.

UNDERSTANDING THE "PROBLEM"

This study was motivated by a desire to understand how residents lived in the Boardwalk Motel, a space where the effects of criminal justice and social policies were made visible. Understanding requires a deep appreciation of where residents came from and what role the motel played in their daily lives. It was this appreciation of how others lived that discourse about the Boardwalk tragically missed. The stigma of the motel was so blinding that many were unable to see the residents as human beings with their own history, behavior, and culture. These aspects of motel life are illustrated in the following summaries of this book's findings.

How Did Residents Come to Live at the Boardwalk?

Throughout this book, I have drawn on Erving Goffman's conceptualization of stigma as "an attribute that is deeply discrediting" to the point "where we tend to impute a wide range of imperfections on the basis on the original one."[21] The stigma attached to the Boardwalk Motel was so powerful that outsiders viewed its residents as nothing but a social problem. This stereotype masked the complex ways in which life experiences and social forces combined to lead individuals to the Boardwalk. To describe why residents ended up at the Boardwalk, I conceptualized them as "social refugees" or persons who were forced to relocate within their own country of citizenship because of the influence of social context and/or social policy. Because the Riverfort County DSS designated the motel as an "emergency shelter," the social refugee metaphor is quite apt to describe this experience.

Many Boardwalk residents were returning to society from prison, and their residences had to be approved by parole. For registered sex offenders, the Boardwalk was often the only option because of local residence restrictions and/or parole prohibitions on residing with family or friends. Other parolees simply could not afford another residence and were placed at the motel by the Homeless and Traveler's Aid Society until they could find work and a suitable place to live. In this respect, the criminal justice system directed these residents to the Boardwalk as part of the reentry process.

Some residents "stepped up" to the Boardwalk after living in boarding houses, shelters, or literally the backseat of their car. These residents were pulled toward the motel because it represented better living conditions than what they had endured previously. Another group of residents "stepped down" to the motel after their living situations became untenable. This displacement was usually the result of some sort of vulnerability, such as losing a job, and residents intended to use the motel to get back on their feet. These typologies demonstrated that the paths that brought residents to the motel played an important role in how residents viewed the motel.

HATAS and the Riverfort County DSS (including Adult Protective Services) placed other residents at the motel because they lacked appropriate housing for one reason or another. These residents often had some sort of disability that rendered them unable to work and/ or take care of themselves. These placements illustrated the myriad conditions experienced by residents before they arrived at the motel. Exploration into these experiences revealed that the majority of residents had histories of trauma, criminal behavior, substance use, disability, and previous bouts of transience and residential instability. By parting the clouds of stigma shrouding the motel, we see that the lives of many marginalized populations were shaped by a multitude of factors both in and out of their control. When we consider the complex histories of vulnerability, we gain better insight as to how policies can be directed to help those in similar situations.

How Did Residents Interact with the Local Community?

The Boardwalk was located within a Dutchland community that was demographically white, affluent, and residentially stable. By contrast, motel residents were racially diverse, poor, and transient. Because of this, Dutchland residents viewed the motel as an eyesore and worried about how the motel residents affected their community. This was problematic because what made the Boardwalk so attractive to social refugees was the sustaining habitat that provided numerous amenities within walking distance.

While the tensions between both communities never erupted into physical violence, Boardwalk residents were often subject to verbal abuse and could not sit peacefully outside of their rooms without hearing insults shouted out from passing cars. These insults made it clear that motel residents were unwanted in Dutchland, despite the fact that many received emergency housing assistance and had no control over where they were placed. A few female residents shoplifted from local businesses, but other than these property crimes, motel residents did not prey on the Dutchland community in the ways that Dutchland residents feared.

Despite those transgressions, the majority of motel residents had a mutually beneficial relationship with the sustaining habitat. They purchased food at the local grocery store and fast-food locations, and some residents, such as Jake and Sky, had legitimate jobs within the community. Other residents embarked into what Jeff Ferrell calls "the empire of scrounge" by collecting scrap metal and other discarded consumer items from dumpsters or public areas.[22] This underground environmental action gave motel residents income and meaningful goods while reducing the amount of visible waste in Dutchland and saving valuable landfill space.

How Did Motel Residents Interact with One Another?

Of all the findings that emerged from this study, the most surprising was the discovery of the motel's vibrant culture. This culture revolved around satisfying the wants and needs of residents through social interaction. These needs were both material and social, and addressing them created community among motel residents. Residents satisfied their material needs by fostering an underground economy where goods such as cigarettes and food, as well as services, were exchanged on a daily basis. Some enterprising residents realized the importance of this exchange and sold items such as drugs or individual cigarettes for substantial profit. Because many residents lacked cash, the underground economy was a web of exchange that allowed them to negotiate prices based on the resources that each participant brought to the table.

Another surprising aspect of the Boardwalk community was the way that residents went out of their way to care for one another. Despite the fact that residents functioned with few resources, many recognized that some were more vulnerable than others. It was common to see residents donate food and clothing to those who lacked the means to care for themselves. The residents who engaged in care work often provided for disabled residents placed at the motel by DSS with little financial or social support. These efforts were motivated by a widespread belief that case workers simply placed clients at the motel and left them "to die." Other instances of care involved summer cookouts and parties celebrating special occasions like holidays or birthdays. Despite their meager resources, residents understood that the effort of preparing and sharing food was a universally accepted symbol of care. By caring for one another, the relationships among residents progressed beyond underground business transactions to emotional connections.

Conspicuously absent at the motel were robberies, burglaries, and other visible interpersonal crimes characteristic of locations that scholars may consider socially disorganized.[23] Inspections of police records indicated that most calls to the motel were to check on disabled individuals and resolve interpersonal conflict. These confrontations were not random acts of violence but arose instead from community interactions gone wrong. This conflict was created when social interactions created feelings of disrespect between residents. Such occasions often occurred when residents attempted to care for others by sharing resources and did not receive material or emotional support in return.

The primary culture of the motel was one of community, which unavoidably led to conflict. Because residents had so few resources, threats to those resources were taken very seriously. Conflict arose out of and created fragility, which was a shortage of material goods and social capital that left residents vulnerable to unexpected or self-inflicted disruptions to short- and long-term goals. This hallmark of motel life created a cycle that began when residents were displaced from previous environments in a state of fragility and arrived at the motel from prison, or after stepping up or down. When they arrived, residents engaged in acts of community to satisfy their material and social needs. These actions often led to conflict, which increased fragility and left residents in greater need of material resources and social support. Residents fluctuated between community and conflict until the living environment became untenable, at which point they were displaced from the motel and became social refugees in search of another settlement.

Where Are They Now?

Upon leaving the motel, residents either stepped up or stepped down, depending on their social situations and the available housing options. The locations that residents migrated to depended on the circumstances that led to their displacement from the Boardwalk. The transient nature of the motel and its chaotic shutdown made it difficult to keep in touch with the residents who contributed to this book. Many residents, such as Ed and Anthony, simply disappeared and left no indication as to where they went or why. For those residents whose moves were known to me, migration from the motel was either by force or by choice. In the next pages, I relate how, to the best of my knowledge, several residents left the motel and where they are as of this writing.

The government shutdown of the motel was the ultimate forced move, and the social refugees involved in that situation scattered to any settlement that would take them. Closing the Boardwalk was a modern-day version of the response to "urban nomads," who, according to sociologist James Spradley, live largely hidden from society and are "run out," "*pushed from* a destination," and told to "keep moving" when discovered by citizens and police.[24] The other common form of displacement by force was eviction for nonpayment of rent. To their credit, Elizabeth and the owner were fairly accommodating of the financial needs of residents. Residents were in such dire straits that coming up with $205 a week was a challenge that often came down to the wire. In these instances, management allowed some residents to get days, sometimes even weeks, behind on rent before starting eviction proceedings.[25] This policy appeared to be reserved for long-term residents, as short-term residents such as Burt and Tat were sent packing days after they failed to pay.

Removing residents who had been at the motel for over thirty days was a more involved process that required the aid of the county sheriff. Roy was evicted in July 2012 after he failed to secure a job and fell behind with his rent. His eviction caused quite a stir because he had a verbal altercation with Elizabeth in the parking lot over items that he claimed were missing from his room. Elizabeth told me later that she gave him time to clean out his room before the sheriff placed a lock on the door but he did not use the opportunity. Roy eventually took the owner of the motel to court, and Elizabeth claimed that the owner settled with him for an unspecified amount. After Roy was evicted, Natalie claimed that she saw him sleeping in bus stops in the fall and then eventually ran into him during the winter at another hotel used by social services. Roy was arrested in early February 2013 in a statewide bust of a large cocaine ring and sent to jail. As of January 2016, records revealed that his earliest release date would be July 2016.

Because the root of eviction was nonpayment of rent, evicted residents lacked the financial means to find other housing, and without social support, they became literally homeless. This was the situation that the older resident Love, her son Ben, and his girlfriend Lisa ran into in early January 2014, just weeks before the motel was shut down.

Ben had been out of jail for a week, and he and Lisa were staying with Love at the Boardwalk because they had no other place to live. The news of the Boardwalk's closing stressed Ben. "Shit is fuckin' drivin' me crazy. I don't know what's gonna happen now, this place is closing, I'm sure my probation officer is gonna be like, where the fuck you gonna go now?" DSS told him to go to the mission, but Ben felt that he would be better in an apartment because the mission was "just not what I need." He seemed less worried about his mother because DSS would "put her in a nice little shelter that's all women. They'll look out for her." However, the closing of the Boardwalk posed a problem because as long as it was open, Ben, Lisa, and Love could stay together as a family unit in the room that Love paid for. If the motel closed, then they would be separated, and Ben said that Love had no resources to pay for an apartment: "She's been there six months payin' two hundred dollars a week but she only gets like 650 for fuckin', stupid social security or SSI or whatever the shit is that she has. And then fuckin', like she blew through all of her savings that she had."

This situation came to a head a week later when Elizabeth started eviction proceedings against Love. The date of their eviction was a brutally cold Friday in January, and two sheriff's deputies arrived to force Love, Ben, and Lisa out of their room. They lacked a housing option other than DSS and had no mode of transportation, so I offered to drive them to DSS. The family filled as many garbage bags and canvas tote bags as they could, but they were still forced to leave belongings in the room when they left.

One item that they did not leave behind was a small, gray, one-year-old cat, who Love brought down to my car in a cardboard carrier that was falling apart. Love pleaded with me through her tears to take care of the cat, and I assured her that I would find her a good home. As we drove down Main Street toward DSS, Love sobbed uncontrollably in my front seat, only pausing to apologize to her son Ben, wailing, "I fucked up my life. I fucked up everything by living there." Ben was far less emotional and instructed her, "You can't do this shit down at DSS. You can't be cryin' in front of them." Love worried that they were going to be split up and could not bear of the thought of being separated. Ben assured her that she would probably be placed in a good living situation, while he would have to fend for himself in a mission. Lisa was unable to go on DSS because of an earlier sanction due to Ben dealing marijuana out of her apartment. Ben told me that the motel's closing would likely end their relationship. I dropped them off at DSS and we exchanged phone numbers, although all three of them told me that they had no more minutes on their prepaid phones. Since then I have not been able to get in touch with them, although I honored my promise to Love by adopting her cat.

Other residents were removed from the motel by their caseworkers. After Reg and Larry complained to Curtis's family and caseworker, he was moved to an apartment and then the same motel where Natalie had seen Roy. Natalie remarked to me, "So yeah, I couldn't believe it. It was like a fuckin' Boardwalk reunion." Steve was moved to an adult care facility by his caseworker after Reg contacted DSS about Steve's living conditions. Vito worked with his caseworker to get moved out of the motel and left mere weeks before the motel was shut down. He was placed in an adult care facility that I suspect was the same one that Steve went to. After I visited him at the facility a few times, Vito's phone was shut down and I lost contact with him.

Residents who were placed by DSS and violated their conditions of emergency housing were also forced to leave. In these instances,

DSS called Elizabeth, who then instructed the residents to leave peacefully without police involvement. This happened to Jasper and Patch, who were both kicked out on the same day in April. I saw Jasper standing next to the second stairwell wearing a gray hooded sweatshirt and guarding half a dozen bags of belongings. He told me he was waiting for his coworkers to arrive because he was going to stay with them. When they pulled up in a black minivan with stenciled advertising for a cleaning service, I helped Jasper put his bags in the van and he gave me a hug and told me to take care. I was never able to reconnect with Jasper or Patch, and I am unsure what happened to them.

Because Darryl was paroled as a registered sex offender, he had to work with both his parole officer and a caseworker from DSS to find alternative housing. DSS's goal was to move him to a location that was cheaper than the Boardwalk, and a few options were available, including a rooming house with an awful reputation outside of Riverfort. In January 2013 Darryl's parole officer moved him to a motel in downtown Riverfort, which Darryl hated because he had to share a room with two other men. He told me, "I'm not good with this, I'm not good with living with other people, I freak out." He and his partner hoped to get an apartment together, and Digital searched Craigslist postings for locations that would accept DSS payments, but ultimately Darryl's parole officer had to approve any move.

At the end of January Darryl was approved to move into a twelve-room boarding house outside of Riverfort. Digital soon moved into the same boarding house but in a different room, and they were happy to be only a hallway apart. This rooming house was an hour and a half bus ride from Riverfort and at the end of a pockmarked dirt road. When I visited, Darryl told me, "This is like slum city," and he admitted he thought it was worse than the Boardwalk. On each of my numerous visits, the same two men sat in the living room huddled under blankets watching a tiny television with the lights off. There was one working bathroom, one working shower, and a shared kitchen. Residents often turned on the oven to 450 degrees and then left the door open in order to heat the first floor. The only working bathroom had a toilet full of murky water, and scattered across the floor were the carcasses of expired air fresheners. A nugget of soap sat on a sink basin covered in so much grime that using the soap was probably more hazardous than not.

In April 2013 Darryl told me that a park was under construction behind the building and because he could not live within 1,000 feet of a park, he was being evicted from the boarding house.[26] He and Digital found an apartment in a nearby city and asked me to help them move. It was fortunate that I did help because on moving day, Darryl's nephew was supposed to provide additional transportation but never showed; without me, Darryl and Digital would not have been able to move.

Their new apartment was located in an unassuming two-story white building with four units. They felt good about this step up and were eager to decorate and spruce it up with a fresh coat of paint. Digital told me that it was a lot of space for the $600 they paid, and it was quiet in all directions. Unfortunately, less than a month later, parole informed Darryl that he could not live there because there was a daycare within 1,000 feet. Darryl and Digital again went on the hunt for apartments and found a list of ten that they brought to parole, out of which four were approved. Darryl complained that the local police department did not say anything about the daycare when he registered. His displacement was due to a statewide law restricting where registered sex offenders could live, which trumped any decisions by local government.

I was out of town when Digital and Darryl moved to their new apartment in downtown Riverfort so I was unable to assist them. Darryl's nephew did come through this time to drive the moving van, but the move was not without hardship, as Darryl later told me: "Moving was a crazy day. We were supposed to move to a two bedroom, the day we were supposed to move the landlord canceled on us. He rented it to somebody else. So we ran around all day finding a different apartment and moved in the evening." Digital called it a "desperate move" because each address had to be given to the parole officer and checked out in a period of just a few hours. "It was just so hard. It wasn't just it had to be a vacant apartment and we could move there, it had to be within, ya know, the guide-lines." The apartment they ended up taking was the only one that parole approved, and they showed up at 7:00 PM with a truckload of their belongings, praying that the landlord still had the apartment, which he did.

Despite their dramatic arrival, Dig and Darryl were very happy with their new apartment, and it provided them with the stability and security to improve their lives. Darryl started working with a local company that unloaded freight cars, and he quickly earned an administrative position. Sadly, when I spoke to Darryl in May 2014, he had lost his job because a supervisor did not agree with the company's policy of hiring registered sexual offenders. His relationship with Digital was also crumbling, and Darryl was giving consideration to moving to New York City or Florida for a fresh start. Things turned around in the fall of 2014, when Darryl got a new job and received a car from a close friend.

In April 2015 Darryl ended his relationship with Digital and moved into an apartment a few miles away in Riverfort. This new apartment was a one bedroom that cost $650 and included all utilities. Darryl was happy that he had the money to pay for it on his own and did not need DSS to assist with rent. When I asked why he ended his relationship with Digital, Darryl told me that "I could not deal with his craziness anymore" but spoke of his affection for Digital: "I still love him and I try to help him out the best I can." According to Darryl, Digital was self-medicating with alcohol and marijuana and was about to get evicted. In May 2015 Darryl started a new job as a low-level manager in a warehouse, making $25 an hour. This money allowed him to purchase a new car with the help of an auto loan. When I spoke to him in July 2015, he was cheerful and told me that he was still involved with the AIDS council and other community organizations.

I was finally able to make contact with Larry in the summer of 2015, when he called me from a new phone number. He told me that after the Park Place was shutdown, the owner allowed him to live at another motel for free in exchange for doing maintenance. He lived at that motel for a year, making $40 a week, and then moved to downtown Riverfort with a friend he had known for years. Larry was excited because his disability was approved and set to kick in in November, which would give him almost $1,500 a month. He told me that living would be tight until then, because he was only receiving $300 a month from his retirement. However, he was happy to be where he was and said, "As long as I'm above ground, I'm okay."

Most of the residents I encountered at the Boardwalk had the goal of stepping up to a better location when their resources permitted. Numerous residents expressed the desire to move but admitted that since they arrived at the motel, all their resources had gone toward survival, and they had no money to save for a new home. Because of this, those who moved out on their own terms never did so without a drastic change in life circumstances. This high cost of being poor has been well documented by Barbara Ehrenreich, who calls being poor "a perpetual high-wire act."[27]

It was only after securing two jobs that Sam was able to save enough to move into an apartment with his partner Justine. We spoke via phone on several occasions about me coming to see it, and Sam seemed genuinely excited to show how his circumstances had improved. Sadly, he stopped returning my calls, and I was never able to find out what happened to him, though rumors abounded that he fell back into drug use.

The young couple Avery and Elisha had a relatively short stay at the motel of several weeks and moved out into a newly purchased trailer, thanks to an influx of money from Avery's worker's compensation case. Without it they would have stayed at the Boardwalk.

Biggie and Deirdre moved into a trailer park in December 2012 after months of planning. Their move was facilitated by the purchase of a car that allowed them to move their possessions. The car purchase was made possible by the owner and Elizabeth giving the couple leeway on rent payments so they could save enough for the car. Sadly, Reg and Sky claimed that they ran into Biggie on July 4, 2013, and he told them that Deirdre had died of a stroke and that he was back to living in a motel after spending some time living out of his car.

Dee and Toby moved out of the motel in March 2013 into an apartment in Pinewood that cost $450 a month. This move was facilitated by financial resources from their limited social networks. Toby's sister offered to pay the first month's rent as long as Dee and Toby could come up with the security deposit. Without this offer, they would not have been able to move, and Dee told me, "You know we got no savings, all our savings went to rent for this place at $205 a week." Dee and Toby recognized how lucky they were to receive this financial aid because they felt they had burned all of their social bridges through their addictions. Like Biggie and Deirdre, Dee and Toby benefited from some managerial wiggle room when they were short on rent. Furthermore, Dee's friend and ex-client, Guy, paid their week's rent on over a dozen occasions. Without this support from Guy and motel management, Dee and Toby would have been evicted from the motel long before they moved out by choice.

In August 2013 Jake, Reg, and Sky moved out of the motel and into a two-bedroom apartment in Pinewood for $675 a month. As a makeshift family unit, they had planned on moving out for quite some time, especially since most of their friends had left. Reg told me, "I had enough, fricken tired a livin' there, tired a da people, the place is changed so much from what it used to be, bro. From when it used to be Sam and all a us, it changed so much, man." Another impetus for the move was the fact that the owner wanted to charge them an extra $30 a month because Jake shared the room. Reg complained, "The second you tell me you're gonna jack my rent up, keep taking stuff away, nothing works, then you tell me you wanna jack my rent up, it's the last straw."

The three of them pulled together enough money to move. Jake was indebted to Reg and Sky, and although they were angry at him for delaying his payments, he did finally offer a large sum that could be put toward the move. Ironically, Sky's loss of her job was also a blessing in disguise because her unemployment payments were initially delayed, so the lump sum she then received helped to pay for the apartment. The move was a huge step up, and in the weeks leading up to the move, Sky giddily said, "I'm just so excited, to get the hell outta here. We need stability is what it is. Especially tryin' to get outta a motel, it's hard to save money." This speaks to how punishing it was for residents to live week to week at the motel while draining any sort of savings. Because of this, lump-sum entitlements such as the Earned Income Tax Credit are lifesavers for people looking to improve their circumstances. Carol Stack notes that "random fluctuations in the meager flow of available cash and goods tend to be of considerable importance to the poor."[28] These random fluctuations are incredibly important when it comes to finding housing. Urban planning specialist Chester Hartman states: "One pays for housing well in advance. The entire month's rent must be paid on the first day of any rental period. One pays for food only a few days before it is consumed, and one always has the option of delaying food expenditures until just prior to eating. Housing is a nondivisible and not easily adjustable expenditure."[29]

Despite their increased financial resources, Reg, Jake, and Sky still needed other moving support. None of them had a valid license or credit card, so they required someone to rent and drive the moving van. That someone turned out to be me, and Reg admitted that without me, he would have had nowhere else to turn. They also needed bodies to move all the possessions from their room and storage unit. Reg recruited several individuals with motel connections after bribing them with cash and marijuana. Without these social networks, it is likely that they would not have been able to move.

Almost a year after they moved, Reg, Sky, and Jake were still living in the same apartment and had turned it into a comfortable home. Reg adopted a dog from a family who used to live at the motel, and he found a purpose in helping an older gentleman who ran a store nearby, although this relationship ended several months later. Sky found a job working at a local fast-food restaurant, and Jake got a job at a clothing store. When I visited them in the spring of 2014, Sky proudly showed me an impressive scrapbook that Reg had given her for Valentine's Day, which contained pictures, cutouts from magazines, and other totems of his love for her. Fran reappeared out of the blue in the summer of 2014 and moved into this apartment. I was saddened to hear that Sky's father passed away in the early summer of that year as well. The four of them moved into a new apartment about a mile away in 2015, and I visited them in July. Jake and Sky were still working, and Reg had adopted another dog from the neighbors at their previous apartment. This apartment had even more space than their previous apartment, and I was impressed by their continued ability to step up.

It is important to note that all these instances involved couples who were able to pull together resources through expanded social capital that single residents lacked. Despite these success stories of

Dee and Toby, Biggie and Deirdre, Digital and Darryl, and Reg, Sky, and Jake, the majority of residents who left the motel continued their lives as vulnerable social refugees. Like the urban nomad culture, motel life was characterized by *"mobility, alienation, poverty,* and a unique set of *survival strategies."*[30] Residents migrated to the motel with histories of transience and vulnerability and left rarely having improved their situations. This was due largely to the cycle of community, conflict, and fragility that existed at the motel. Although social services used the motel as an emergency shelter, it did nothing to prevent or fix the transient careers that many of its clients faced. The residents who arrived at the motel without the assistance of DSS or HATAS often turned to DSS when they were displaced because their financial resources and social capital had been drained.

If there is one thing that this book should make clear, it is that the story of the Boardwalk is a story of homelessness. It is a story of how people lose their homes, where they go to find shelter, and how they create identity and meaning in their lives through interactions with other homeless populations and middle-class society. Although the residents of the Boardwalk represent a drop in the bucket of the overall homeless population in the United States, their stories offer an invaluable look into what it means to be homeless. In the next section I will show how their experiences can translate into meaningful public policy that addresses the plight of the over 500,000 social refugees who struggle to survive each and every day.[31]

TURNING PROBLEMS INTO POLICY

From a policy standpoint, the first question to ask is, was using the Boardwalk as a housing solution for social refugees a good idea? The answer is clearly no. The motel housed so many types of social refugees that it failed to serve as a stable settlement for any of them. By exploring the ways in which the motel failed, we can get an idea of how motels could care for vulnerable populations in ways that meet their needs without creating cycles of displacement.

The most obvious universal factor that affected the Boardwalk was the uninhabitable physical condition of the motel. Code violations existed long before I began my fieldwork and were constant sources of stress that endangered residents' health and well-being. The other universal factor that impeded residents of the Boardwalk was the hostility from the local Dutchland community. Over time, the Boardwalk became synonymous with deviance to the point where motel residents were powerless to overcome the motel's master status. It is easy to see why the Boardwalk was so threatening to residents of Dutchland. In essence, the motel brought characteristics of the city—minorities, poverty, and residential instability—into the suburbs. Dutchland residents moved to the suburbs precisely to escape these urban problems. Although motel residents largely kept to themselves as they interacted with the local sustaining habitat, they acted with the constant knowledge that their presence was undesired. As Nelson Mandela writes in his autobiography, "If wealth is a magnet, poverty is some kind of repellant."[32]

Aside from these universal factors that afflicted every resident of the motel, specific populations of social refugees experienced life differently because of their social positions. From a criminal justice standpoint, placing parolees and sex offenders at the motel did nothing to promote successful reentry. Conditions of parole prohibited parolees from interacting with anyone with criminal history. At the Boardwalk, this constituted the majority of residents, so parolees risked violating their parole in their attempts to meet their resource deprivations. Parolees were also instructed to abstain from alcohol and drugs, which was difficult because drug use was a common coping mechanism and form of social currency at the Boardwalk. By the same token, those with drug addictions found it difficult to ignore the temptations around them. Likewise, parolees and sex offenders had to meet with parole officers and attend treatment locations that were several miles away. Meeting those requirements involved taking buses that were not always reliable and used valuable monetary resources. Because of this, the temptation to skip a meeting was always present, and the immediate benefits of not attending, such as having money for food, outweighed the long-term costs. While such decisions may appear to be gross errors in judgment, research finds that poverty and scarcity actually reduces cognitive function, leading to choices that favor short-term benefits.[33]

Finally, because of their stigma, sex offenders became targets of abuse from other motel residents. One day I sat outside with new resident Jonny, who told me that he was staying for a few days on his own volition because he was visiting the area and did not want to burden his relatives with his presence. He was unaware that sex offenders lived at the motel, and when I mentioned this, he bolted upright in his chair, almost knocking his sunglasses off his face, and asked if I could point any out. I denied knowing any, and he spat, "Fucking kiddy touchers. I can take people on parole, that's fine, but I can't handle fucking kiddy touchers."

For populations that DSS placed at the Boardwalk, especially those with mental health issues and other disabilities, the motel was a dangerous environment. Some residents were unable to articulate when living conditions became hazardous, and this was problematic because management did not proactively inspect rooms to make them inhabitable. Furthermore, for many residents with mental health issues, their social interactions quickly developed into conflict. The sad irony is that many of them were sent to the motel because their caseworkers worried that they would be unsafe in shelters. Those placed by agencies were not in control of their housing and therefore were powerless to move when hostility or unsafe living conditions arose. As the calamity of code violations at the Boardwalk indicated, the agencies that placed individuals at the motel suffered from a lack of oversight. Residents who were not placed by DSS consistently told me, "They shouldn't be here," referring to those with mental health issues. It was recognized that there was too much danger and too little supervision to make the motel a safe environment for those unable to care for themselves.

Residents who stepped up or down to the Boardwalk to regain stability found that the stigma attached to the motel negatively affected their lives. What distinguished these residents was that they had the most to work with and offer in terms of material resources and social capital. Over time, these resources were drained as long-term residents fought a losing battle against the motel's living environment (figure 16). Many of my colleagues pointed out that someone could rent a decent apartment for the $820 monthly rent that residents paid at the Boardwalk. This $820 a month did not guarantee heat, air conditioning, a fridge, kitchen, or even drinkable water. Offsetting these conditions exacted so much material cost to buy fans, space heaters, refrigerators, microwaves, and bottled water that once residents settled at the motel they found it very hard to leave. They struggled to make monthly, even weekly, rent payments, and because of this, putting down a security deposit and first month's rent for an apartment was nearly impossible. The paying residents were also resentful toward those whose stay was paid for by DSS or HATAS. Roy had a hard time understanding why sex offenders were "rewarded" with free housing while he struggled to pay for his room.

Microlevel Policy Implications

Given this knowledge, what sort of policy recommendations could be made regarding motels that house social refugees? Although the Boardwalk and Park Place were shut down, DSS continued to send individuals to other area motels. If motels are going to serve as settlements, how should they be used? One idea would be to segregate different populations in different locations. While citizens might be concerned that clustering sex offenders in one location would lead to increased crime, there is little evidence that spatial clustering increases recidivism.[34] On the contrary, clustering may actually make it easier for law enforcement to monitor sex offenders' behavior. Significant problems could arise if a motel was dedicated to strictly housing those placed by DSS, especially individuals with mental health issues. What was impressive at the Boardwalk was how the diffusion of residents created an environment that kept some populations in check. Many residents attempted to help those with mental health issues by giving them food and clothing, helping them shower, and helping clean their rooms. While it is undeniable that a hierarchy existed at the motel, care, support, and community triumphed despite it. Therefore motel-related policies should tap into the support structures that residents create and should reinforce that culture to improve their lives.

At the motel level, this would involve a private/public partnership among the motel, the criminal justice system, and social services. All parties have an interest because motel owners want sources of income, and the justice system and social services are looking for housing options. Motels like the Boardwalk represent a captive audience of citizens with similar vulnerabilities and therefore similar needs. Public policies should wrap these residents in support so that, whenever possible, they can move to more stable living conditions and regain a foothold in society.

The first step would be to create a better connection between the motel and social services. This could be accomplished by placing social workers at the motel on a twenty-four-hour basis. These social workers would serve as non–criminal justice authority figures, who could act as liaisons between residents and DSS. This would allow residents to have questions and concerns addressed immediately and save them from traveling to or calling DSS. Social workers could also attempt to resolve disputes before police were called, and they could provide a watchful eye over vulnerable residents.

In addition to bringing social workers to the motel, an array of other services should be brought to the motel on a regular basis. Residents at the Boardwalk lacked experience with many social institutions that allow people to live autonomously. Financial planning was almost nonexistent at the motel (Sam told me how he wanted to set up a bank account for the first time in his life). Budget counseling would assist residents in rationing their funds, much of which arrived on the first of every month and led to spending binges that left residents scrambling at the end of the month. Residents could also benefit from life skills courses on how to cook and care for themselves. At the Boardwalk in particular, a shuttle service to and from the grocery store would have spared residents the danger of crossing Main Street, and one could imagine that having a dietician on hand would be equally beneficial. Bringing other services to the motel, such as drug and alcohol counseling, psychological counseling to teach conflict resolution and resilience, and general health advice, would help address residents' vulnerabilities while incurring little cost to residents themselves. Many residents wished to move but lacked the necessary funds and driver's licenses to rent moving vans if they did not have vehicles. If social services worked with residents to find affordable housing, it would be ideal to provide moving support as well, because it would be tragic if a resident could not leave simply because he or she lacked transportation.

There is precedent for this sort of policy that wraps vulnerable populations in support and care instead of subjecting them to scrutiny and stigma. Project Homeless Connect brings homeless people to one location on a single day in order to "obtain as many services in one day as would otherwise take months." The federal government's Interagency Council on Homelessness declared this program a national best practice model, and fairs include services such as dental care, eyeglasses, HIV testing, housing, food, hygiene products, medical care, mental health services, SSI benefits, legal advice, California identification cards, voice mail accounts, employment counseling/job placement, wheelchair repair, addiction services, and more.[35] Local governments that use motels to house the homeless should strive to bring residents to Project Homeless Connect events or create something similar at the actual motel.[36]

Another example of care occurred in the late 1980s, when a single-room occupancy motel called Wood Street Commons opened in Pittsburgh that was specifically designed in partnership with social services "to provide safe, affordable, and supportive housing" to its residents. The project came about through collaboration with the Community Human Services Corporation, a nonprofit that worked with private philanthropic groups, government agencies, and service providers. In stark contrast to the Boardwalk, this location had a strong presence of social workers and community partners who supported residents. Furthermore, poor living conditions were viewed as "pathological" and a threat to social stability, so efforts were made to fix problems whenever they arose.[37] Wood Street Commons still exists today (now called the Residences at Wood Street) and provides 258 SRO units for the homeless and those at risk of homelessness.

Consider the mindset and success of Wood Street Commons versus that of the Boardwalk and another clear policy recommendation emerges. If a motel is supported by government funding, such as the Boardwalk, some of that funding should go directly toward making the motel a safe living environment. This funding should bypass the owner and involve a direct contract between the government and building repair companies. This would avoid the code issues that plagued the Boardwalk, ensure that living conditions did not disrupt lives, and also help to combat the stigma from surrounding communities.

Before it was closed down, the Boardwalk Motel represented a golden opportunity to change how vulnerable populations were served. The Boardwalk was a for-profit halfway house/shelter with none of the structure and support provided from a nonprofit organization. Despite the Boardwalk's closure, the need for locations like it persists. With this need comes the opportunity to optimize such locations to empower and support the social refugees who live there. The policy recommendations that I have outlined are important steps to operating shelters that support those in need.

Macrolevel Policy Implications

The Boardwalk Motel was born out of the necessity to house those who would otherwise be homeless. On a societal level, our duty is to correct policies that create homelessness while enacting policies that provide residential stability. I described motel residents as suffering from fragility, or a lack of financial and social support, that left them vulnerable to unintended or self-inflicted disruptions to short- and long-term goals. This fragility was the root of homelessness for the social refugees who fled to the Boardwalk. Effective macrolevel policy must then address the deterioration of financial and social resources that lead to homelessness.

One major institution that contributes to homelessness in the United States is the criminal justice system. Part of the need for the Boardwalk was created by sex-offender residence restrictions that barred many registered sex offenders from other housing options. Study after study has determined that these policies are ineffective at preventing sex crimes.[38] The unintended consequence of such legislation is that residence restrictions limit housing options for registered sex offenders and create residential instability.[39] In light of these findings, jurisdictions should consider alternative or modified forms of residence restrictions, if they are going to use them at all. One idea is to enforce targeted residence restrictions that focus on specific types of offenders (such as those with child victims), instead of blanket policies that affect all sex offenders.[40] Another option would be to rely on risk assessments to determine the length of time that offenders are subjected to residence restrictions.[41]

Research indicates that the connection between homelessness and incarceration is a two-way street. Those who are incarcerated have higher histories of previous homelessness than the general population, and a significant portion of the homeless have histories of incarceration.[42] Remember that while residents left the motel only because of increased financial and social support, many reentering ex-offenders experience a lack of these resources. In fact, it could be said that while incarceration does not prevent crime, its collateral consequences include financial and social disruption.[43] It is estimated that incarceration reduces former male inmates' earnings by 40 percent.[44]

Therefore several courses of action need to be taken. In an era of budget concerns, there is an increased focus on the costs and benefits of punitive sanctions. From 1998 to 2009, state correctional budgets increased from $12 billion to more than $50 billion per year, with little utilitarian benefit to show for it.[45] Incarceration should be an option of last resort because it is a costly endeavor that strips inmates of social networks and the ability to work. Whenever possible, those sanctioned by the criminal justice system should remain in their communities. A report by the Vera Institute of Justice (2013) demonstrates that diversion programs are an effective alternative to jail and incarceration.[46] Jail diversion programs provide treatment to individuals with behavioral health issues, instead of sending them to jail. A Massachusetts jail diversion program saved an estimated $1.3 million in costs, while a New York diversion program saved $39,518 per participant. Specialized court programs that divert people with mental health and drug issues from incarceration to treatment are similarly effective. A meta-analysis of courts in four jurisdictions found that mental health court participants were less likely to be arrested and had a larger reduction in arrest rates than similar individuals who only went to jail.

If an individual must be incarcerated, there needs to be increased attention on reentry planning so that ex-offenders are released to stable living situations that address their vulnerabilities instead of exacerbating them. The Second Chance Act is an important component of this focus on reentry. This national legislation was signed into law in 2008 and allocates grant money to state and local programs that are designed to reduce recidivism and support ex-prisoners.[47] Since 2009 the Second Chance Act has made over six hundred grant awards, serving more than 92,000 formerly incarcerated individuals.[48] Funded programs include the Allegheny County Reentry Initiative, which reduced rearrest rates among participants by more than 50 percent. Furthermore, we must continue to encourage employers to provide jobs to ex-offenders so that they can become financially independent and avoid residential displacement. One such program funded by the Second Chance Act is Tennessee's Project Return, which has provided temporary employment to more than 125 men and women as they prepare for stable employment.[49]

Many of the homeless residents of the Boardwalk were military veterans.[50] It was estimated that on a single night in January 2013 there were 57,849 homeless veterans in the United States, representing 12 percent of the homeless population.[51] The Veteran's Administration announced a plan to end veteran homelessness by 2015, and although it did not eradicate homelessness among veterans, the number of homeless veterans decreased by 33 percent since 2010.[52] While the issue of how to support veterans is well outside the scope of this book, hiring able-bodied veterans of all ages must be encouraged if they are to build financial and social nest eggs.[53] For those veterans who lack stable housing, programs such as the Department of Housing and Urban Development and Veterans Affairs Supportive Housing (HUD-VASH) program, which provides housing vouchers to veterans, must continue to be implemented and refined.[54] Veterans must also be given the social support and mental health treatment that they require to adjust to civilian lives.

The aforementioned policy recommendations focus on empowering individuals to improve their financial stability so that they may find affordable housing and insulate themselves against life events that drain their financial resources. This can be achieved by increasing streams of income and decreasing burdens on savings. One way to achieve this goal would be a substantial increase in the minimum wage. It was estimated that in order to rent a two-bedroom apartment in Riverfort County, a person must earn $13.06 an hour, while the minimum wage of the state was less than $9 an hour.[55] There also needs to be a substantial increase in the availability of affordable housing. In 2000 Riverfort County estimated that among renters making less than $10,000 a year, 81 percent directed more than the HUD-recommended ratio of 35 percent of their income toward housing.[56] This is precisely what kept many motel residents from leaving the Boardwalk and is perhaps the single biggest determinant of fragility because any destabilizing event, such as the loss of work or health related crisis, could lead to displacement. On a related note, extending affordable health care to vulnerable populations must be a priority if we intend to stem the creation of social refugees.

There does remain the question of how to serve and empower homeless populations with disabilities that render them unable to work and/or live autonomously. Without strong social networks, these individuals will likely rely on public assistance throughout their lives. Therefore when it comes to housing and caring for these individuals, we must ask ourselves, what are the minimum standards of living that all citizens deserve? The living conditions of the Boardwalk Motel were morally offensive to say the least, but more disconcerting was the fact that they were allowed to get to that point. County government was responsible for inspections, but local government was responsible for code enforcement, and both entities failed to communicate and act in ways that protected the most vulnerable of citizens. There needs to be some sort of discussion at all levels of government about what this country is willing to accept in terms of housing standards and how building codes can be more effectively enforced.

When one considers these policy recommendations, it becomes clear that addressing homelessness is a complex task. Changes in the criminal justice system, the veteran's affairs administration, and the labor market can significantly improve the lives of many. Furthermore, the complexity of the problem presents unique opportunities for innovative programs that think outside the box to address the web of problems that vulnerable populations face. One example of a program that attempts to address the intricate web of problems that vulnerable populations face is Health Leads, which envisions a health care model "that addresses all patients' basic resource needs as a standard part of quality care."[57] The Health Leads model recognizes that health issues are often related to other life conditions, such as a lack of food, money, and basic utilities like heat and air conditioners. In Health Leads clinics, doctors assess the basic needs of their patients and then "prescribe food, heat, and other basic resources their patients need to be healthy, alongside prescriptions for medication." Patients then work with college-student advocates who connect them with community resources that address their needs. While Health Leads does not cater to the homeless specifically, the program is a powerful example of wrapping the vulnerable in care, instead of isolating them on islands of marginalization.

Considering the complexities of homelessness creates policies like the one found in the state of Utah. In eight years, Utah reduced its rate of chronic homelessness by 74 percent through a program that simply gave apartments to the homeless without stipulations. The impetus behind it was research that concluded that the annual emergency room and jail costs for an average homeless person were $16,670, compared to the $11,000 required to house them and pair them with a social worker.[58] Other positive programs include the Downtown Street Team in Daytona Beach, which hires the homeless to clean up the downtown area while giving them a place to stay at the Salvation Army; A Key Not a Card in Portland, which provides immediate permanent housing so the homeless can stabilize their lives; and 1811 Eastlake Project in Seattle, where homeless addicts are housed while receiving 24/7 support. These programs have achieved tangible results. A Key Not a Card housed 936 people from 2005 through 2009, and in the first year of the 1811 East Lake Project, the county was saved $2.5 million, compared to the program's cost of $1.1 million, and 66 percent of residents remained housed after one year.[59] The 1811 Eastlake Project is an example of the "Housing First" model. This model provides immediate permanent housing to "people experiencing homelessness, especially for people with long histories of homelessness and co-occurring health challenges while providing the supportive services people need to keep their housing and avoid returning to homelessness."[60] Housing First programs show high rates of housing retention and housing stability, as well as public savings costs for hospital care, addiction treatment centers, and jails.

ETHNOGRAPHY'S ROLE

This book is the result of over a year of fieldwork that involved intense observation and close relationships with participants. Therefore it is important to consider how this endeavor and ethnography in general contribute to our understanding of the world that we share. By relying on the observation of human experience, ethnography creates knowledge in ways that other methodologies cannot.

The driving purpose behind this study was my desire to understand what life was really like at the Boardwalk Motel. The story of the Boardwalk could be told only by those living there. Ethnography's power rests in its ability to capture the voices of underground populations in order to dissolve stereotypes and humanize those labeled as less than human. Residents of the motel were fueled to participate in the study because they had a burning desire to retain control over their humanity. When Dee and I talked about the reputation of the motel, she said, "Slowly but surely we're getting the crackheads and prostitutes out of here. Hi, we're real people living here. That's why we put our plants outside, to show that real people live here."

By observing people and behavior over time, I was able to examine the Boardwalk Motel not at a cross-sectional moment in time but instead over what turned out to be the tail end of its lifespan. Therefore this book chronicled not only the lives of motel residents but the culmination of social forces that had affected them over time and which eventually led to their displacement. This was a watershed moment in the lives of the Boardwalk's residents and the Dutchland community. Because the closing occurred at the end of my research, this study captured a story that otherwise may not have been told. In that respect, this book is not just research. It is history.

In his classic work, *A People's History of the United States*, Howard Zinn writes: "If history is to be creative, to anticipate a possible future without denying the past, it should, I believe, emphasize new possibilities by disclosing those hidden episodes of the past when, even if in brief flashes, people showed their ability to resist, to join together occasionally to win."[61]

While I hoped to conduct a study that would ultimately help the lives of the Boardwalk's residents, the motel's closing made that impossible. However, it cannot be denied that motel residents did indeed show brilliant flashes of resistance to stigma, and the ability to join together and care for one another. Because residents had the courage to share those flashes with me and ultimately the world, they can claim a victory. They can claim a victory because their voices, as they should be, are a testament to their existence as human beings. Ethnography can claim victory because it captures the lived experience of people and preserves their memories as a historical record of their universal right to exist. As Zinn reminds us, "History which keeps alive the memory of people's resistance suggests new definitions of power."[62] In consideration of this power, I will close by reflecting on the possibilities that arise through new definitions of the past.

A CALL FOR A FRESH PERSPECTIVE

When President Barack Obama was elected to a second term in November 2012, I asked residents what they thought about this development. After all, President Obama marched to victory on the back of "hope" and "yes we can." I was saddened, but not surprised, to hear residents tell me, "It doesn't matter," and, "Nothing is going to change for people like us." These beliefs were symbolic of a larger societal pandemic that can be conceptualized as widespread disenchantment with the American Dream.

Those feelings of motel residents are evidence of the significant barriers to action in their defense. Many powerful voices continue to rally against the most vulnerable citizens of this country. Parts of the political machine have been hijacked into a destructive force, as demonstrated by recent cuts to food stamps and the behavior of politicians such as Democratic state representative Tom Brower of Hawaii, who walked the streets in an Armani Exchange hat while smashing the shopping carts of the homeless with a sledgehammer in an effort to "clean up the streets."[63] Political action against the homeless has included instructing the homeless to relocate or be arrested, granting police the power to arrest those sleeping in public and storing personal property in public, and banning the feeding of the homeless in local parks.[64] In 2013–2014 thirty-one cities across the United States took action to restrict or ban food sharing with homeless populations.[65] Business owners have taken steps such as putting bleach on food in dumpsters and designing gutters to drip onto the street so the homeless cannot take shelter.[66] Such actions "ensure that homeless populations are perpetually in the wrong place, that they are perpetually and unavoidably occupying space that has been legally defined as outside their rights and control."[67] Therefore perhaps the most pressing need is to change the public perception of homelessness. While policies must be compartmentalized to different institutions, the cultural zeitgeist of stigmatizing social refugees amounts to institutionalized violence, or what Jonathan Kozol calls "state terrorism as social welfare policy" that requires nationwide attention.[68]

This zeitgeist also suggests that a far more radical social change that attends to the foundation of America and the ways in which inequality is created through capitalism and consumerism is required. The efforts of the Dutchland community to sanitize its social space of the Boardwalk and its residents are clear evidence that the melting pot of America is indeed a myth.[69] English vagrancy laws have evolved into U.S. ordinances that "are a reflection of society's perception of a continuing need to control some of its 'suspicious' or 'undesirable' members."[70] That these labels have been affixed to those on the economic and social margins is an artifact of a capitalist society that equates explicit material consumption and buying power with human worth and dignity. Sociologist Jeff Ferrell describes this cultural process as "the regulation of public interaction, the restoration of exclusionary community, the reencoding of cultural space along the lines of order and privilege."[71]

The warning signs have existed for decades. In 1890 journalist Jacob Riis asked, "When another generation shall have doubled the census of our city, and to that vast army of workers, held captive by poverty, the very name of home shall be as a bitter mockery, what will the harvest be?"[72] Over a century later sociologist Joel Blau wrote that homelessness is "one of the clearest examples of the new willingness to write off the poor." He further questioned the organization of the United States economy, saying, "Conservatives argue that the United States 'won' the Cold War; it triumphed over communism in Eastern Europe and the Soviet Union. But the economy that won this victory cannot house its own people and condemns a significant percentage of the population to a life of poverty and struggle. If this is victory, it is a hollow victory indeed."[73]

Marginalization will continue as long as stark class inequality exists and as long as capitalism creates commodity from basic human needs that some would consider rights.[74] It will continue as long as the economically and politically wealthy continue to build up symbolic and real walls in social space. The borders of shared social space will continue to be drawn by those with the economic clout to ensure that their notions of "quality of life," "civility," and "order" are not disrupted by the presence of those who make them uncomfortable, echoing the words of philosopher Friedrich Engels who declared, "The breeding places of disease, the infamous holes and cellars in which the capitalist mode of product confines our workers night after night are not abolished; they are merely shifted elsewhere."[75]

Sanitization will continue until everyday efforts are made to take back public space in the name of outsiders, efforts like pouring concrete over "anti-homeless spikes" outside London businesses and challenging the criminalization of sidewalk use via sit-ins.[76] There is a call for those who are inclined to act, and that call is to resist the corporate culture of control, whereby "the destruction of order and privilege, the cracking open of closed spaces, results not in mean-spirited recrimination, not in the revenge of the oppressed—but in the festival of the oppressed."[77]

The changes that I have proposed regarding homelessness and social refugees may seem too daunting, as if the cultural infrastructure is too sound to dismantle and repair. However, every action must begin with an idea, so I propose that it is a human right to sit equally in the horizontal and vertical dimensions of social space. When I first introduced the social refugee, I stated that motel residents were quite different from those crossing international borders because of crisis in their homelands. The National Law Center on Homelessness and Poverty and the National Coalition for the Homeless might disagree. In 2009 these organizations published a report arguing that criminalization of the homeless in the United States violated international human rights law, claiming that the "human rights framework can serve as a useful tool in the fight against criminalization as it recognizes a full range of rights that protect the fundamental human dignity of people experiencing homelessness."[78] After spending time in welfare motels, writer Jonathan Kozol states, "We do appear to feel a home must somehow be deserved or earned. We do seem to regard it as a 'gift' of sorts, which now and then may be awarded for correct behavior."[79] Joel Blau writes: "Since homelessness cannot be solved alone, it would be short-sighted to put forth single-issue proposals on housing without tying them, for example, to campaigns for higher wages and national health care, all united through the theme of common economic—read human—rights. Then, and only then, will it be possible to make some real progress."[80]

If we view social refugees as a humanitarian issue, then policy ceases to be Democratic or Republican, conservative or liberal. Instead, it is transformed into the defense of human rights. Social policies need to be considered in terms of the ontological harm they either cause or prevent to the basic rights of human citizens. Within this framework, we can identify the most fundamental of these rights as the right to a home. As the German/Jewish philosopher Hannah Arendt argues in *The Origins of Totalitarianism* (1958): "The first loss which the rightless suffered was the loss of their homes, and this meant the loss of the entire social structure into which they were born and in which they established for themselves a distinct place in the world."[81]

To address the social issues of homelessness and marginalization, perhaps we need to revisit a symbol rooted in the past. The Statue of Liberty reaches 305 feet into the sky, its torch lighting the way for the millions of immigrants who have arrived in New York harbor since it was dedicated in 1886. Inside the statue's pedestal is a plaque, engraved with the words of Emma Lazarus's "The New Colossus." The final words of this poem symbolize the statue's call: "Give me your tired, your poor, your huddled masses yearning to breathe free, the wretched refuse of your teeming shore. Send these, the homeless, tempest-tost to me, I lift my lamp beside the golden door!" It is time for us to face that plaque, acknowledge the inequality that cripples so many citizens, and make a decision. Either we tear down these hollow words, or we make a commitment to restore them to their full power.

APPENDIX 1

List of Participants

Name	Sex	Age	Race	Room	Notes	Tenure
Nolan	Male	70s	Black	1	Veteran who drank often and carried a knife. Elizabeth told me he was taken to the hospital and died in winter 2013.	Revolving
Jerry	Male	60s	White	2	Veteran who was confined to a wheelchair	Long-term
Ed	Male	52	White	3	Placed by DSS; sold/used pills	Revolving
Vito	Male	Late 30s	White	3	Placed by DSS; in a wheelchair because of a spider bite that damaged his nerves	Long-term
Slash	Male	30s	White	3	On parole; lived with Vito	Long-term
Reg	Male	30	White	4	Level 1 sex offender not on parole; Sky's partner and my gatekeeper	Long-term
Sky	Female	29	White	4	Reg's partner; worked at KFC with Jake	Long-term
Fran	Female	41	White	4	Friend of Sky's; history of attempted suicide	Long-term
Jake	Male	36	White	5	Friends with Reg and Sky; intense transient history	Long-term
Marc	Male	24	Guatemalan	6	Worked at a local car dealership and sent money home	Long-term
Steve	Male	57	White	7	Placed by DSS; veteran and chain smoker	Long-term
Patch	Male	Early 60s	Black	7	Placed by DSS; on parole	Short-term
Biggie	Male	44	Black	9	Deirdre's partner; smoked marijuana; received disability	Long-term
Deirdre	Female	53?	White	9	Biggie's partner; received retirement	Long-term
Trim	Male	61	White	10	Recovering addict with many tattoos; worked construction	Long-term
Sarah	Female	40s	White	10	Knew Reg and Sky; placed candles and plants in her windows	Long-term
Mike	Male	40s	White	14	Natalie's partner; did maintenance and drove a cab	n/a
Kelly	Female	Late 50s	White	14	Rudy's partner; worked the desk at one time	Long-term

Name	Sex	Age	Race	Room	Notes	Tenure
Rudy	Male	Late 50s	White	14	Kelly's partner; worked maintenance at one time	Long-term
Shawn	Male	Late 30s	White	14	Registered nurse; marijuana user	Short-term
Avery	Male	Late 20s	White	15	Elisha's partner; received worker's comp from a leg injury	Short-term
Elisha	Female	Late 20s	White	15	Avery's partner; became friendly with Deirdre and Biggie	Short-term
Lane	Male	62	White	23	Friends with Larry	Long-term
Dusty	Male	50s	White	23	Quite religious	Short-term
Nora	Female	20s	White	23	Justin's partner; arrested for stealing	Short-term
Justin	Male	20s	White	23	Nora's partner; drug user	Long-term
Curtis	Male	31	White	24	Placed by DSS; substantial mental health issues	Short-term
Spike	Male	37	Puerto Rican	24	Placed by DSS; wore bracelets to promote condom use	Short-term
Mary Anne	Female	Late 20s	White	24	Spike's partner; avid fan of soda	Long-term
Thomas	Male	Late 40s	White	24	Lived with his diabetic wife	Long-term
Dee	Female	36	White	25	Ex-stripper/escort; recovering addict; Toby's partner	Long-term
Toby	Male	40s	White	25	Dee's partner; recovering addict; had a young estranged daughter	Long-term
Jasper	Male	62	White	25	Registered sex offender on parole	Short-term
Ned	Male	50s	Black	26	Was missing toes; offered to pay bills by phone	Short-term
Larry	Male	55	White	26	Moved in from his car and became a manager; sports fan	Long-term
Sonny	Male	27	Korean	26	Parolee	Short-term
Tat	Male	35	Dominican	26	Parolee and registered sex offender who was quite upfront about it	Short-term
Rob	Male	30s	White	26	Placed by his father who was a mailman; inhaled aerosol	Short-term
Sam	Male	54	Black	27	Older veteran who valued employment; recovering addict	Long-term

(continued)

Name	Sex	Age	Race	Room	Notes	Tenure
Digital	Male	39	Black	27	Darryl's partner; wanted to open a restaurant	Short-term
Roy	Male	43	Black	29	Unemployed drug seller and marijuana user; very friendly	Short-term
Cinque	Male	35	Black	29	Parolee and registered sex offender; employed with Waste Management	Long-term
Price	Male	26	Hispanic	29	Veteran on parole; registered sex offender	Short-term
Jonny	Male	40s	White	29	Veteran with extreme animosity toward sex offenders	Short-term
Riley	Male	50s	White	29	Placed by DSS; came from a shelter	Short-term
Darryl	Male	47	Hispanic	30	RSO on parole; Digital's partner	Long-term
Love	Female	60s	White	30	Lived with a small cat named Missy	Long-term
Ben	Male	Late 20s	White	30	Returned from jail for selling marijuana	Short-term
Lisa	Female	Late 20s	White	30	Ben's partner; lost her DSS apartment when Ben went to jail	Short-term
Anthony	Male	25	Puerto Rican	31	Placed by DSS; marijuana seller and user	Short-term
Ryan	Male	30s	White	32	On parole; tried to find a job at KFC	Short-term
Burt	Male	Late 50s	White	32	Known as "Mr. Clean" because of his appearance	Short-term
Derek	Male	20s	White	33	Rumored to have been removed because of a mental breakdown	Long-term
Ellen	Female	Mid-50s	White	34	Arrived with Trim; eventually moved to the Park Place	Long-term
Noonan	Male	40s	White	34	Parolee and union worker	Revolving
Lenny	Male	Late 30s	White	35	Lived with his partner and dog; worked driving trucks	Long-term
Walt	Male	30	Black	36	Registered sex offender on parole	Long-term
Dale	Male	41	White	38	Registered sex offender on parole; veteran and nurse	Long-term

Name	Sex	Age	Race	Room	Notes	Tenure
Paul	Male	63	White	39	Veteran in a wheelchair who became friends with Love	Short-term
Clive	Male	19	White	40	Elisha's brother; moved in with his parents; on probation for drugs	Short-term
Harry	Male	67	White	40	RSO on parole; had work history as an electrician	Long-term
Gene	Male	40s	White	42	Placed by DSS, arrived on a bike, which he traded to Shawn for a microwave	Short-term
Elizabeth	Female	Late 60s	White	n/a	Afternoon and evening manager; wore a wig; lived in house next to the Park Place	n/a
Natalie	Female	Late 40s	White	n/a	Elizabeth's daughter; Mike's partner; battled drug addiction; desk worker	n/a
Neal	Male	Late 40s	White	n/a	Park Place resident; friends with Reg, Sky, and Jake	Long-term
Ramón	Male	32	Puerto Rican	n/a	Used to live in 5; worked at KFC; friends with Reg, Sky, and Jake	Long-term
Justine	Female	51	Black	n/a	Sam's partner; worked at a girl's residential facility	n/a
Petey	Male	Late 30s	White	n/a	Park Place resident	Revolving
Randy	Male	50	White	n/a	Parolee and registered sex offender; lived at the Park Place	Long-term
Eric	Male	20s	White	n/a	Lived at the Park Place; marijuana user; lived previously with his grandmother	Short-term
Bernie	Male	30s	White	n/a	Park Place resident; friends with Reg and Sky; worked at a beverage center	Long-term
Wallace	Male	20s	Black	n/a	Lived nearby; friends with Reg; marijuana user	n/a
Brad	Male	20s	White	n/a	Worked at Giant Foods; bought marijuana from Reg	n/a
Guy	Male	Early 50s	White	n/a	Dee's friend and former client; occasionally helped her with rent	n/a

APPENDIX 2

A Reflection on Method

The preceding analysis focused its ethnographic lens on motel residents and how they organized themselves in the context of social forces that made their lives incredibly unstable. In this appendix, I would like to turn the lens on myself to examine how I confronted and negotiated several methodological issues. While I touched on some of these topics in the introduction, I hope that offering deeper reflection here will clarify things for readers and contribute to the larger discourse on how scholars use ethnographic methods to examine social behavior.

Like many ethnographers, I entered my research site from a position of considerable power. Therefore it is important to discuss how I managed issues of power and privilege between myself and research participants. Several aspects of my fieldwork showed clearly how motel residents and I occupied very different social positions. Consider my decision on the first day of fieldwork to wear a "field outfit" of a plain white t-shirt and shorts, clothes that, in my view, were damaged enough to forgo wearing in my usual daily activities. This was just one of many situations that emphasized the difference between my middle-class resources and the fragility of social refugees at the Boardwalk.

My privilege was most apparent when I decided not to become a full-time resident of the motel. Coming to and going from the motel drove home the fact that I had a stable residence to go to and that I viewed the motel as a location to go from. From a migratory perspective, it underscored the values that I imposed on the motel as a setting to be pushed from and pulled to. Residents told me that they respected my choice (see Reg's comment in the introduction), but I worried that my behavior continually reminded them of what they lacked or where they had been. I did not see any evidence that this aspect of my fieldwork psychologically harmed any residents or created substantial rifts between us. However, had I toughed it out as a full-time resident, this closeness and solidarity might have led participants to open up in ways not captured in this study.

This conscious decision on my part was an overt declaration of where my priorities lay throughout the study. In hindsight, I wish that I had made a better attempt to endure the conditions that my participants experienced every day. My experience should demonstrate that the mentality of "you gotta do you" does not apply only to those on the margins, and that the balance between personal comfort and care for others must be balanced by all.

My absences from the field had profound implications for my data collection and findings. Not only did it increase social distance between me and participants, there were several instances when important events (such as Reg's arrest and Roy's eviction) transpired without my presence.[1] Had I been there to observe them, my data on these moments would have been more situated in the event itself, rather than relying on residents' recollections of how circumstances unfolded. These recollections are important and useful, but my data would surely have been richer if I were present for the event itself. In retrospect, I wish that I had spent more time in the field, because I kicked myself mentally every time I was not present for an event that seemed important.

The difference in social positions and resources was further emphasized whenever residents requested loans from me. Sky called me the "richest" person she and Reg knew because I owned a vehicle. My social position represented a stability that motel residents severely lacked, and while they called on one another for loans, my stability represented dependability and hope when all else seemed lost. This aspect of my fieldwork deserves further exploration.

A discussion on loans in the field can be aided by considering the following question. What were the meanings attached to the action of asking me for loans? Residents approached me for loans when they felt they had no other options, and they were often apologetic in their requests. This signified that they were aware of our different social planes and conscious of the connections we had made that went beyond researcher and participant. Reg often prompted his requests with, "Brother, I hate to ask you." While residents needed my help, they did not want me to feel that they simply viewed me as a source of money, echoing my own concerns that residents would feel that they were simply sources of data. These concerns demonstrate that we all had to consider the intricate ways that my research benefited those involved.

Requests for loans often came with justifications, and residents were very clear about what the money would be used for. This suggested that they feared I might reject their request without this justification. Public discourse is rife with stereotypes and myths about how the poor spend their money. When residents offered the reasons for their financial need, they were trying to confront and allay these concerns.

When residents approached me for loans, those acts spoke clearly to our different social positions. Therefore I had to consider the effects of my response. Residents often expected an answer on the spot, probably because they had encountered many situations when they were told, "I'll get back to you" and then were ignored. I never rejected a loan request during my fieldwork. This is due in part to the fact that requests were never made for amounts larger than $40, and I viewed that as a reasonable amount. However, I also realized that rejecting loans in principle would have created an even starker contrast in social position and called into question the power dynamics of the study. By studying residents' lives, I was asking them to open themselves up to incredible scrutiny and entrust their stories to my hands. This level of trust and vulnerability cannot be given monetary value, but it obviously helped me achieve an important goal. In that respect, giving loans was my way to help residents achieve some of their own goals in times of need.

Therefore I did not hound residents about paying the loans back. Although I told residents that I could not offer a second loan until the first was paid back, this issue never arose. Residents always repaid me and were often apologetic about how long it took. I did not want residents to view me as some sort of loan-shark, so I told them not to worry about it when they referenced such delays. This was an effort on my part to decrease social distance and treat our relationships as more communal than transactional. I also decreased social distance by blurring the lines between research at the motel and my life outside of the setting. As I mentioned in the introduction, Reg and Sky visited my office on campus and met several colleagues. Friends of mine also visited me at the motel and enjoyed a day at the lake with Reg, Sky, Jake, and Sky's mother.

Despite these efforts, social distance did exist between motel residents and me. One of the obvious ways concerned the fact that I do not consider myself an active smoker or user of any drugs other than alcohol. However, there were times when I engaged in certain behaviors because they made me feel closer to residents in the heat of the moment. These instances of solidarity were enjoyable for me because I felt like I was embracing the culture of the motel instead of simply observing it. In these seductive moments, the pleasure that I gained from celebrating daily life allowed me to see how particular activities created the illusion of care-free living. I would like to explore these moments in greater detail.

I am not a habitual smoker of marijuana, and the last time I actually inhaled a cannabis product before going to the motel was as a junior in college in 2004. Marijuana use was common at the motel, and in my early days of seeking acceptance, I declined it whenever it was offered. However, when Anthony arrived in June, I allowed myself to be seduced by the experience of the moment.[2]

It was a late afternoon in June and I was hanging out with Reg, Mike, Jake, and Anthony. We sat at the bottom of the middle landing because it offered shade while we enjoyed the fresh air. Anthony was looking to establish a customer base for his marijuana dealing, so he let us all smoke for free. A turquoise pipe was passed around, and I declined it on the first go-around. But after watching other residents take hits while we laughed and joked, I had an "oh, what the hell" moment where I reached out and asked for the pipe on the next round.

I knew that this action would generate buzz among residents and break some of the residual ice around my role as a researcher and possible police informant. Indeed it did, as Reg put his fist to his mouth and yelled, "Oh!" Jake and Anthony then commented that I was surely not a cop, and Reg cracked a joke about "corrupting" me. Although this action helped allay the fears of residents as intended, I also participated because the community activity between us was enticing and enjoyable. Sharing this behavior during that moment enhanced my appreciation of the solidarity created by motel residents as they coped with their living situation. I smoked marijuana on only a handful of other occasions when I was similarly seduced, but I largely avoided smoking mostly because I did not enjoy the smell.

Likewise, I do not consider smoking cigarettes to be part of my public identity, but because cigarettes were an integral part of community at the Boardwalk, I smoked a fair share of them during my fieldwork. On these occasions, the act again enhanced my feelings of solidarity and community in the moment. I did not inhale the smoke deeply but took light drags and blew the smoke out quickly. If residents picked up on this behavior, they never mentioned it, and I did not get the sense that it affected our relationships in a negative way.

Many motel residents were similar to James Spradley's urban nomads in that they viewed alcohol as a "symbol of social solidarity and friendship and where group drinking and collective drunkenness is an acceptable aspect of the culture."[3] While they often drank to the point of drunkenness, I viewed alcohol as a social activity that did not require getting drunk. I discussed alcohol as a coping mechanism in chapter 4, and perhaps if I had been a full-time resident, drinking to get drunk would have been a more significant part of my experience. On occasions when I happened to be leaving the field later that day, residents actively monitored the amount that I drank, and Reg told me several times that my career was not worth "fucking up" by driving drunk. This effort on their part demonstrates that despite some social distance between us, I was vested in their lives, and they were in mine as well.

The phrase "vested in their lives" may raise some eyebrows, but there is almost no other way to put it. When a study is conducted using the voices of others, a level of trust and respect needs to be established in order for those voices to come through. A researcher can rarely accomplish this without becoming vested in the lives of participants. Two major concerns about ethnography are that becoming involved with participants means the researcher not only significantly influences the life outcomes of those under study but also loses the ability to present findings in a balanced way. I would like to conclude this appendix by discussing my involvement with participants and addressing concerns about how that involvement affected my presentation of their lives.

There is no doubt that my actions had effects on the lives of my subjects. Residents were psychologically boosted by being able to call me a friend. When I visited Reg and Sky in the summer of 2014 for Jake's birthday, Reg made it a point to tell others that I was going to be a professor and that he had "important friends." The resources that I shared were sometimes very important. Reg, Jake, and Sky may not have been able to move without my help, and I wonder what could have happened to Sam and Larry had I not given them loans.

That said, my involvement in the lives of residents did not do much to change their fragility overall. My presence could do nothing to help registered sex offenders overcome the labels that hindered them from finding jobs and housing. My resources could not help me get back in contact with residents who disappeared without a trace. My influence could not get Jake and Sky better-paying jobs or improve the safety of the neighborhood they moved to. When Love and her son Ben were evicted from the motel, all I could do was drive them to DSS and give their cat a safe home. When the motel was shut down and residents scattered into the cold, I was powerless to change anything about their situation. This evidence demonstrates that the social forces that affect those on the margins of society are often considerably more powerful than ethnographers in the field.

I now want to address how I presented motel residents in terms of their behavior and character. If anything undeniable emerged during my fieldwork, it was that motel residents were three-dimensional. The people I encountered at the Boardwalk were not mirror opposites of the stereotypes applied to them. They were not saints, but they were not sinners either, just complex human beings. Residents surprised me with their care, humor, and insights, but they also acted in ways that were violent, vindictive, and illegal. I have portrayed these dimensions of what I observed to the best of my ability.

Throughout this book I clearly use a theoretical lens that pays particular attention to how political, economic, and criminal justice systems exacerbate inequality. Even so, I tried to give equal and descriptive attention to how residents behaved and made decisions in their daily lives. Readers are free to make judgments about the residents of the Boardwalk Motel and the context in which they lived their lives, and to come to their own conclusions. Perhaps I would have come to similar conclusions had I employed a different theoretical lens, talked to different people, or come from a different background of social position and life experience. Such is the nature of ethnography as a research method. It starts with a researcher and a research setting, and the interaction between them molds and produces the results.

In closing, it would be disingenuous to imply that there were not important issues of differential resources and social position that arose throughout my fieldwork, especially given how close I became to motel residents. Nor can I deny that an explicit goal of this work was to confront the social stereotypes applied to the Boardwalk and its residents. What I can do is acknowledge these issues and explain how I worked through them in my research and writing. I hope that this reflection illustrates how I did my best to negotiate my role as a researcher in ways that respected my subjects, as well as readers of this book.

NOTES

PREFACE

1. LeAlan Jones, Lloyd Newman, and David Isay, *Our America: Life and Death on the South Side of Chicago* (New York: Scribner, 1997), 17.
2. Erving Goffman, *Stigma: Notes on the Management of Spoiled Identity* (Englewood Cliffs, N.J.: Prentice Hall, 1963), 3.
3. Allison D. Redlich, "Community Notification: Perceptions of Its Effectiveness in Preventing Child Sexual Abuse," *Journal of Child Sexual Abuse* 10, no. 3 (January 2001): 91–116, http://www.ncbi.nlm.nih.gov/pubmed/17522002.
4. See Anthony J. Petrosino and Carolyn Petrosino, "The Public Safety Potential of Megan's Law in Massachusetts: An Assessment from a Sample of Criminal Sexual Psychopaths," *Crime & Delinquency* 45, no. 1 (January 1999): 140–58, doi:10.1177/0011128799045001008; Jeffrey C. Sandler, Naomi J. Freeman, and Kelly M. Socia, "Does a Watched Pot Boil? A Time-Series Analysis of New York State's Sex Offender Registration and Notification Law," *Psychology, Public Policy, and Law* 14, no. 4 (2008): 284–302; and Bob Edward Vasquez, Sean Maddan, and Jeffery T. Walker, "The Influence of Sex Offender Registration and Notification Laws in the United States: A Time-Series Analysis," *Crime & Delinquency* 54, no. 2 (October 26, 2007): 175–92, doi:10.1177/0011128707311641.
5. See Keri B. Burchfield and William Mingus, "Not in My Neighborhood: Assessing Registered Sex Offenders' Experiences with Local Social Capital and Social Control," *Criminal Justice and Behavior* 35, no. 3 (March 2008): 356–74, doi:10.1177/0093854807311375; Jill S. Levenson, "The Effect of Megan's Law on Sex Offender Reintegration," *Journal of Contemporary Criminal Justice* 21, no. 1 (February 2005): 49–66, doi:10.1177/1043986204271676;

Jill S. Levenson and Leo P. Cotter, "The Impact of Sex Offender Residence Restrictions: 1,000 Feet from Danger or One Step from Absurd?," *International Journal of Offender Therapy and Comparative Criminology* 49, no. 2 (May 2005): 168–78, doi:10.1177/0306624X04271304; Jill S. Levenson, David A. D'Amora, and Andrea L. Hern, "Megan's Law and Its Impact on Community Re-Entry for Sex Offenders," *Behavioral Sciences & the Law* 25 (2007): 587–602, doi:10.1002/bsl; Monica L. P. Robbers, "Lifers on the Outside: Sex Offenders and Disintegrative Shaming," *International Journal of Offender Therapy and Comparative Criminology* 53, no. 1 (February 2009): 5–28, doi:10.1177/0306624X07312953; Richard Tewksbury, "Experiences and Attitudes of Registered Female Sex Offenders," *Federal Probation* 68, no. 3 (2000): 30–34; Richard Tewksbury, "Collateral Consequences of Sex Offender Registration," *Journal of Contemporary Criminal Justice* 21, no. 1 (February 2005): 67–81, doi:10.1177/1043986204271704; Richard Tewksbury and Matthew B. Lees, "Perceptions of Sex Offender Registration: Collateral Consequences and Community Experiences," *Sociological Spectrum* 26, no. 3 (May 2006): 309–34, doi:10.1080/02732170500524246; Richard G. Zevitz and Mary Ann Farkas, "Sex Offender Community Notification: Managing High Risk Criminals or Exacting Further Vengeance?," *Behavioral Sciences & the Law* 18 (2000): 375–91.

6.   All names and locations mentioned in the text are pseudonyms.

7.   Christine Benedict, *Resolution No. 353-a Requesting Albany County Remove Families and Individuals from Certain Motels on Route 5, Town of Colonie* (Colonie, N.Y.: Albany County Legislature, 2007).

8.   Elliot Liebow, *Tally's Corner: A Study of Negro Streetcorner Men* (Boston: Little, Brown, 1967); Philippe Bourgois, *In Search of Respect: Selling Crack in El Barrio* (Cambridge: Cambridge University Press, 1996); David A. Snow and Leon Anderson, *Down on Their Luck: A Study of Homeless Street People* (Berkeley: University of California Press, 1993); Elijah Anderson, *Code of the Street: Decency, Violence, and the Moral Life of the Inner City* (New York: Norton, 1999); Mitchell Duneier, *Sidewalk* (New York: Farrar, Straus and Giroux, 1999).

9.   Jonathan Kozol, *Rachel and Her Children: Homeless Families in America* (New York: Crown, 1988), 11.

10. Erving Goffman, "Symbols of Class Status," *British Journal of Sociology* 2, no. 4 (1951): 295.

INTRODUCTION

1.   For an excellent source of information on motels in America, see John A. Jakle, Keith A. Sculle, and Jefferson S. Rogers, *The Motel in America* (Baltimore: Johns Hopkins University Press, 1996).

2. "Old-Style Motels Fading Out," *USA Today*, December 3, 2003, http://www.usatoday.com/travel/hotels/2003–12–02-motels_x.htm.

3. Norman S. Hayner, *Hotel Life* (Chapel Hill: University of North Carolina Press, 1936).

4. Paul Groth, *Living Downtown: The History of Residential Hotels in the United States* (Berkeley: University of California Press, 1994).

5. American Hotel & Lodging Association, "History of Lodging," 2012, http://www.ahla.com/content.aspx?id=4072.

6. Kristin Jackson, "The World's First Motel Rests Upon Its Memories," *Seattle Times*, April 25, 1993, http://community.seattletimes.nwsource.com/archive/?date=19930425&slug=1697701.

7. American Hotel & Lodging Association, "History of Lodging."

8. Jakle, Sculle, and Rogers, *The Motel in America*.

9. Hayner, *Hotel Life*.

10. Jakle, Sculle, and Rogers, *The Motel in America*.

11. American Hotel & Lodging Association, "History of Lodging."

12. Jakle, Sculle, and Rogers, *The Motel in America*.

13. "Old-Style Motels Fading Out."

14. American Hotel & Lodging Association, "History of Lodging."

15. Eric Krell, "Inside Extended Stay Hotels," *HR Magazine*, 2012, http://www.shrm.org/publications/hrmagazine/editorialcontent/2012/1012/pages/1012krell1.aspx.

16. "Old-Style Motels Fading Out."

17. Even chain hotels bring a fair amount of controversy as companies such as Motel 6 and Econolodge have been accused of denying rooms to African Americans or giving them specially designated rooms in poorer condition than those given to whites. This stems from the famous 1994 case *Heart of Atlanta Motel v. United States*. See United States District Court, Southern District of Florida, *United States of America v. Ghanashyambhai M. Patel and Joyitshana G. Patel, d/b/a Econo-Lodge Motel Defendants*, http://www.justice.gov/crt/housing-and-civil-enforcement-cases-documents-16.

18. Groth, *Living Downtown*.

19. Mara L. Keire, "The Committee of Fourteen and Saloon Reform in New York City, 1905–1920," *Business and Economic History* 26, no. 2 (1997): 573–83.

20. Hayner, *Hotel Life*, 8.

21. Elliot Ness, "How to Curb Prostitution in Hotels," *Southern Hotel Journal* (February 1943): 1–5.

22. Jakle, Sculle, and Rogers, *The Motel in America*.

23. Donald J. Bogue, *Skid Row in American Cities* (Chicago: University of Chicago Press, 1963), 1.

24. For studies on skid rows, see ibid.; James P. Spradley, *You Owe Yourself a Drunk: An Ethnography of Urban Nomads* (Boston: Little, Brown, 1970);

Ronald J. Miller, *The Demolition of Skid Row* (Lexington, Mass.: Lexington Books, 1982).

25. Peter H. Rossi, *Down and Out in America: The Origins of Homelessness* (Chicago: University of Chicago Press, 1989).

26. J. Kevin Eckert, *The Unseen Elderly: A Study of Marginally Subsistent Hotel Dwellers* (San Diego: Campanile Press, 1980).

27. Harvey A. Siegal, *Outposts of the Forgotten: Socially Terminal People in Slum Hotels and Single Room Occupancy Tenements* (New Brunswick, N.J.: Transaction Publishers, 1978).

28. Hayner, *Hotel Life*; Eckert, *The Unseen Elderly*; Robert C. Prus and Steve Vassilakopoulos, "Desk Clerks and Hookers: Hustling in a 'Shady' Hotel," *Urban Life* 8, no. 1 (1979): 52–71; Robert C. Prus and Styllianoss Irini, *Hookers, Rounders, and Desk Clerks: The Social Organization of the Hotel Community* (Toronto: Gage, 1980).

29. Hayner, *Hotel Life*.

30. J. Robert Lilly and Richard A. Ball, "No-Tell Motel: The Management of Social Invisibility," *Urban Life* 10, no. 2 (1981): 179–98.

31. Ibid.

32. Siegal, *Outposts of the Forgotten*.

33. Ibid.; Hayner, *Hotel Life*.

34. Eckert, *The Unseen Elderly*.

35. Siegal, *Outposts of the Forgotten*.

36. Chris Jones, "Why the Chicago Heat Wave of 1995 Needs a 20-Year Remembrance," *Chicago Tribune*, March 12, 2015, http://www.chicago tribune.com/entertainment/theater/ct-1995-heat-wave-anniversary-2015 0312-story.html.

37. Eric Klinenberg, *Heat Wave: A Social Autopsy of Disaster in Chicago* (Chicago: University of Chicago Press, 2002).

38. Leslie A. Brownrigg, *People Who Live in Hotels: An Exploratory Overview, Survey Methodology #2006–3* (Washington, D.C.: U.S. Census Bureau, 2006), https://www.census.gov/srd/papers/pdf/ssm2006-03.pdf.

39. American Hotel & Lodging Association, *2013 Lodging Industry Profile*.

40. E. Ann Carson and Daniela Golinelli, *Prisoners in 2012: Trends in Admissions and Releases, 1991–2012 (rev.)* (Washington, D.C.: Bureau of Justice Statistics, 2013), http://www.bjs.gov/index.cfm?ty=pbdetail&iid=4842.

41. Lauren E. Glaze and Erinn J. Herberman, *Correctional Populations in the United States, 2012* (Washington, D.C.: Bureau of Justice Statistics, 2013), http://www.bjs.gov/index.cfm?ty=pbdetail&iid=4909.

42. Joan Petersilia, "From Cell to Society: Who Is Returning Home?," in *Prisoner Reentry and Crime in America*, ed. Jeremy Travis and Christy Visher (New York: Cambridge University Press, 2005), 15–49.

43. Carson and Golinelli, *Prisoners in 2012*.

44. Robert J. Sampson and John H. Laub, *Crime in the Making: Pathways and Turning Points Through Life* (Cambridge, Mass.: Harvard University Press, 1993); Sara Wakefield and Christopher Wildeman, *Children of the Prison Boom* (New York: Oxford University Press, 2013); Bruce Western, *Punishment and Inequality in America* (New York: Russell Sage, 2006).

45. E. Ann Carson, *Prisoners in 2013* (Washington, D.C.: Bureau of Justice Statistics, 2014), http://www.bjs.gov/index.cfm?ty=pbdetail&iid=5109. Estimates were calculated using the data from p. 17, indicating that in 2012, 21,800 inmates whose most serious offense was rape/sexual assault were released from prison.

46. Jill S. Levenson and Leo P. Cotter, "The Impact of Sex Offender Residence Restrictions: 1,000 Feet from Danger or One Step from Absurd?," *International Journal of Offender Therapy and Comparative Criminology* 49, no. 2 (May 2005): 168–78, doi:10.1177/0306624X04271304; Gwenda M. Willis and Randolph C. Grace, "The Quality of Community Reintegration Planning for Child Molesters: Effects on Sexual Recidivism," *Sexual Abuse: A Journal of Research and Treatment* 20, no. 2 (June 2008): 218–40, doi:10.1177/1079063208318005.

47. Lorine A. Hughes and Keri B. Burchfield, "Sex Offender Residence Restrictions in Chicago: An Environmental Injustice?," *Justice Quarterly* 25, no. 4 (December 2008): 647–73, doi:10.1080/07418820802119976; Lorine A. Hughes and Colleen Kadleck, "Sex Offender Community Notification and Community Stratification," *Justice Quarterly* 25, no. 3 (September 2008): 469–95, doi:10.1080/07418820701710941; Richard Tewksbury and Elizabeth E. Mustaine, "Where Registered Sex Offenders Live: Community Characteristics and Proximity to Possible Victims," *Victims & Offenders* 3, no. 1 (January 15, 2008): 86–98, doi:10.1080/15564880701752371; Elizabeth E. Mustaine, Richard Tewksbury, and Kenneth M. Stengel, "Residential Location and Mobility of Registered Sex Offenders," *American Journal of Criminal Justice* 30, no. 2 (2006): 177–92, http://www.springerlink.com/index/jw36q71267358395.pdf; Elizabeth E. Mustaine, Richard Tewksbury, and Kenneth M. Stengel, "Social Disorganization and Residential Locations of Registered Sex Offenders: Is This a Collateral Consequence?," *Deviant Behavior* 27, no. 3 (July 2006): 329–50, doi:10.1080/01639620600605606; Kelly M. Socia and Janet P. Stamatel, "Neighborhood Characteristics and the Social Control of Registered Sex Offenders," *Crime & Delinquency* 58, no. 4 (November 8, 2011): 565–87, doi:10.1177/0011128711420111.

48. J. C. Barnes et al., "Analyzing the Impact of a Statewide Residence Restriction Law on South Carolina Sex Offenders," *Criminal Justice Policy Review* 20, no. 1 (July 8, 2008): 21–43, doi:10.1177/0887403408320842; Paul A. Zandbergen and Timothy C. Hart, "Reducing Housing Options for Convicted Sex Offenders: Investigating the Impact of Residency Restriction Laws

Using GIS," *Justice Research and Policy* 8, no. 2 (September 1, 2006): 1–24, doi:10.3818/JRP.8.2.2006.1.

49. Kelly M. Socia, "The Policy Implications of Residence Restrictions on Sex Offender Housing in Upstate NY," *Criminology & Public Policy* 10, no. 2 (May 3, 2011): 351–89, doi:10.1111/j.1745–9133.2011.00713.x.

50. United States Census Bureau, *Income, Poverty and Health Insurance Coverage in the United States: 2010* (Washington, D.C., 2011), https://www.census.gov/newsroom/releases/archives/income_wealth/cb11–157.html.

51. Carmen DeNavas-Walt, Bernadette D. Proctor, and Jessica C. Smith, *Income, Poverty, and Health Insurance Coverage in the United States: 2012* (Washington, D.C.: U.S. Census Bureau, 2013), https://www.census.gov/prod/2013pubs/p60-245.pdf.

52. Joint Center for Housing Studies of Harvard University, *The State of the Nation's Housing* (Cambridge, Mass., 2011), http://www.jchs.harvard.edu/sites/jchs.harvard.edu/files/son2011.pdf.

53. Erik Eckholm, "As Jobs Vanish, Motel Rooms Become Home," *New York Times*, March 11, 2009, http://www.nytimes.com/2009/03/11/us/11motel.html.

54. National Coalition for the Homeless, *Foreclosure to Homelessness: The Forgotten Victims of the Subprime Crisis, Health Care* (Washington, D.C., 2009).

55. Terri Wingate-Lewinson, June Gary Hopps, and Patricia Reeves, "Liminal Living at an Extended Stay Hotel: Feeling 'Stuck' in a Housing Solution," *Journal of Sociology & Social Welfare* 37, no. 2 (2010): 9–35.

56. Terri Lewinson, "Capturing Environmental Affordances: Low-Income Families Identify Positive Characteristics of a Hotel Housing Solution," *Journal of Community & Applied Social Psychology* 21 (2011): 55–70, doi:10.1002/casp, 55.

57. Siegal, *Outposts of the Forgotten*.

58. Brownrigg, *People Who Live in Hotels*.

59. Rupa Shenoy and New England Center for Investigative Reporting, "State Seeks to Move Homeless from Hotel Rooms to Group Homes," *WGBH*, 2014, http://wgbhnews.org/post/state-seeks-move-homeless-hotel-rooms-group-homes.

60. Randy Billings, "Homelessness Hits Record High in Portland," *Press Herald* (Maine), October 27, 2013, http://www.pressherald.com/news/Homelessness_hits_record_high_in_Portland_.html.

61. Giving Children Hope, "Statistics of Homeless Children in Orange County, CA," 2010, http://gchope.org/statistics-of-homeless-children-in-orange-county-ca/.

62. Siegal, *Outposts of the Forgotten*, 7.

63. Tim O'Brien, "Colonie Approves Motel Limits, 6–0," *Times Union*, July 25, 2013, http://www.timesunion.com/local/article/colonie-approves-motel-limits-6-0-4687845.php.

64. Tim O'Brien, "Crackdown Urged at Problem Motels," *Times Union*, July 11, 2013, http://www.timesunion.com/default/article/crackdown-urged-at-problem-motels-4661057.php.

65. Tim O'Brien, "Colonie Motel Owners Gain by Housing the Poor," *Times Union*, September 6, 2013, http://blog.timesunion.com/colonie/colonie-motel-owners-gain-by-housing-the-poor/1455/.

66. Kozol, *Rachel and Her Children.*

67. Jeff Ferrell, *Tearing Down the Streets: Adventures in Urban Anarchy* (New York: Palgrave Macmillan, 2002), 17, 6, 8, 13.

68. John Lofland et al., *Analyzing Social Settings: A Guide to Qualitative Observation and Analysis*, 4th ed. (Belmont, Ca.: Wadsworth, 2006).

69. Robert M. Emerson, Rachel I. Fretz, and Linda L. Shaw, *Writing Ethnographic Fieldnotes* (Chicago: University of Chicago Press, 1995).

70. See, in order, William F. Whyte, *Street Corner Society* (Chicago: University of Chicago Press, 1943); Elliot Liebow, *Tally's Corner: A Study of Negro Streetcorner Men* (Boston: Little, Brown, 1967); Spradley, *You Owe Yourself a Drunk*; Carol Stack, *All Our Kin: Strategies for Survival in a Black Community* (New York: Basic Books, 1974); Bettylou Valentine, *Hustling and Other Hard Work: Life Styles in the Ghetto* (New York: Free Press, 1978); David A. Snow and Leon Anderson, *Down on Their Luck: A Study of Homeless Street People* (Berkeley: University of California Press, 1993); Philippe Bourgois, *In Search of Respect: Selling Crack in El Barrio* (Cambridge: Cambridge University Press, 1996); John Hagan and Bill McCarthy, *Mean Streets: Youth Crime and Homelessness* (Cambridge: Cambridge University Press, 1998); Mitchell Duneier, *Sidewalk* (New York: Farrar, Straus and Giroux, 1999); Elijah Anderson, *Code of the Street: Decency, Violence, and the Moral Life of the Inner City* (New York: Norton, 1999); Mary Patillo-McCoy, *Black Picket Fences: Privilege and Peril Among the Black Middle Class* (Chicago: University of Chicago Press, 1999); Katherine S. Newman, *No Shame in My Game: The Working Poor in the Inner City* (New York: Vintage, 2000); Jamie J. Fader, *Falling Back: Incarceration and Transitions to Adulthood Among Urban Youth* (New Brunswick, N.J.: Rutgers University Press, 2013).71.

Perhaps the most modern example is Barbara Ehrenreich, *Nickel and Dimed: On (Not) Getting By in America* (New York: Metropolitan Books, 2001). For a criminal justice example, see Ted Conover, *Newjack: Guarding Sing Sing* (New York: Vintage, 2000). Another recent example is Tracie McMillan, *The American Way of Eating: Undercover at Walmart, Applebee's, Farm Fields and the Dinner Table* (New York: Scribner, 2012). Both Ehrenreich and McMillan mention living in cheap motels because of the financial constraints they intentionally placed on themselves. However, neither discusses the culture of living there.

72. Patricia A. Adler and Peter Adler, *Membership Roles in Field Research*, Sage University Papers Series on Qualitative Research Methods, vol. 6 (Newbury Park, Ca.: Sage, 1987), 32.

73. Ibid.

74. Robert S. Weiss, *Learning from Strangers: The Art and Method of Qualitative Interview Studies* (New York: Simon & Schuster, 1994), 54.

75. There is the possibility that framing the study to Biggie in terms of "social inequality" primed him to discuss particular topics, but after reflecting on our interactions, I do not believe that was the case as he rarely discussed anything related to social stratification. As I proceeded to disclose my study to other participants, I framed the study as an examination of what motel life was really like, as told by those who lived there. Residents were drawn to this framework because it empowered them to educate me about their lives at the motel, and I do not believe it presented a problematic frame of reference for observation.

76. Despite the Boardwalk's reputation, I rarely felt that I was in any immediate physical danger. There are several reasons for this. First, I made it a point to trust my instincts, and in some instances I simply avoided certain people who I thought might be unstable and removed myself from situations that seemed volatile and involved people I had just met. Second, I often retreated to my room during the late night and early morning hours, unless I was with someone I trusted. Third, once my research role became apparent and accepted by many long-term residents, they vouched for me, and I had the feeling that they would not allow me to be put in danger, even if they themselves were involved in a physical altercation. The only times I feared for my safety involved Nolan, who carried a knife and became easily agitated. However, he was fairly frail in stature, and residents such as Reg told me not to worry about him. Regardless, while he was around I made a point to never turn my back to him. Finally, as I will show, random violence was simply not a characteristic of the Boardwalk.

77. This incident with Reg was the only time I recall getting fairly intoxicated. After this incident, I became much more aware of my alcohol use. While many residents of the motel went on frequent alcohol binges, I attempted to be more of a social drinker. My motivation was to avoid further situations that would cloud my judgment and recollection as a researcher. In this incident with Reg, two aspects stuck out clearly enough in my head for me to record them. The first was his admonishment of me, and the second was the fact that after I got home, I cried in fear that I had ruined my study.

78. When I began the study I did not park my car in the motel parking lot because I did not want to begin my stay being asked for rides. I also was initially concerned about something happening to it because I was not

sure what the environment was like. Eventually, when I disclosed this, Reg chastised me, telling me that I was stereotyping. Sam told assured me that nothing would happen to it but added that I would be asked for a lot of rides.

79. Early on I felt that because of the limited resources available to many residents and my social position, I did not want to take from what they had. However, I eventually changed my opinion after an experience with Larry. He gave me money to buy him some beers from the gas station and told me to get something for myself. When I came back with only his beers, he looked genuinely hurt. I realized then that when residents offered me food or other items, it was rude not to accept what they chose to share, considering what little they had.

80. Adler and Adler, *Membership Roles in Field Research*, 36.

81. Lois Presser, *Been a Heavy Life: Stories of Violent Men* (Urbana: University of Illinois Press, 2008), 9.

82. Shadd Maruna, *Making Good: How Ex-Convicts Reform and Rebuild Their Lives* (Washington, D.C.: American Psychological Association, 2001).

83. Marvin B. Scott and Stanford M. Lyman, "Accounts," *American Sociological Review* 33, no. 1 (1968): 46–62.

84. Presser, *Been a Heavy Life*, 3.

85. Erving Goffman, *The Presentation of Self in Everyday Life* (New York: Anchor Books, 1959), 242.

1. BIOGRAPHY OF A RESIDENTIAL MOTEL

1. Reg claimed to receive $915 a month from disability as well as his father's death benefits. By combining this with the financial resources of Sky, Fran, and Jake, it was not unrealistic to think that they could save enough for an apartment's first month's rent and security deposit.

2. "Town of Colonie Building Department Files," n.d.

3. Planning and Economic Development Department, *Central Avenue Corridor Inventory Study* (Colonie, N.Y., 2011).

4. Ibid., 7.1.

5. The other motel was purchased in 1997 for $1.25 million. James Denn, "Hotelier Pays $1.25 Million to Acquire Colonie Super 8," *Times Union*, August 13, 1997. Nearly half the motels in America are owned by Indian Americans, mostly Gujaratis. The first Gujarati motel owner ran what was actually called a "residential hotel" in the 1940s that catered to the poor. For an in-depth examination of this phenomenon, see Pawan Dhingra, *Life Behind the Lobby: Indian American Motel Owners and the American Dream* (Stanford, Ca.: Stanford University Press, 2012).

6. "Investigators Seek Clues in Motel Fire," *Times Union*, March 22, 1986.

7. Nancy Hass, "Motel Industry Changes, Indian Owners Carve Niche," *Times Union*, November 16, 1986.
8. Mary Chris Kuhr and Peter Werhwein, "Motel Hit by 3rd Fire in 2 Years," *Times Union*, April 3, 1988.
9. Ken Thurman, "Police Grab Suspected 'Cat Burglar' in Shower," *Times Union*, December 17, 1988; "Man Held on Shoplifting, Knife Charges," *Times Union*, June 23, 1988.
10. "Colonie Man Charged with Raping Girl," *Times Union*, September 5, 1990.
11. "Jury Convicts Man Who Fled from Trial," *Times Union*, February 2, 1991.
12. Michael Lopez, "Culture Clash: Deadhead's High Living Shot Down by the Law," *Times Union*, March 29, 1993; Laura Suchowolec, "Illegal Asbestos Workers Face Deportation," *Daily Gazette*, September 2, 1993, http://news .google.com/newspapers?nid=1957&dat=19930902&id=intGAAAAIBAJ&sj id=1OgMAAAAIBAJ&pg=4592,240279.
13. "Motel Manager Held in Mate's Stabbing," *Times Union*, March 14, 1995.
14. Rich Karlin, "$25-a-Night Sanctuary on Desolation Row," *Times Union*, March 22, 1996, http://albarchive.merlinone.net/mweb/wmsql.wm.request ?oneimage&imageid=5806451, A3.
15. Lawrence M. Brin, "Story Did Disservice to Central Avenue," *Times Union*, March 29, 1996, http://albarchive.merlinone.net/mweb/wmsql.wm.request? oneimage&imageid=5807449.
16. "Colonie's Secrecy Is Indefensible," *Times Union*, January 10, 1997.
17. Jeremy Boyer, "Motel a Home of Last Resort," *Daily Gazette*, April 14, 2002, http://news.google.com/newspapers?nid=1957&dat=20020414&id=TnshA AAAIBAJ&sjid=IYoFAAAAIBAJ&pg=5668,3103782.
18. Carol DeMare, "Across the Hall, a Sex Offender," *Times Union*, July 3, 2007, http://alb.merlinone.net/mweb/wmsql.wm.request?HIT_00000000 _6466455.1.
19. Christine Benedict, *Resolution No. 353-a Requesting Albany County Remove Families and Individuals from Certain Motels on Route 5, Town of Colonie* (Colonie, N.Y.: Albany County Legislature, 2007).
20. Ibid.
21. Carol DeMare, "Safety Checks Begin at Motels: Central Avenue Inspections Prompted by Lawmaker's Concerns Over Code Violations," *Times Union*, August 26, 2007.
22. Michael F. Conners II, *Review Department of Social Services Temporary Assistance Division Motel Placement* (Albany, N.Y., 2008).
23. Ryan Hutchins, "Colonie May Restrict Where Some Sex Offenders Can Stay," *Times Union*, February 11, 2009, http://www.knowledgeplex.org /news/3029021.html?p=1.
24. CBS 6, "Colonie Considers Sex-Offender Solutions," *CBS 6 WRGB*, 2009, http://www.cbs6albany.com/news/colonie-1264601-police-chief.html.

25. CBS 6, "Colonie Approves Sex Offender Limits," *CBS 6 WRGB*, 2009, http://www.cbs6albany.com/articles/approves-1265354-colonie-limits.html.

26. Robert Gavin, "Lawyer: Colonie Law 'Defects' Likely," *Times Union*, August 8, 2009.

27. *License Required to House Registered Sex Offenders* (Colonie, N.Y.: Town of Colonie, 2009).

28. Tim O'Brien, "Two Motels to Stop Housing Sex Offenders," *Times Union*, October 31, 2009; Tim O'Brien, "Checking in on Motels Housing Offenders," *Times Union*, December 15, 2009, http://www.timesunion.com/local/article/Checking-in-on-motels-housing-offenders-555788.php. One other reason for the decline in the number of sex offenders was that the Riverfort County residence restriction law was struck down in 2009, so offenders were then placed in the city of Riverfort.

29. Tim O'Brien, "Motel Owner: License a Bad Deal," *Times Union*, January 25, 2010.

30. Tim O'Brien, "When Sex Offenders Check In," *Times Union*, September 29, 2009.

31. Ibid.

32. O'Brien, "Two Motels to Stop Housing Sex Offenders."

33. During my time at the Boardwalk, the trailer park next to the motel was home to at least two registered sex offenders whose victims were under the age of sixteen. No actions were taken against the trailer park. Both Reg and Sam were aware of these offenders and the young kids who got picked up and dropped off by a school bus each day, with Reg telling me, "That's not kosher."

34. Tim O'Brien, "Checkout Time on Central Ave.?," *Times Union*, May 21, 2010, http://albarchive.merlinone.net/mweb/wmsql.wm.request?oneimage&imageid=10673071.

35. Nancy Strang-Vadebogart, "Fuller Road Motel 33 Fuller Road Review Request for Waiver of Moratorium" (2011), 24.

36. Planning and Economic Development Department, *Central Avenue Corridor Inventory Study*.

37. Mitchell Duneier, *Sidewalk* (New York: Farrar, Straus and Giroux, 1999), 123.

38. Both Sam and Natalie claimed that the motel owner attempted to buy the trailer park at one point but did not like the terms so he pulled out and left $10,000 on the table.

39. Reg and Sky claim that they looked at living at this motel before the Boardwalk, but the place only rented rooms to Chinese who worked at the restaurant.

40. The tobacco shop was shut down in summer 2013. Rumor among residents was that the owner was selling individual cigarettes, or "loosies."

41. I saw residents leave mail here as well, but one day Sky complained that "Every time I put something in the office, the mailman never takes it. He

just goes in, throws the stuff on the counter and leaves. Pain in my ass." She then made a habit of using mailboxes around the neighborhood near the grocery store and KFC. On a few occasions I mailed things from campus for her.

42. On more than one occasion they ran out of receipts, so I was given a receipt written on a torn square of paper with an ink stamp. I saw one of these in Reg and Sky's room as well.

43. The number of points is determined by the risk level of the offender, which can be between 1 and 3. The motel can house any combination of offenders as long as their cumulative risk levels do not exceed 6. It is interesting to note that the license expired in early 2013 yet remained up for over three months before it was replaced by an updated license. During this time registered sex offenders continued to reside at the motel.

44. According to Dee, "Yeah, that's where all the fuckin' cats came from. It was a house for stray cats 'cause it was just open, open area. They stopped using it and it all caved in." Noonan told me that the union he worked for put in a bid on the demolition project, but it went to another company.

45. Biggie told me that the first-floor rooms were used for long-term residents. I never received any indication from any other residents or staff that this was the case, and from what I observed the assignment of rooms was simply based on what was open and relatively clean. The larger first-floor rooms provided more living space, and this was enjoyed by many long-term residents and couples such as Reg and Sky, Dee and Toby, and Biggie and Deirdre. I never observed any conflict between residents over occupying upstairs versus downstairs rooms, and even for long-term residents, other living conditions besides room size, such as air conditioning, heat, and general appearance, often took precedence in choosing living spaces.

46. When I asked Elizabeth about this she advised me, "You just gotta shove it in there."

47. All told I spent about $100 on supplies for my room (purchases included a remote, a fan, caulk to fix my toilet, and screen netting so I could leave my door open in the summer while keeping bugs out). I would have spent more if my social networks had not provided me with a fridge and a space heater.

48. I passed this on to new residents who on several occasions asked me how to turn things on. Usually this involved them complaining to Elizabeth and her shouting up at me to show them how to work things.

49. I got rid of the couch after a week because there were signs of mice living inside it (such as droppings on my table), and I did not want them taking over my room. In fairness to Jake, he told me before he left that he suspected as much. In this instance, I was guilty of contributing to the mess at the rear of the motel because I could not lift the couch into the dumpster. A few days later Reg flagged down the garbage truck and called me over to

help lift the couch into the dumpster so it could be removed. It was a messily disgusting task, as the couch had soaked up quite a bit of water from the rain and was dirty, smelly, wet, and heavy as we lifted it into the dumpster. We also threw a soggy blanket into the dumpster and tried to do the same with a carpet, but it was too waterlogged to lift.

50. When I told Elizabeth about the problem and that I wanted a new room, she asked, "You don't want that room no more?" I found this to be incredibly funny, given the severity of the situation.

2. PATHWAYS TO MOTEL LIFE

1. Egon F. Kunz, "The Refugee in Flight: Kinetic Models and Forms of Displacement," *International Migration Review* 7, no. 2 (1973): 127.

2. Everett S. Lee, "A Theory of Migration," in *Migration*, ed. John Archer Jackson (Cambridge: Cambridge University Press, 1969), 286–87.

3. See Nels Anderson, *The Hobo: The Sociology of the Homeless Man* (Chicago: University of Chicago Press, 1923).

4. Dale, Price, Tat, Walt, Jasper, and Harry were returning from prison for sex offense convictions. Darryl and Cinque were registered sex offenders but claimed to be returning from a parole revocation and a weapons and gun charge, respectively. I am unsure as to exact criminal histories of Ryan, Slash, Noonan, Patch, and Sonny.

5. Erving Goffman, *Asylums* (Garden City, N.Y.: Anchor Books, 1961), 4.

6. Ibid.

7. Gresham M. Sykes, *The Society of Captives: A Study of a Maximum Security Prison* (Princeton, N.J.: Princeton University Press, 1958).

8. Joan Petersilia, *When Prisoners Come Home: Parole and Prisoner Reentry* (New York: Oxford University Press, 2003), 3.

9. For a qualitative examination of the struggles of finding food and shelter after prison, see David J. Harding et al., "Making Ends Meet After Prison," *Journal of Policy Analysis and Management* 33, no. (2014): 440–70, doi:10.1002/21741.

10. Martha R. Burt et al., *Strategies for Improving Homeless People's Access to Mainstream Benefits and Services* (Washington, D.C.: U.S. Department of Housing and Urban Development, Office of Policy Development and Research, 2010).

11. Devah Pager, "The Mark of a Criminal Record," *American Journal of Sociology* 108, no. 5 (2003): 937–75.

12. For similar notions about scaling back expectations explored from a female offender's perspective, see Andrea M. Leverentz, *The Ex-Prisoner's Dilemma: How Women Negotiate Competing Narratives of Reentry and Desistance* (New Brunswick, N.J.: Rutgers University Press, 2014).

13. David M. Altschuler and Rachel Brash, "Adolescent and Teenage Offenders Confronting the Challenges and Opportunities of Reentry," *Youth Violence and Juvenile Justice* 2, no. 1 (January 2004): 72–87, doi:10.1177/1541204003260048, 72.

14. American Fact Finder, *Financial Characteristics* (Washington, D.C., 2013), http://factfinder.census.gov/faces/tableservices/jsf/pages/productview.xhtml?src=CF.

15. Riley's opinion probably changed a few days later when he went to push open a window to cool off his room and the entire glass pane shattered on contact.

16. This statement came with a fair amount of foreshadowing because Biggie soon found himself embroiled in drama with Reg.

17. When residents such as Reg, Sky, and Sam stepped down from previous environments, they placed many belongings in storage units.

18. What happened to Vito's sister remained unclear as he refused to elaborate about her.

19. Terri Wingate-Lewinson, June Gary Hopps, and Patricia Reeves, "Liminal Living at an Extended Stay Hotel: Feeling 'Stuck' in a Housing Solution," *Journal of Sociology & Social Welfare* 37, no. 2 (2010): 19.

20. For more on flopping and ways to analyze flop locations, see James P. Spradley, *You Owe Yourself a Drunk: An Ethnography of Urban Nomads* (Boston: Little, Brown, 1970).

21. It is interesting that Roy made this distinction. In a 2009 report on the criminalization of the homeless, a list of the ten cities with the most punitive policies toward the homeless was presented, and five were in the South, four in the state of Florida. See National Law Center on Homelessness and Poverty and National Coalition for the Homeless, *Homes Not Handcuffs: The Criminalization of Homelessness in U.S. Cities* (Washington, D.C., 2009).

22. I asked Fran to elaborate on these events, but she would not go into more detail, and I decided not to press the issue.

23. They bought the minivan for $500 but never registered or insured it, and the front plates did not match the back ones. They got a flat tire on the highway and someone called the police to help them fix it. When the police arrived they noticed the unmatched plates, impounded the van, and fined Sky $600.

24. This move was one of the few examples of residents moving for work, which harkens back to the early lives of hobos who moved across the American frontier in search of work. See Anderson, *The Hobo*.

25. This finding is very similar to what Snow and Anderson found in their study of homeless street people. See David A. Snow and Leon Anderson, *Down on Their Luck: A Study of Homeless Street People* (Berkeley: University of California Press, 1993).

26. There was no evidence that Biggie was a registered sex offender, given these claims of early sexual victimization.

27. It is interesting to note that Darryl's alleged victim was also eight years old.

28. The lack of further detail about drug use at the motel is due to my role as a researcher. Because I did not engage in drug use with residents besides drinking alcohol, they came to view me as fairly straightlaced. As a result, I was not invited to observe or partake in harder drug use, and I did not press the issue.

29. A fair number of residents had military histories. Sam, Larry, Price, Dale, Darryl, Steve, Ramòn, Dee, Jerry, Paul, and Rob all claimed to have been in some form of military service.

30. Robert J. Sampson and John H. Laub, "Crime and Deviance Over the Life Course: The Salience of Adult Social Bonds," *American Sociological Review* 55, no. 5 (1990): 609–27.

31. In all my time at the Boardwalk, Dee's story was the only instance that I heard of a woman being assaulted.

32. Thomas J. Dishion, Joan McCord, and François Poulin, "When Interventions Harm: Peer Groups and Problem Behavior," *American Psychologist* 54, no. 9 (1999): 755.

33. Joan McCord, "Cures That Harm: Unanticipated Outcomes of Crime Prevention Programs," *Annals of the American Academy of Political and Social Science* 587, no. 1 (May 1, 2003): 16–30, doi:10.1177/0002716202250781.

34. I was able to verify several claims of disability by looking at official paperwork, listening to conversations between residents and case workers, and observing the medications residents took. However, I was unable to verify other claims (especially of severe mental illness) because those residents lacked paperwork and connections to social services that I could pursue.

35. I was skeptical of this claim but did not pursue the issue further.

36. Biggie and Deirdre's relationship with the program began to deteriorate over time. I asked Deirdre what she thought about it and she said, "'Cause they used to come when they felt like it, every time they took us somewhere, oh you gotta hurry up, you gotta hurry up, I only got a certain time with you guys, I gotta see other client. We got tired of that stuff, I mean after a while, you get sick of that garbage, can be a pain right in the butt. Instead of Biggie getting two hours with them a week, he was getting nothing. S'posed to spend with him two hours a week. Then when they bring his meds, they come out with half of the medicine or they didn't bring it all out, so that didn't help any either. So you can't depend on people like that." Once they purchased a car, they did not have to rely on the program as much, and Deirdre felt relieved that they did not have to depend on anyone else.

3. MANAGING STIGMA AND IDENTITY

1. Erving Goffman, *Stigma: Notes on the Management of Spoiled Identity* (Englewood Cliffs, N.J.: Prentice Hall, 1963), 3, 5, 30.
2. Philippe Bourgois, *In Search of Respect: Selling Crack in El Barrio* (Cambridge: Cambridge University Press, 1996), 8.
3. Jocelyn A. Hollander and Rachel L. Einwohner, "Conceptualizing Resistance," *Sociological Forum* 19, no. 4 (2004): 538.
4. Victor M. Rios, *Punished: Policing the Lives of Black and Latino Boys* (New York: NYU Press, 2011), 21.
5. Goffman, *Stigma*.
6. Michèle Lamont, *The Dignity of Working Men: Morality and the Boundaries of Race, Class, and Immigration* (Cambridge, Mass.: Harvard University Press, 2001), 7. For examples, see Elijah Anderson, *Code of the Street: Decency, Violence, and the Moral Life of the Inner City* (New York: Norton, 1999); Heith Copes, Andy Hochstetler, and J. Patrick Williams, "'We Weren't Like No Regular Dope Fiends': Negotiating Hustler and Crackhead Identities," *Social Problems* 55, no. 2 (2008): 254–70, doi:10.1525/sp.2008.55.2.254.
7. Lois Presser, *Been a Heavy Life: Stories of Violent Men* (Urbana: University of Illinois Press, 2008), 3.
8. George C. Rosenwald and Richard L. Ochberg, eds., *Storied Lives: The Cultural Politics of Self-Understanding* (New Haven, Conn.: Yale University Press, 1992), 1.
9. Presser, *Been a Heavy Life*, 2.
10. Shadd Maruna, *Making Good: How Ex-Convicts Reform and Rebuild Their Lives* (Washington, D.C.: American Psychological Association, 2001), 87.
11. See Anderson, *Code of the Street*; Albert K. Cohen, *Delinquent Boys* (Glencoe, N.Y.: Free Press, 1955); Walter B. Miller, "Lower Class Culture as a Generating Milieu for Gang Delinquency," *Journal of Social Issues* 14 (1958): 5–19; Marvin E. Wolfgang and Franco Ferracuti, *The Subculture of Violence: Towards an Integrated Theory in Criminology* (London: Tavistock, 1967).
12. This is part of a larger societal tendency to equate sexual offenders with sexual predators who victimize children, when in reality child sexual predators are a small subset of all sexual offenders. See James Quinn, Craig Forsyth, and Carla Mullen-Quinn, "Societal Reaction to Sex Offenders: A Review of the Origins and Results of the Myths Surrounding Their Crimes and Treatment Amenability," *Deviant Behavior* 25, no. 3 (May 2004): 215–32, doi:10.1080/01639620490431147.
13. Goffman, *Stigma*, 92.
14. The newspaper article detailing this story listed the girl as fourteen, but Reg claimed the reporter got the age wrong.

15. The visits by local law enforcement gave Elizabeth knowledge about all the sex offenders at the motel. Elizabeth also outed Walt's status to me, and Tat claimed that she outed him during his previous stay at the Boardwalk.
16. Roy F. Baumeister, Karen Dale, and Kristin L. Sommer, "Freudian Defense Mechanisms and Empirical Findings in Modern Social Psychology: Reaction Formation, Projection, Displacement, Undoing, Isolation, Sublimation, and Denial," *Journal of Personality* 66, no. 6 (1998): 1089.
17. Ibid.
18. Some research finds five-year recidivism rates for most sex offenders to be 7 percent or less, and ten-year rates between 6 and 22 percent. See Leslie Helmus et al., "Absolute Recidivism Rates Predicted By Static-99R and Static-2002R Sex Offender Risk Assessment Tools Vary Across Samples: A Meta-Analysis," *Criminal Justice and Behavior* 39, no. 9 (May 21, 2012): 1148–71, doi:10.1177/0093854812443648. Other studies find rates around 14 percent. See Timothy Fortney et al., "Myths and Facts About Sexual Offenders: Implications for Treatment and Public Policy," *Sexual Offender Treatment* 2, no. 1 (2007): 1–17.
19. Maruna, *Making Good*, 117.
20. Ibid., 11, 118.
21. Ibid., 74.
22. Ibid., 87.
23. Dee told me as well that she thought being on unemployment made her lazy.
24. Steve did similar work when he lived at the motel and received cigarettes from Elizabeth in return.
25. Donald Black, "The Epistemology of Pure Sociology," *Law and Social Inquiry* 20, no. 3 (1995): 829–70.
26. Matthew Desmond, "Disposable Ties and the Urban Poor," *American Journal of Sociology* 117, no. 5 (2012): 1311.
27. Jack Katz, *Seductions of Crime* (New York: Basic Books, 1988), 97.
28. This is similar to what Gresham Sykes found in the prison world, where men are not able to assert masculinity through sexual conquest with women, so physical aggression becomes the marker of the male role. See Gresham M. Sykes, *The Society of Captives: A Study of a Maximum Security Prison* (Princeton, N.J.: Princeton University Press, 1958).
29. Jeffrey A. Schaler, *Addiction Is a Choice* (Chicago: Open Court, 2000).
30. Katz, *Seductions of Crime*, 80.
31. See, in order, Davina Allen, "Narrating Nursing Jurisdiction: 'Atrocity Stories' and 'Boundary-Work,'" *Symbolic Interaction* 24, no. 1 (2001): 75–103; Regula V. Burri, "Doing Distinctions: Boundary Work and Symbolic Capital in Radiology," *Social Studies of Science* 38, no. 1 (February 1, 2008): 35–62, doi:10.1177/0306312707082021; Matthew B. Ezzell, "'Barbie Dolls' on the Pitch: Identity Work, Defensive Othering, and Inequality in Women's Rugby," *Social Problems* 56, no. 1 (2009): 111–31, doi:10.1525/sp.2009.56.1.111.

SP5601; Grace Yukich, "Boundary Work in Inclusive Religious Groups: Constructing Identity at the New York Catholic Worker," *Sociology of Religion* 71, no. 2 (2010): 172–96; Carla D. Shirley, " 'You Might Be a Redneck If . . . ': Boundary Work Among Rural, Southern Whites," *Social Forces* 89, no. 1 (September 1, 2010): 35–61, doi:10.1353/sof.2010.0081; Mindy Stombler, " 'BUDDIES' OR 'SLUTTIES': The Collective Sexual Reputation of Fraternity Little Sisters," *Gender & Society* 8, no. 3 (September 1, 1994): 297–323, doi:10.1177/089124394008003002; Daniel L. Wann and Nyla R. Branscombe, "Die-Hard and Fair-Weather Fans: Effects of Identification on BIRGing and CORFing Tendencies," *Journal of Sport & Social Issues* 14, no. 2 (September 1, 1990): 103–17, doi:10.1177/019372359001400203.

32. Terri Lewinson, "Residents' Coping Strategies in an Extended-Stay Hotel Home," *Journal of Ethnographic and Qualitative Research* 4, no. 2001 (2010): 180–96.

33. Goffman, *Stigma*, 20.

4. COMMUNITY, CONFLICT, AND FRAGILITY

1. Tim O'Brien, "Town Seeks to Make It Harder to Build Motels on Central Avenue," *Times Union*, July 8, 2013, http://blog.timesunion.com/colonie/town-seeks-to-make-it-harder-to-build-motels-on-central-avenue/1411/.

2. Carol Stack, *All Our Kin: Strategies for Survival in a Black Community* (New York: Basic Books, 1974).

3. Matthew Desmond, "Disposable Ties and the Urban Poor," *American Journal of Sociology* 117, no. 5 (2012): 1296.

4. Sudhir Venkatesh frames the underground economy as a "widespread set of activities, usually scattered and not well integrated, through which people earn money that is not reported to the government and that, in some cases, may entail criminal behavior." The culture of the Boardwalk was not organized solely around earning money off the books, but because a substantial amount of social interaction involved buying and selling resources (including drugs), I feel this is an apt conceptualization. See Sudhir Alladi Venkatesh, *Off the Books: The Underground Economy of the Urban Poor* (Cambridge, Mass.: Harvard University Press, 2006), 8.

5. There were occasions when I was unable to give rides, and I noticed that Jake had gotten quite adept at biking to the grocery store while carrying a trash bag full of cans. He was equally skilled at biking back with a twelve-pack of beer.

6. I was happy that Tat did not take offense to my rebuffing his offer for a tattoo. I enjoyed spending time with him, and one of my favorite memories is when he walked over to me with his cell phone and asked, "You hang out with a lotta white people in your life, right? What does this mean?" He had

gotten a text from a girl saying she was at her "buffs" and I surmised that it meant her best friend's. He thanked me and walked away laughing.

7. Reg bought loose tobacco and tubes from the local tobacco store in order to sell his cigarettes. When Ed asked him about this process, Reg offered to teach him if Ed purchased the materials: "You put the thirty dollars in my hand, I'll get you three fricken things of tubes, the tobacco, and the machine and I'll teach you to do it." Reg claimed that he made almost $600 a month selling cigarettes to support his beer habit. This seemed to me like a bit of an exaggeration.

8. Eric's habits of selling stolen goods caught up to him when he stole a bicycle from a local drug dealer named Rav and then sold it to Reg, who then sold it to someone else. When the previous owner found out about it, he confronted Reg and threatened to shoot him unless Reg came up with $400 or a bike equal to the one he lost. Reg was able to purchase a bike from a local shop for $189 and give it to Rav, avoiding any retaliation.

9. Ed once offered me Xanax for free and I turned him down. I told Reg about this later and he said, "Take 'em, somebody here will buy them from ya. Money in the bank."

10. One interesting situation occurred on Thanksgiving afternoon as I sat in Reg's room with Clive. Clive was nineteen and lived upstairs with his mother and father. On that afternoon, Clive came down to buy marijuana from Reg and ended up staying in the room to smoke. There was a knock on the door, and when Reg opened the door, Clive's father stood outside. Upon seeing Clive, he asked, "What are you doin' here?" Clive sheepishly replied, "Smoking." His father nodded and then ended up buying marijuana himself.

11. Marjorie L. DeVault, *Feeding the Family: The Social Organization of Caring as Gendered Work* (Chicago: University of Chicago Press, 1994).

12. Berenice Fisher and Joan Tronto, "Toward a Feminist Theory of Caring," in *Circles of Care: Work and Identity in Women's Lives*, ed. Emily K. Able and Margaret K. Nelson (Albany: State University of New York Press, 1990), 35–62.

13. Sam told me something similar—that he would knock on a resident's door if he had not seen them for week or so to make sure they were not dead.

14. Nels Anderson, *The Hobo: The Sociology of the Homeless Man* (Chicago: University of Chicago Press, 1923).

15. When Biggie first fired up the grill there were flames shooting out of the bottom and he, Randy, and Avery spent several minutes trying to figure out why. Seeing as Biggie lived directly below me, I worried about him having an accident with the grill, but he assured me that he would not "blow everyone up" because he had put so many grills together that he knew what he was doing.

16. Reg mentioned that he saw Biggie eating tuna salad that had been sitting out in his room for days. Sam told me about one day when he observed Biggie grilling, "dripping sweat and shit, digging all in his nose. He had some rag and he cleaned the fuckin' spatchula with it and it's black as my fuckin' shoe dirty. And he wiping the spatchula, he's flippin' burgers. Yo, come get a plate? I said, no I'm good brotha. Sweat dripping off his fat chest, it's drippin' all over the food. I said, oh my god, oh. People just don't think about what they doin', man. Oh, I'm the grill master, just wiping sweat all over the, and he's standin' right over our food. Not our food, it's his food, but I didn't eat none of it. Then he wiping his face, digging in his nose, with the same rag that he cleaned that spatchula with. He done slung it over his shoulder like a real professional chef, like he watchin' shit on TV. I said, I couldn't believe he did that. This guy's nasty. I couldn't believe he did that shit, Chris. I'm lookin at him like, I know he just didn't do that." I also observed this sort of behavior when I spent time inside Biggie's room. The air inside often smelled like grease, and flies buzzed around on a constant basis. On many occasions I saw food such as baked beans or pasta in sauce sitting out on tables for days.

17. In some ways, this new resident cannot be blamed for this transgression, as the transient nature of the motel made it quite difficult for residents to enter into caring relationships. Long-term residents acknowledged that they often did not even make the effort to remember names. Reg summed it up by saying, "People come and go so quick around here."

18. This episode made my relationships with Biggie and Reg somewhat awkward. Both were openly feuding with each other, but I did not want to appear as if I was taking sides when I spoke with each of them. When each would rant about the other, I would not affirm or deny their positions. Instead, I simply listened and recorded their words. Furthermore, Biggie began openly collecting empty bottles and cans in large trash cans outside of his room and often urged me to give any empties to him. I knew that Reg was also on the lookout for empties and, in a way, expected that I would give him some. I tried to address this by alternating my empty bottles and cans between Biggie and Reg, without telling them that I was doing so.

19. Reg became openly hostile to Darryl, and anytime I mentioned Darryl, Reg would comment, "Oh, that fucking pedophile?" Darryl was relatively mature about the situation and gave Reg a card with ten dollars in it for his birthday.

20. This can be seen in other instances as well. After their "can wars," Reg invited Biggie to share in his Thanksgiving and also invited him to his birthday party. Jake and Gene got into a violent encounter one night when Gene would not leave a party when he was told to, but a few days later they smoked marijuana together.

21. Marcel Mauss, *The Gift* (New York: Free Press, 1954).

22. Stack, *All Our Kin*, 34.

23. These norms that Burt describes echo Nels Anderson's examination of the "code of etiquette" that existed in jungle camps and the way that older residents enforced discipline. See Anderson, *The Hobo*.

24. Elijah Anderson, *Code of the Street: Decency, Violence, and the Moral Life of the Inner City* (New York: Norton, 1999), 66, 32.

25. Elizabeth told me that she tried to avoid calling the police whenever possible because the police would ask her a bunch of questions over the phone and it made her feel like she was the one engaging in deviant behavior. She mostly used the threat of calling the police to control behavior.

26. Maria Kefalas, Patrick J. Carr, and Susan Clampet-Lundquist, "To Snitch or Not to Snitch: The Crisis of Trust in the City of Brotherly Love," *Contexts* 10, no. 3 (2011): 56.

27. Gresham M. Sykes, *The Society of Captives: A Study of a Maximum Security Prison* (Princeton, N.J.: Princeton University Press, 1958).

28. Ibid.

29. It is important to note that the aforementioned analysis of aggressive verbal posturing is rooted in a symbolic interactionist perspective, which is based in temporal blocks of behavior that are then mined for meaning. In that regard, one might argue from a phenomenological perspective that these somewhat fantastical examples of aggressive posturing border are just that: fantasies that exist in the present without explicit and intended functionality. Sociologists Jack Katz and Thomas Csordas argue that one aspect of participant observation is that it "usually cannot hope to grasp meanings of the present that are rooted in vast and idiosyncratic temporal reaches." The strong seductions of the moment in residents' lives must be acknowledged as explanations for their actions, particularly because the researcher is unable to determine exactly how respondents construct their notions of the present and future. See Jack Katz and Thomas J. Csordas, "Phenomenological Ethnography in Sociology and Anthropology," *Ethnography* 4, no. 3 (September 1, 2003): 283, doi:10.1177/146613810343001.

30. Marc was in fact from Guatemala, and even if Reg did harbor hatred for Latinos, he did not let it get in the way of socializing and engaging in community with Marc.

31. Venkatesh, *Off the Books*.

32. Stack, *All Our Kin*; Desmond, "Disposable Ties and the Urban Poor."

33. Anderson, *Code of the Street*.

34. Kefalas, Carr, and Clampet-Lundquist, "To Snitch or Not to Snitch."

35. For discussions of social disorganization theory, see Clifford R. Shaw and Henry McKay, *Juvenile Delinquency and Urban Areas* (Chicago: University of Chicago Press, 1942); Robert J. Bursik Jr., "Social Disorganization and Theories of Crime and Delinquency: Problems and Prospects," *Criminology* 26, no. 4 (November 1988): 519–52, doi:10.1111/j.1745–9125.1988.tb00854.x;

Jeffrey D. Morenoff, Robert J. Sampson, and Stephen W. Raudenbush, "Neighborhood Inequality, Collective Efficacy, and the Spatial Dynamics of Urban Violence," *Criminology* 39, no. 3 (2001): 517–58, http://online library.wiley.com/doi/10.1111/j.1745–9125.2001.tb00932.x/full; Robert J. Sampson, Stephen W. Raudenbush, and Felton Earls, "Neighborhoods and Violent Crime: A Multilevel Study of Collective Efficacy," *Science* 277, no. 5328 (August 15, 1997): 918–24, doi:10.1126/science.277.5328.918; Charis E. Kubrin and Ronald Weitzer, "New Directions in Social Disorganization Theory," *Journal of Research in Crime and Delinquency* 40, no. 4 (November 1, 2003): 374–402, doi:10.1177/0022427803256238.

36. William F. Whyte, *Street Corner Society* (Chicago: University of Chicago Press, 1943), 269.

5. INTERACTIONS WITH THE COMMUNITY

1. Harvey A. Siegal, *Outposts of the Forgotten: Socially Terminal People in Slum Hotels and Single Room Occupancy Tenements* (New Brunswick, N.J.: Transaction, 1978), 7.

2. Jeff Ferrell, *Tearing Down the Streets: Adventures in Urban Anarchy* (New York: Palgrave Macmillan, 2002), 8.

3. Ibid., 229, 8.

4. Tim O'Brien, "Town Will Seek to Shutter Skylane Motel—the Colonie Blog," *Times Union*, December 17, 2013, http://blog.timesunion.com/colonie /town-will-seek-to-shutter-skylane-motel/1550/.

5. Tim O'Brien, "Colonie Motel Owners Gain by Housing the Poor," *Times Union*, September 6, 2013, http://blog.timesunion.com/colonie/colonie -motel-owners-gain-by-housing-the-poor/1455/.

6. Ibid.

7. The public grossly overestimates the recidivism rate for sexual offenders, putting it at 75 percent when research indicates it is likely around 14 percent. See Timothy Fortney et al., "Myths and Facts About Sexual Offenders: Implications for Treatment and Public Policy," *Sexual Offender Treatment* 2, no. 1 (2007): 1–17.

8. James Quinn, Craig Forsyth, and Carla Mullen-Quinn, "Societal Reaction to Sex Offenders: A Review of the Origins and Results of the Myths Surrounding Their Crimes and Treatment Amenability," *Deviant Behavior* 25, no. 3 (May 2004): 215–32.

9. Human Rights Watch, *No Easy Answers* (New York, 2007), http://www.hrw .org/node/10685/section/6.

10. Christine Benedict, "Colonie Motels—Corporate Welfare at Its Finest!," *Times Union*, September 6, 2013, http://blog.timesunion.com/christine benedict/colonie-motels-corporate-welfare-at-its-finest/40/.

11. Nels Anderson, *The Hobo: The Sociology of the Homeless Man* (Chicago: University of Chicago Press, 1923); Clifford R. Shaw, *The Jack-Roller: A Delinquent Boy's Own Story* (Chicago: University of Chicago Press, 1930).

12. For a discussion on the various definitions of order maintenance policing and its theoretical and practical implications, especially in light of "broken windows," see David Thacher, "Order Maintenance Reconsidered: Moving Beyond Strong Causal Reasoning," *Journal of Criminal Law & Criminology* 94, no. 2 (2004): 381–414.

13. This explanation from the police that seeing us drinking in the parking lot could somehow harm someone passing by fits clearly with the notions of sanitization of social space. It also echoes Spradley's work in that tramps find it hard to drink without violating social norms. See James P. Spradley, *You Owe Yourself a Drunk: An Ethnography of Urban Nomads* (Boston: Little, Brown, 1970).

14. Benedict, "Colonie Motels—Corporate Welfare at Its Finest!"

15. It is interesting that all these observed examples involved women as the perpetrators. Of course, my fieldwork is limited in scope so it is possible and likely that men were involved in crimes within the local community. However, I did submit a FOI Act request to the Dutchland Police for any arrests that occurred during my fieldwork involving an individual whose listed residence was the Boardwalk Motel, and I was given only a single report that did not actually involve a crime or arrest. Therefore I am unable to elaborate on this finding or the scope of crimes that motel residents committed in the community.

16. Benedict, "Colonie Motels—Corporate Welfare at Its Finest!"

17. Erving Goffman, *Stigma: Notes on the Management of Spoiled Identity* (Englewood Cliffs, N.J.: Prentice Hall, 1963).

18. Dee and Toby occasionally did laundry in their tub to save money and the trip.

19. Roy used this phrase with almost every unknown woman he interacted with. We passed by a bus stop on our walk back to the motel and he greeted the older black woman sitting inside with "How are you, Miss Lady?"

20. The owner of the Boardwalk also owned the Park Place and the Home Cooking buffet restaurant. I often wondered if owning these locations together was a strategic decision, with the assumption that motel residents would visit the buffet because they were unable to cook in their rooms.

21. Biggie, Deirdre, Toby, Dee, Reg, and Sky were the only residents who told me that they used this pantry. Pickups were every other Thursday, and to enroll residents needed picture ID and proof of residence, in this case a receipt from the motel.

22. Unlike some low-income communities, the Boardwalk was not located in what many would call a "food desert," or a location devoid of fresh and nutritious food. The Giant Foods located within walking distance had a

substantial variety of fruits, vegetables, and nutritious items. Dee also visited the Veggie Mobile, which was a community garden vehicle that drove through the Riverfort area to sell fresh fruits and vegetables in locations with many elderly and low-income residents. However, the Veggie Mobile did not stop near the motel, so residents had to travel into downtown Riverfort or Pinewood to visit it.

23. Because of this, residents who received food stamps but lacked the means to prepare food were at a significant disadvantage when it came to eating in the sustaining habitat.

24. Many of the working poor make just enough money to disqualify them from receiving food stamps. This was the case for Sky, who worked forty hours a week at $7.85 an hour. Reg said they would gladly trade whatever income put her over in exchange for $200 of food stamps each month.

25. O'Brien, "Colonie Motel Owners Gain by Housing the Poor."

26. Jake told me that Rob would frequent this McDonald's and try to panhandle. He was eventually kicked out and banned for this. Vito also panhandled on a daily basis along Main Street. He told me that on good days he came home with around thirty dollars.

27. Sam called me the next day and laughed while he told me that his boss was surprised to see me with him, because workers were not supposed to bring friends or family to work. Sam said his boss did not understand who I was and thought that maybe Sam was "slow" and I was there to assist him. Sam then showed him my business card and further explained my project to clarify our relationship.

28. When it became obvious to Sam that the Marriott was not giving him enough hours to live on, he got a job at a Wendy's near downtown Riverfort.

29. Roy had been working at this restaurant for eight months before he was fired. He also said that the supervisor stole trash bags, and at this moment I stupidly exclaimed, "Who steals trash bags?" Reg, who was listening to the conversation, laughed and said, "We do." He shrugged and continued, "She takes 'em from her job" (meaning Sky). This was an early moment where my own middle-class judgments were lucky to not get me in trouble.

30. Jeff Ferrell, *The Empire of Scrounge: Inside the Urban Underground of Dumpster Diving, Trash Picking, and Street Scavenging* (New York: NYU Press, 2005), 3.

31. Ibid., 9.

32. Biggie also collected scrap metal. However, his scrapping career was cut short in the winter when a building inspector came by the motel and told him that his room was unsanitary. The owner and Elizabeth then told Biggie that they would kick him out if he continued to scrap metal in his room.

33. Ferrell, *The Empire of Scrounge*, 126.

34. Anderson, *The Hobo*, 136.

35. Unfortunately, Jake did end up selling this collection after he moved out of the motel and into an apartment with Reg and Sky.

36. Tim O'Brien, "Toll: 8 Dead, 300 Injured," *Times Union*, April 11, 2013, http://www.timesunion.com/local/article/toll-8-dead-300-injured-4415337 .php#page-3.

CONCLUSION: POLICY FAILURE IN THE AGE OF SOCIAL SANITIZATION

1. Elijah Anderson, *Streetwise: Race, Class, and Change in an Urban Community* (Chicago: University of Chicago Press, 1990), 72.

2. Tim O'Brien, "Colonie Approves Motel Limits, 6–0," *Times Union*, July 25, 2013, http://www.timesunion.com/local/article/Colonie-approves-motel -limits-6-0-4687845.php.

3. Tim O'Brien, "Town Will Seek to Shutter Skylane Motel—the Colonie Blog," *Times Union*, December 17, 2013, http:timesunion.com/colonie /town-will-seek-to-shutter-skylane-motel/1550/.

4. Tim O'Brien, "Colonie to Close Skylane Motel Over Code Violations," *Times Union*, January 14, 2014, http://www.timesunion.com/local/article/colonie -to-close-Skylane-Motel-over-code-5140116.php.

5. Tim O'Brien, "Colonie to Close Skylane Motel Next Week," *Times Union*, January 14, 2014, http://blog.timesunion.com/colonie/colonie-to-close-skylane -motel-next-week/1559/.

6. Tim O'Brien, "Skylane Motel Is Empty Now, Except Maybe for a Dog," *Times Union*, January 27, 2014, http://blog.timesunion.com/colonie/skylane -motel-is-empty-now-except-maybe-for-a-dog/1575/.

7. Tim O'Brien, "Colonie Motel Emptied, but Unauthorized Repairs Upset Town," *Times Union*, January 27, 2014, http://www.timesunion.com /default/article/colonie-motel-emptied-but-unauthorized-repairs-5179813 .php.

8. Tim O'Brien, "Owner Faces Added Code Charges," *Times Union*, February 22, 2014, http://www.timesunion.com/local/article/owner-faces-added -code-charges-5256473.php.

9. Tim O'Brien, "Motels' Case Will Go to Trial," *Times Union*, November 14, 2014, http://blog.timesunion.com/colonie/motels-case-will-go-to-trial/1765/.

10. Tim O'Brien, "Owner of Colonie Motels Offers to Close One, Convert Other to Offices," *Times Union*, 2014, http://www.timesunion.com/local/article /owner-offers-to-convert-closed-motel-5976272.php.

11. Keshia Clukey, "Blu-Bell, Skylane Motels in Colonie to Be Razed," *Times Union*, March 19, 2015, http://www.timesunion.com/news/article/Alex -Patel-owner-of-troubled-Colonie-motels-due-6144570.php.

12. Tim O'Brien and Keshia Clukey, "Colonie Approves Law Limiting Some Motel Stays," *Times Union*, February 26, 2015, http://www.timesunion.com /news/article/Central-Avenue-motel-case-adjourned-owner-in-6103317. php.

13. Paul Nelson, "Bogus Report Brings Penalty," *Times Union*, January 31, 2014, http://www.timesunion.com/default/article/bogus-report-brings -penalty-5194015.php.

14. Tim O'Brien, "Colonie Motel Owners Gain by Housing the Poor," *Times Union*, September 6, 2013, http://blog.timesunion.com/colonie/colonie -motel-owners-gain-by-housing-the-poor/1455/.

15. Tim O'Brien, "Skylane Motel Owner Pleads Not Guilty but Won't Stop Shut-down," *Times Union*, January 23, 2014, http://blog.timesunion.com/colonie /skylane-motel-owner-pleads-not-guilty-but-wont-stop-shutdown/1573/.

16. Christine Benedict, "Colonie Motels—Corporate Welfare at Its Finest!," *Times Union*, September 6, 2013, http://timesunion.com/christinebenedict /colonie-motels-corporate-welfare-at-its-finest/40/.

17. Nelson, "Bogus Report Brings Penalty."

18. O'Brien, "Colonie Approves Motel Limits, 6–0."

19. Ibid.

20. Nels Anderson, *The Hobo: The Sociology of the Homeless Man* (Chicago: University of Chicago Press, 1923), xxi.

21. Erving Goffman, *Stigma: Notes on the Management of Spoiled Identity* (Englewood Cliffs, N.J.: Prentice Hall, 1963), 3, 5.

22. Jeff Ferrell, *The Empire of Scrounge: Inside the Urban Underground of Dumpster Diving, Trash Picking, and Street Scavenging* (New York: NYU Press, 2005), 3.

23. See Charis E. Kubrin and Ronald Weitzer, "New Directions in Social Disorganization Theory," *Journal of Research in Crime and Delinquency* 40, no. 4 (November 1, 2003): 374–402, doi:10.1177/0022427803256238.

24. James Spradley, *You Owe Yourself a Drunk: An Ethnography of Urban Nomads* (Boston: Little, Brown, 1970), 98, 254, 98.

25. This is in stark contrast to what residents encountered in New York City's Martinique Hotel, where the owner showed up at residents' doors with a gun. See Jonathan Kozol, *Rachel and Her Children: Homeless Families in America* (New York: Crown, 1988).

26. Darryl felt that this was an intentional decision by local government to push sex offenders out of the area.

27. Barbara Ehrenreich, "It Is Expensive to Be Poor," *Atlantic*, 2014, http:// www.theatlantic.com/business/archive/2014/01/it-is-expensive-to-be -poor/282979/. See also Ehrenreich, *Nickel and Dimed: On (Not) Getting By in America* (New York: Metropolitan Books, 2001).

28. Carol Stack, *All Our Kin: Strategies for Survival in a Black Community* (New York: Basic Books, 1974), 107.

29. Kozol, *Rachel and Her Children*, 15.

30. Spradley, *You Owe Yourself a Drunk*, 253.

31. Estimating the homeless population in the United States is difficult because it relies on capturing those in shelters or on the street. It is estimated that in January 2014, 578,424 people were homeless on a given night. Some 69 percent were staying in residential programs, while 31 percent were in unsheltered locations. See Meghan Henry, Alvaro Cortes, Azim Shivji, and Katherine Buck, *The 2014 Annual Homeless Assessment Report (AHAR) to Congress* (Washington, D.C.: U.S. Department of Housing and Urban Development, Office of Community Planning and Development, 2014).

32. Nelson Mandela, *Long Walk to Freedom: The Autobiography of Nelson Mandela* (New York: Back Bay Books, 1995), 77.

33. Anandi Mani et al., "Poverty Impedes Cognitive Function," *Science* 341, no. 6149 (August 30, 2013): 976–80, doi:10.1126/science.1238041; Anuj K. Shah, Sendhil Mullainathan, and Eldar Shafir, "Some Consequences of Having Too Little," *Science* 338, no. 6107 (November 2, 2012): 682–85, doi:10.1126/science.1222426.

34. I can find only one study that found a significant relationship between sex-offender clustering and recidivistic sex crimes, and this held true only for crimes against adults. See Kelly M. Socia, "Too Close for Comfort? Registered Sex Offender Spatial Clustering and Recidivistic Sex Crime Arrest Rates," *Sexual Abuse: A Journal of Research and Treatment* 25, no. 6 (December 2013): 531–56, doi:10.1177/1079063212469061.

35. Project Homeless Connect, "Project Homeless Connect," San Francisco, 2014, http://www.projecthomelessconnect.com/mission.

36. In Kozol's *Rachel and Her Children*, hotel resident Kim makes a similar call for action when she says, "You could do some good things in those empty rooms. Lectures. Movies. Every night you could have education going on. Doctors could come and talk, explain things women need to learn. Imagine all the decent things you could do with just a little common sense if you were not thinking of this situation as a penalty for failure" (126).

37. Bruce A. Arrigo, "Rooms for the Misbegotten: On Social Design and Deviance," *Journal of Sociology & Social Welfare* 21, no. 4 (1994): 98, 106.

38. For a comprehensive analysis of findings, see Kelly M. Socia, "Residence Restrictions Are Ineffective, Inefficient, and Inadequate: So Now What?," *Criminology & Public Policy* 13, no. 1 (2014): 1–9.

39. Lorine A. Hughes and Colleen Kadleck, "Sex Offender Community Notification and Community Stratification," *Justice Quarterly* 25, no. 3 (September 2008): 469–95, doi:10.1080/07418820701710941; Jill S. Levenson and Leo P. Cotter, "The Impact of Sex Offender Residence Restrictions: 1,000 Feet from Danger or One Step from Absurd?," *International Journal of Offender Therapy and Comparative Criminology* 49, no. 2 (May 2005): 168–78, doi:10.1177/0306624X04271304; Elizabeth E. Mustaine, Richard

Tewksbury, and Kenneth M. Stengel, "Social Disorganization and Residential Locations of Registered Sex Offenders: Is This a Collateral Consequence?," *Deviant Behavior* 27, no. 3 (July 2006): 329–50; Mustaine, Tewksbury, and Stengel, "Residential Location and Mobility of Registered Sex Offenders," *American Journal of Criminal Justice* 30, no. 2 (2006): 177–92, http://www .springerlink.com/index/jw36q71267358395.pdf; Paul A. Zandbergen and Timothy C. Hart, "Reducing Housing Options for Convicted Sex Offenders: Investigating the Impact of Residency Restriction Laws Using GIS," *Justice Research and Policy* 8, no. 2 (September 1, 2006): 1–24, doi:10.3818/ JRP.8.2.2006.1.

40. Beth M. Huebner et al., "The Effect and Implications of Sex Offender Residence Restrictions," *Criminology & Public Policy* 13, no. 1 (February 11, 2014): 139–68, doi:10.1111/1745–9133.12066.

41. Ibid.

42. Stephen Metraux, Caterina G. Roman, and Richard S. Cho, "Incarceration and Homelessness," paper presented to the National Symposium on Homelessness Research, Washington, D.C., 2007.

43. For an in-depth discussion of collateral consequences of incarceration, see Marc Mauer and Meda Chesney-Lind, *Invisible Punishment: The Collateral Consequences of Mass Imprisonment* (New York: New Press, 2003).

44. Bruce Western and Becky Pettit, *Collateral Costs: Incarceration's Effect on Economic Mobility* (Washington, D.C.: Pew Charitable Trusts, 2010).

45. Office of National Drug Control Policy, *Alternatives to Incarceration: A Smart Approach to Breaking the Cycle of Drug Use and Crime* (Washington, D.C., 2011).

46. David Cloud and Chelsea Davis, *Treatment Alternatives to Incarceration for People with Mental Health Needs in the Criminal Justice System: The Cost-Savings Implications* (New York: Vera Institute of Justice, 2013).

47. Council of State Governments Justice Center, *Reentry Matters: Strategies and Successes of Second Chance Act Grantees Across the United States* (New York, 2013), http://scholar.google.com/scholar?hl=en&btnG=Search&q=in title:Reentry+Matters#0.

48. Council of State Governments Justice Center, *The Second Chance Act Fact Sheet* (New York, 2015).

49. Ibid.

50. The motel was ill-equipped to serve disabled veterans, as evidenced by the fact that when Jerry was placed there in March 2013, he was the first resident I had ever seen in a wheelchair. There were no elevators up to the second floor, so Jerry was given a room on the first floor. Even this was problematic, however, because the concrete sidewalk of the motel had no wheelchair ramps. For Jerry to access his room, Larry had to assemble several planks of wood into a makeshift ramp from the parking lot onto the

sidewalk. The timing could not have been better, as Vito (a nonveteran) arrived in a wheelchair a week later.

51. Meghan Henry, Alvaro Cortes, and Sean Morris, *The 2013 Annual Homeless Assessment Report (AHAR) to Congress: Part 1 Point-in-Time Estimates of Homelessness* (Washington, D.C.: U.S. Department of Housing and Urban Development, Office of Community Planning and Development, 2013).

52. White House, "Ending Veteran Homelessness," n.d., https://www.white house.gov/issues/veterans/ending-homelessness.

53. Employment data for veterans are often broken down into those who have served since September 2001 (known as Gulf War Era II veterans) and those who served prior to that date. Among Gulf War Era II veterans, the unemployment rate in 2013 for males was 8.8 percent compared to 7.5 percent in the general population. Female Gulf War Era II veterans were unemployed at a rate of 9.6 percent compared to 6.8 percent in the general population. It should also be noted that in 2013 the unemployment rate for Gulf War Era II veterans with a disability was not statistically significantly different from that of their counterparts with no disability. See Bureau of Labor Statistics, *Employment Situation of Veterans Summary* (Washington, D.C., 2014), http://www.bls.gov/news.release/vet.nro.htm.

54. One landmine in HUD-VASH implementation that should be addressed is that it excludes veterans who are lifetime sex-offender registrants. This stipulation should be removed because when used in conjunction with sex-offender residence restrictions, it makes finding housing for veterans with sex-offense histories nearly impossible. For a discussion of HUD-VASH best practices, see United States Department of Housing and Urban Development, *HUD-VASH Best Practices—Version 1.0: A Working Document* (Washington, D.C., 2012).

55. Executive Committee, Albany Ten Year Plan to End Homelessness Executive Committee, *Albany County Ten-Year Plan to End Homelessness* (Albany, N.Y., 2005).

56. Ibid.

57. Health Leads, "What We Do for Changes in Healthcare," 2014, https://healthleadsusa.org/what-we-do/.

58. Jenny Shank, "Utah Is on Track to End Homelessness by 2015 with This One Simple Idea," *NationSwell*, 2013, http://www.nationswell.com/one-state-track-become-first-end-homelessness-2015/.

59. National Law Center on Homelessness and Poverty and National Coalition for the Homeless, *Homes Not Handcuffs: The Criminalization of Homelessness in U.S. Cities* (Washington, D.C., 2009).

60. United States Interagency Council on Homelessness, "Housing First," accessed September 2, 2015, http://usich.gov/usich_resources/solutions/explore/housing_first/.

61. Howard Zinn, *A People's History of the United States* (New York: HarperCollins, 1980), 11.

62. Ibid., 574.

63. Scott Keyes, "State Rep. Uses Sledgehammer to Destroy Homeless People's Possessions," *Think Progress*, November 19, 2013, http://thinkprogress.org/economy/2013/11/19/2966371/hawaii-homeless-smash/.

64. Scott Keyes, "Florida City About to Make It Illegal for Homeless People to Have Possessions in Public," *Think Progress*, April 21, 2014, http://thinkprogress.org/economy/2014/04/21/3428899/fort-lauderdale-criminalize-homelessness/; Terrance Heath, "Utah Is Ending Homelessness by Giving People Homes," *Nation of Change*, 2014, http://www.nationofchange.org/utah-ending-homelessness-giving-people-homes-1390056183.

65. National Coalition for the Homeless, *Share No More: The Criminalization of Efforts to Feed People in Need* (Washington, D.C., 2014).

66. Kozol, *Rachel and Her Children*.

67. Jeff Ferrell, *Tearing Down the Streets: Adventures in Urban Anarchy* (New York: Palgrave Macmillan, 2002), 43.

68. Kozol, *Rachel and Her Children*, 183.

69. Ferrell, *Tearing Down the Streets*.

70. William J. Chambliss, "A Sociological Analysis of the Law of Vagrancy," *Social Problems* 12, no. 1 (1964): 75.

71. Ferrell, *Tearing Down the Streets*, 17.

72. Jacob A. Riis, *How the Other Half Lives: Studies Among the Tenements of New York* (New York: Sagamore Press, 1957), 20.

73. Joel Blau, *The Visible Poor: Homelessness in the United States* (New York: Oxford University Press, 1992), 178, 180.

74. Ibid.

75. Neil Smith, "Social Justice and the New American Urbanism: The Revanchist City," in *The Urbanization of Injustice*, ed. Andy Merrifield and Erik Swyngedouw (London: Lawrence and Wishart, 1997), 130.

76. Chris Caesar, "Activists Pour Concrete on Store's 'Anti-Homeless' Spikes, Win," *Boston.com*, 2014, http://www.boston.com/news/nation/2014/06/12/activists-pour-concrete-store-anti-homeless-spikes-win/2YXnYKonz6y2T75pizlC3L/story.html.

77. Ferrell, *Tearing Down the Streets*, 325.

78. National Law Center on Homelessness and Poverty and National Coalition for the Homeless, *Homes Not Handcuffs*.

79. Kozol, *Rachel and Her Children*, 91.

80. Blau, *The Visible Poor*, 182.

81. Hannah Arendt, *The Origins of Totalitarianism* (Cleveland: World, 1958), 293.

APPENDIX 2. A REFLECTION ON METHOD

1. See Donald Black, "The Epistemology of Pure Sociology," *Law and Social Inquiry* 20, no. 3 (1995): 829–70; Ruth Horowitz, *Teen Mothers: Citizens or Dependents?* (Chicago: University of Chicago Press, 1996).
2. Jack Katz, *Seductions of Crime* (New York: Basic Books, 1988).
3. James P. Spradley, *You Owe Yourself a Drunk: An Ethnography of Urban Nomads* (Boston: Little, Brown, 1970), 117.

BIBLIOGRAPHY

Adler, Patricia A., and Peter Adler. *Membership Roles in Field Research*. Sage University Papers Series on Qualitative Research Methods, Vol. 6. Newbury Park, Ca.: Sage, 1987.

Allen, Davina. "Narrating Nursing Jurisdiction: 'Atrocity Stories' and 'Boundary-Work.'" *Symbolic Interaction* 24, no. 1 (2001): 75–103.

Altschuler, David M., and Rachel Brash. "Adolescent and Teenage Offenders Confronting the Challenges and Opportunities of Reentry." *Youth Violence and Juvenile Justice* 2, no. 1 (January 2004): 72–87. doi:10.1177/1541204 003260048.

American Fact Finder. *Financial Characteristics*. Washington, D.C.: United States Census Bureau, 2013. http://factfinder.census.gov.

American Hotel & Lodging Association. "History of Lodging," 2012. http://www .ahla.com/content.aspx?id=4072.

——. "2013 Lodging Industry Profile," 2013. https://www.ahla.com/content .aspx?id=35603.

Anderson, Elijah. *Code of the Street: Decency, Violence, and the Moral Life of the Inner City*. New York: Norton, 1999.

——. *Streetwise: Race, Class, and Change in an Urban Community*. Chicago: University of Chicago Press, 1990.

Anderson, Nels. *The Hobo: The Sociology of the Homeless Man*. Chicago: University of Chicago Press, 1923.

Arendt, Hannah. *The Origins of Totalitarianism*. Cleveland: World, 1958.

Arrigo, Bruce A. "Rooms for the Misbegotten: On Social Design and Deviance." *Journal of Sociology & Social Welfare* 21, no. 4 (1994): 95–113.

Barnes, J. C., Tony Dukes, Richard Tewksbury, and Timothy M. De Troye. "Analyzing the Impact of a Statewide Residence Restriction Law on South

Carolina Sex Offenders." *Criminal Justice Policy Review* 20, no. 1 (July 8, 2008): 21–43. doi:10.1177/0887403408320842.

Baumeister, Roy F., Karen Dale, and Kristin L. Sommer. "Freudian Defense Mechanisms and Empirical Findings in Modern Social Psychology: Reaction Formation, Projection, Displacement, Undoing, Isolation, Sublimation, and Denial." *Journal of Personality* 66, no. 6 (1998): 1081–1124.

Benedict, Christine. *Resolution No. 353-a Requesting Albany County Remove Families and Individuals from Certain Motels on Route 5, Town of Colonie.* Colonie, N.Y.: Albany County Legislature, 2007.

Black, Donald. "The Epistemology of Pure Sociology." *Law and Social Inquiry* 20, no. 3 (1995): 829–70.

Blau, Joel. *The Visible Poor: Homelessness in the United States.* New York: Oxford University Press, 1992.

Bogue, Donald J. *Skid Row in American Cities.* Chicago: University of Chicago Press, 1963.

Bourgois, Philippe. *In Search of Respect: Selling Crack in El Barrio.* Cambridge: Cambridge University Press, 1996.

Brownrigg, Leslie A. *People Who Live in Hotels: An Exploratory Overview.* Survey Methodology #2006–3. Washington, D.C.: U.S. Census Bureau, 2006. https://www.census.gov/srd/papers/pdf/ssm2006-03.pdf.

Burchfield, Keri B., and William Mingus. "Not in My Neighborhood: Assessing Registered Sex Offenders' Experiences with Local Social Capital and Social Control." *Criminal Justice and Behavior* 35, no. 3 (March 2008): 356–74. doi:10.1177/0093854807311375.

Bureau of Labor Statistics. *Employment Situation of Veterans Summary.* Washington, D.C., 2014. http://www.bls.gov/news.release/vet.nro.htm.

Burri, Regula V. "Doing Distinctions: Boundary Work and Symbolic Capital in Radiology." *Social Studies of Science* 38, no. 1 (February 1, 2008): 35–62. doi:10.1177/0306312707082021.

Bursik Jr., Robert J. "Social Disorganization and Theories of Crime and Delinquency: Problems and Prospects." *Criminology* 26, no. 4 (November 1988): 519–52. doi:10.1111/j.1745-9125.1988.tb00854.x.

Burt, Martha R., Jenneth Carpenter, Samuel G. Hall, Kathryn A. Henderson, Debra J. Rog, John A. Hornik, Ann V. Denton, and Garrett E. Moran. *Strategies for Improving Homeless People's Access to Mainstream Benefits and Services.* Washington, D.C.: U.S. Department of Housing and Urban Development, Office of Policy Development and Research, 2010.

Carson, E. Ann. *Prisoners in 2013.* Washington, D.C.: Bureau of Justice Statistics, 2014. http://www.bjs.gov/index.cfm?ty=pbdetail&iid=5109.

Carson, E. Ann, and Daniela Golinelli. *Prisoners in 2012: Trends in Admissions and Releases, 1991–2012 (rev.).* Washington, D.C.: Bureau of Justice Statistics, 2013. http://www.bjs.gov/index.cfm?ty=pbdetail&iid=4842.

Chambliss, William J. "A Sociological Analysis of the Law of Vagrancy." *Social Problems* 12, no. 1 (1964): 67–77.

Cloud, David, and Chelsea Davis. *Treatment Alternatives to Incarceration for People with Mental Health Needs in the Criminal Justice System: The Cost-Savings Implications.* New York: Vera Institute of Justice, 2013.

Cohen, Albert K. *Delinquent Boys.* Glencoe, N.Y.: Free Press, 1955.

Conners II, Michael F. *Review Department of Social Services Temporary Assistance Division Motel Placement.* Albany, N.Y., 2008.

Conover, Ted. *Newjack: Guarding Sing Sing.* New York: Vintage, 2000.

Copes, Heith, Andy Hochstetler, and J. Patrick Williams. "'We Weren't Like No Regular Dope Fiends': Negotiating Hustler and Crackhead Identities." *Social Problems* 55, no. 2 (2008): 254–70. doi:10.1525/sp.2008.55.2.254.

Council of State Governments Justice Center. *Reentry Matters: Strategies and Successes of Second Chance Act Grantees Across the United States.* New York, 2013. http://scholar.google.com/scholar?hl=en&btnG=Search&q=in title:Reentry+Matters#0.

——. *The Second Chance Act Fact Sheet.* New York, 2015.

DeNavas-Walt, Carmen, Bernadette D. Proctor, and Jessica C. Smith. *Income, Poverty, and Health Insurance Coverage in the United States: 2012.* Washington, D.C.: U.S. Census Bureau, 2013. https://www.census.gov /prod/2013pubs/p60-245.pdf.

Desmond, Matthew. "Disposable Ties and the Urban Poor." *American Journal of Sociology* 117, no. 5 (2012): 1295–1335.

DeVault, Marjorie L. *Feeding the Family: The Social Organization of Caring as Gendered Work.* Chicago: University of Chicago Press, 1994.

Dhingra, Pawan. *Life Behind the Lobby: Indian American Motel Owners and the American Dream.* Stanford, Ca.: Stanford University Press, 2012.

Dishion, Thomas J., Joan McCord, and François Poulin. "When Interventions Harm: Peer Groups and Problem Behavior." *American Psychologist* 54, no. 9 (1999): 755–64.

Duneier, Mitchell. *Sidewalk.* New York: Farrar, Straus and Giroux, 1999.

Eckert, J. Kevin. *The Unseen Elderly: A Study of Marginally Subsistent Hotel Dwellers.* San Diego: Campanile Press, 1980.

Ehrenreich, Barbara. "It Is Expensive to Be Poor." *Atlantic,* 2014. http:// www.theatlantic.com/business/archive/2014/01/it-is-expensive-to-be -poor/282979/.

——. *Nickel and Dimed: On (Not) Getting By in America.* New York: Metropolitan Books, 2001.

Emerson, Robert M., Rachel I. Fretz, and Linda L. Shaw. *Writing Ethnographic Fieldnotes.* Chicago: University of Chicago Press, 1995.

Executive Committee, Albany Ten Year Plan to End Homelessness. *Albany County Ten-Year Plan to End Homelessness.* Albany, N.Y., 2005.

Ezzell, Matthew B. "'Barbie Dolls' on the Pitch: Identity Work, Defensive Othering, and Inequality in Women's Rugby." *Social Problems* 56, no. 1 (2009): 111–31. doi:10.1525/sp.2009.56.1.111.SP5601.

Fader, Jamie J. *Falling Back: Incarceration and Transitions to Adulthood Among Urban Youth*. New Brunswick, N.J.: Rutgers University Press, 2013.

Ferrell, Jeff. *The Empire of Scrounge: Inside the Urban Underground of Dumpster Diving, Trash Picking, and Street Scavenging*. New York: New York University Press, 2005.

——. *Tearing Down the Streets: Adventures in Urban Anarchy*. New York: Palgrave Macmillan, 2002.

Fisher, Berenice, and Joan Tronto. "Toward a Feminist Theory of Caring." In *Circles of Care: Work and Identity in Women's Lives*, edited by Emily K. Able and Margaret K. Nelson, 35–62. Albany: State University of New York Press, 1990.

Fortney, Timothy, Jill S. Levenson, Yolanda N. Brannon, and Juanita N. Baker. "Myths and Facts About Sexual Offenders: Implications for Treatment and Public Policy." *Sexual Offender Treatment* 2, no. 1 (2007): 1–17.

Giving Children Hope. "Statistics of Homeless Children in Orange County, CA." 2010. http://gchope.org/statistics-of-homeless-children-in-orange-county -ca/.

Glaze, Lauren E., and Erinn J. Herberman. *Correctional Populations in the United States, 2012*. Washington, D.C.: Bureau of Justice Statistics, 2013. http:// www.bjs.gov/index.cfm?ty=pbdetail&iid=4909.

Goffman, Erving. *Asylums*. Garden City, N.Y.: Anchor Books, 1961.

——. *The Presentation of Self in Everyday Life*. New York: Anchor Books, 1959.

——. *Stigma: Notes on the Management of Spoiled Identity*. Englewood Cliffs, N.J.: Prentice Hall, 1963.

——. "Symbols of Class Status." *British Journal of Sociology* 2, no. 4 (1951): 294–304.

Groth, Paul. *Living Downtown: The History of Residential Hotels in the United States*. Berkeley: University of California Press, 1994.

Hagan, John, and Bill McCarthy. *Mean Streets: Youth Crime and Homelessness*. Cambridge: Cambridge University Press, 1998.

Harding, David J., Jessica J. B. Wyse, Cheyney Dobson, and Jeffrey D. Morenoff. "Making Ends Meet After Prison." *Journal of Policy Analysis and Management* 33, no. 2 (2014): 440–70. doi:10.1002/pam.

Hayner, Norman S. *Hotel Life*. Chapel Hill: University of North Carolina Press, 1936.

Health Leads. "What We Do for Changes in Healthcare," 2014. https://health-leadsusa.org/what-we-do/.

Heath, Terrance. "Utah Is Ending Homelessness by Giving People Homes." *Nation of Change*, 2014. http://www.nationofchange.org/utah-ending -homelessness-giving-people-homes-1390056183.

Helmus, Leslie, R. Karl Hanson, David Thornton, Kelly M. Babchishin, and Andrew J. R. Harris. "Absolute Recidivism Rates Predicted By Static-99R and Static-2002R Sex Offender Risk Assessment Tools Vary Across Samples: A Meta-Analysis." *Criminal Justice and Behavior* 39, no. 9 (May 21, 2012): 1148–71. doi:10.1177/0093854812443648.

Henry, Meghan, Alvaro Cortes, and Sean Morris. *The 2013 Annual Homeless Assessment Report (AHAR) to Congress: Part 1 Point-in-Time Estimates of Homelessness.* Washington, D.C.: U.S. Department of Housing and Urban Development, Office of Community Planning and Development, 2013.

Henry, Meghan, Alvaro Cortes, Azim Shivji, and Katherine Buck. *The 2014 Annual Homeless Assessment Report (AHAR) to Congress.* Washington, D.C.: U.S. Department of Housing and Urban Development, Office of Community Planning and Development, 2014.

Hollander, Jocelyn A., and Rachel L. Einwohner. "Conceptualizing Resistance." *Sociological Forum* 19, no. 4 (2004): 533–54.

Huebner, Beth M., Kimberly R. Kras, Jason Rydberg, Timothy S. Bynum, Eric Grommon, and Breanne Pleggenkuhle. "The Effect and Implications of Sex Offender Residence Restrictions." *Criminology & Public Policy* 13, no. 1 (February 11, 2014): 139–68. doi:10.1111/1745-9133.12066.

Hughes, Lorine A., and Keri B. Burchfield. "Sex Offender Residence Restrictions in Chicago: An Environmental Injustice?" *Justice Quarterly* 25, no. 4 (December 2008): 647–73. doi:10.1080/07418820802119976.

Hughes, Lorine A., and Colleen Kadleck. "Sex Offender Community Notification and Community Stratification." *Justice Quarterly* 25, no. 3 (September 2008): 469–95. doi:10.1080/07418820701710941.

Human Rights Watch. *No Easy Answers.* New York, 2007. http://www.hrw.org /node/10685/section/6.

Jakle, John A., Keith A. Sculle, and Jefferson S. Rogers. *The Motel in America.* Baltimore: Johns Hopkins University Press, 1996.

Joint Center for Housing Studies of Harvard University. *The State of the Nation's Housing.* Cambridge, Mass., 2011. http://www.jchs.harvard.edu/sites/jchs .harvard.edu/files/son2011.pdf.

Jones, LeAlan, Lloyd Newman, and David Isay. *Our America: Life and Death on the South Side of Chicago.* New York: Scribner, 1997.

Katz, Jack. *Seductions of Crime.* New York: Basic Books, 1988.

Katz, Jack, and Thomas J. Csordas. "Phenomenological Ethnography in Sociology and Anthropology." *Ethnography* 4, no. 3 (September 1, 2003): 275–88. doi:10.1177/146613810343001.

Kefalas, Maria, Patrick J. Carr, and Susan Clampet-Lundquist. "To Snitch or Not to Snitch: The Crisis of Trust in the City of Brotherly Love." *Contexts* 10, no. 3 (2011): 56–63.

Keire, Mara L. "The Committee of Fourteen and Saloon Reform in New York City, 1905–1920." *Business and Economic History* 26, no. 2 (1997): 573–83.

Keyes, Scott. "Florida City About to Make It Illegal for Homeless People to Have Possessions in Public." *Think Progress*, April 21, 2014. http://thinkprogress.org /economy/2014/04/21/3428899/fort-lauderdale-criminalize-homelessness/.
——. "State Rep. Uses Sledgehammer to Destroy Homeless People's Possessions." *Think Progress*, November 19, 2013. http://thinkprogress.org/economy /2013/11/19/2966371/hawaii-homeless-smash/.

Klinenberg, Eric. *Heat Wave: A Social Autopsy of Disaster in Chicago*. Chicago: University of Chicago Press, 2002.

Kozol, Jonathan. *Rachel and Her Children: Homeless Families in America*. New York: Crown, 1988.

Krell, Eric. "Inside Extended Stay Hotels." *HR Magazine*, 2012. http://www.shrm. org/publications/hrmagazine/editorialcontent/2012/1012/pages/1012krell1 .aspx.

Kubrin, Charis E., and Ronald Weitzer. "New Directions in Social Disorganization Theory." *Journal of Research in Crime and Delinquency* 40, no. 4 (November 1, 2003): 374–402. doi:10.1177/0022427803256238.

Kunz, Egon F. "The Refugee in Flight: Kinetic Models and Forms of Displacement." *International Migration Review* 7, no. 2 (1973): 125–46.

Lamont, Michèle. *The Dignity of Working Men: Morality and the Boundaries of Race, Class, and Immigration*. Cambridge, Mass.: Harvard University Press, 2001.

Lee, Everett S. "A Theory of Migration." In *Migration*, edited by John Archer Jackson, 286–87. Cambridge: Cambridge University Press, 1969.

Levenson, Jill S. "The Effect of Megan's Law on Sex Offender Reintegration." *Journal of Contemporary Criminal Justice* 21, no. 1 (February 2005): 49–66. doi:10.1177/1043986204271676.

Levenson, Jill S., and Leo P. Cotter. "The Impact of Sex Offender Residence Restrictions: 1,000 Feet from Danger or One Step from Absurd?" *International Journal of Offender Therapy and Comparative Criminology* 49, no. 2 (May 2005): 168–78. doi:10.1177/0306624X04271304.

Levenson, Jill S., David A. D'Amora, and Andrea L. Hern. "Megan's Law and Its Impact on Community Re-Entry for Sex Offenders." *Behavioral Sciences & the Law* 25 (2007): 587–602. doi:10.1002/bsl.

Leverentz, Andrea M. *The Ex-Prisoner's Dilemma: How Women Negotiate Competing Narratives of Reentry and Desistance*. New Brunswick, N.J.: Rutgers University Press, 2014.

Lewinson, Terri. "Capturing Environmental Affordances: Low-Income Families Identify Positive Characteristics of a Hotel Housing Solution." *Journal of Community & Applied Social Psychology* 21 (2011): 55–70. doi:10.1002 /casp.
——. "Residents' Coping Strategies in an Extended-Stay Hotel Home." *Journal of Ethnographic and Qualitative Research* 4, no. 2001 (2010): 180–96.

License Required to House Registered Sex Offenders. Colonie, N.Y.: Town of Colonie, 2009.

Liebow, Elliot. *Tally's Corner: A Study of Negro Streetcorner Men.* Boston: Little, Brown, 1967.

Lilly, J. Robert, and Richard A. Ball. "No-Tell Motel: The Management of Social Invisibility." *Urban Life* 10, no. 2 (1981): 179–98.

Lofland, John, David Snow, Leon Anderson, and Lyn H. Lofland. *Analyzing Social Settings: A Guide to Qualitative Observation and Analysis.* 4th ed. Belmont, Ca.: Wadsworth, 2006.

Mandela, Nelson. *Long Walk to Freedom: The Autobiography of Nelson Mandela.* New York: Back Bay Books, 1995.

Mani, Anandi, Sendhil Mullainathan, Eldar Shafir, and Jiaying Zhao. "Poverty Impedes Cognitive Function." *Science* 341, no. 6149 (August 30, 2013): 976–80. doi:10.1126/science.1238041.

Maruna, Shadd. *Making Good: How Ex-Convicts Reform and Rebuild Their Lives.* Washington, D.C.: American Psychological Association, 2001.

Mauer, Marc, and Meda Chesney-Lind. *Invisible Punishment: The Collateral Consequences of Mass Imprisonment.* New York: New Press, 2003.

Mauss, Marcel. *The Gift.* New York: Free Press, 1954.

McCord, Joan. "Cures That Harm: Unanticipated Outcomes of Crime Prevention Programs." *Annals of the American Academy of Political and Social Science* 587, no. 1 (May 1, 2003): 16–30. doi:10.1177/0002716202250781.

McMillan, Tracie. *The American Way of Eating: Undercover at Walmart, Applebee's, Farm Fields and the Dinner Table.* New York: Scribner, 2012.

Metraux, Stephen, Caterina G. Roman, and Richard S. Cho. "Incarceration and Homelessness," paper presented to the National Symposium on Homelessness Research, Washington, D.C., 2007.

Miller, Ronald J. *The Demolition of Skid Row.* Lexington, Mass.: Lexington Books, 1982.

Miller, Walter B. "Lower Class Culture as a Generating Milieu for Gang Delinquency." *Journal of Social Issues* 14 (1958): 5–19.

Morenoff, Jeffrey D., Robert J. Sampson, and Stephen W. Raudenbush. "Neighborhood Inequality, Collective Efficacy, and the Spatial Dynamics of Urban Violence." *Criminology* 39, no. 3 (2001): 517–58. http://onlinelibrary.wiley.com/doi/10.1111/j.1745-9125.2001.tb00932.x/full.

Mustaine, Elizabeth E., Richard Tewksbury, and Kenneth M. Stengel. "Residential Location and Mobility of Registered Sex Offenders." *American Journal of Criminal Justice* 30, no. 2 (2006): 177–92. http://www.springerlink.com/index/jw36q71267358395.pdf.

——. "Social Disorganization and Residential Locations of Registered Sex Offenders: Is This a Collateral Consequence?" *Deviant Behavior* 27, no. 3 (July 2006): 329–50. doi:10.1080/01639620600605606.

National Coalition for the Homeless. *Foreclosure to Homelessness: The Forgotten Victims of the Subprime Crisis. Health Care.* Washington, D.C., 2009.

——. *Share No More: The Criminalization of Efforts to Feed People in Need.* Washington, D.C., 2014.

National Law Center on Homelessness and Poverty and National Coalition for the Homeless. *Homes Not Handcuffs: The Criminalization of Homelessness in U.S. Cities.* Washington, D.C., 2009.

Ness, Elliot. "How to Curb Prostitution in Hotels." *Southern Hotel Journal* (February 1943): 1–5.

Newman, Katherine S. *No Shame in My Game: The Working Poor in the Inner City.* New York: Vintage, 2000.

Office of National Drug Control Policy. *Alternatives to Incarceration: A Smart Approach to Breaking the Cycle of Drug Use and Crime.* Washington, D.C., 2011.

Pager, Devah. "The Mark of a Criminal Record." *American Journal of Sociology* 108, no. 5 (2003): 937–75.

Patillo-McCoy, Mary. *Black Picket Fences: Privilege and Peril Among the Black Middle Class.* Chicago: University of Chicago Press, 1999.

Petersilia, Joan. "From Cell to Society: Who Is Returning Home?" In *Prisoner Reentry and Crime in America*, edited by Jeremy Travis and Christy Visher, 15–49. New York: Cambridge University Press, 2005.

——. *When Prisoners Come Home: Parole and Prisoner Reentry.* New York: Oxford University Press, 2003.

Petrosino, Anthony J., and Carolyn Petrosino. "The Public Safety Potential of Megan's Law in Massachusetts: An Assessment from a Sample of Criminal Sexual Psychopaths." *Crime & Delinquency* 45, no. 1 (January 1999): 140–58. doi:10.1177/0011128799045001008.

Planning and Economic Development Department. *Central Avenue Corridor Inventory Study.* Colonie, N.Y., 2011.

Presser, Lois. *Been a Heavy Life: Stories of Violent Men.* Urbana: University of Illinois Press, 2008.

Project Homeless Connect. "Project Homeless Connect." San Francisco, 2014. http://www.projecthomelessconnect.com/mission.

Prus, Robert C., and Styllianoss Irini. *Hookers, Rounders, and Desk Clerks: The Social Organization of the Hotel Community.* Toronto: Gage, 1980.

Prus, Robert C., and Steve Vassilakopoulos. "Desk Clerks and Hookers: Hustling in a 'Shady' Hotel." *Urban Life* 8, no. 1 (1979): 52–71.

Quinn, James, Craig Forsyth, and Carla Mullen-Quinn. "Societal Reaction to Sex Offenders: A Review of the Origins and Results of the Myths Surrounding Their Crimes and Treatment Amenability." *Deviant Behavior* 25, no. 3 (May 2004): 215–32. doi:10.1080/01639620490431147.

Redlich, Allison D. "Community Notification: Perceptions of Its Effectiveness in Preventing Child Sexual Abuse." *Journal of Child Sexual Abuse* 10, no. 3 (January 2001): 91–116. http://www.ncbi.nlm.nih.gov/pubmed/17522002.

Riis, Jacob A. *How the Other Half Lives: Studies Among the Tenements of New York.* New York: Sagamore Press, 1957.

Rios, Victor M. *Punished: Policing the Lives of Black and Latino Boys.* New York: New York University Press, 2011.

Robbers, Monica L. P. "Lifers on the Outside: Sex Offenders and Disintegrative Shaming." *International Journal of Offender Therapy and Comparative Criminology* 53, no. 1 (February 2009): 5–28. doi:10.1177/0306624X07312953.

Rosenwald, George C., and Richard L. Ochberg, eds. *Storied Lives: The Cultural Politics of Self-Understanding.* New Haven, Conn.: Yale University Press, 1992.

Rossi, Peter H. *Down and Out in America: The Origins of Homelessness.* Chicago: University of Chicago Press, 1989.

Sampson, Robert J., and John H. Laub. "Crime and Deviance Over the Life Course: The Salience of Adult Social Bonds." *American Sociological Review* 55, no. 5 (1990): 609–27.

——. *Crime in the Making: Pathways and Turning Points Through Life.* Cambridge, Mass.: Harvard University Press, 1993.

Sampson, Robert J., Stephen W. Raudenbush, and Felton Earls. "Neighborhoods and Violent Crime: A Multilevel Study of Collective Efficacy." *Science* 277, no. 5328 (August 15, 1997): 918–24. doi:10.1126/science.277.5328.918.

Sandler, Jeffrey C., Naomi J. Freeman, and Kelly M. Socia. "Does a Watched Pot Boil? A Time-Series Analysis of New York State's Sex Offender Registration and Notification Law." *Psychology, Public Policy, and Law* 14, no. 4 (2008): 284–302.

Schaler, Jeffrey A. *Addiction Is a Choice.* Chicago: Open Court, 2000.

Scott, Marvin B., and Stanford M. Lyman. "Accounts." *American Sociological Review* 33, no. 1 (1968): 46–62.

Shah, Anuj K., Sendhil Mullainathan, and Eldar Shafir. "Some Consequences of Having Too Little." *Science* 338, no. 6107 (November 2, 2012): 682–85. doi:10.1126/science.1222426.

Shank, Jenny. "Utah Is on Track to End Homelessness by 2015 with This One Simple Idea." *NationSwell,* 2013. http://www.nationswell.com/one-state-track-become-first-end-homelessness-2015/.

Shaw, Clifford R. *The Jack-Roller: A Delinquent Boy's Own Story.* Chicago: University of Chicago Press, 1930.

Shaw, Clifford R., and Henry McKay. *Juvenile Delinquency and Urban Areas.* Chicago: University of Chicago Press, 1942.

Shirley, Carla D. "'You Might Be a Redneck If . . . ': Boundary Work Among Rural, Southern Whites." *Social Forces* 89, no. 1 (September 1, 2010): 35–61. doi:10.1353/sof.2010.0081.

Siegal, Harvey A. *Outposts of the Forgotten: Socially Terminal People in Slum Hotels and Single Room Occupancy Tenements.* New Brunswick, N.J.: Transaction, 1978.

Smith, Neil. "Social Justice and the New American Urbanism: The Revanchist City." In *The Urbanization of Injustice*, edited by Andy Merrifield and Erik Swyngedouw, 117–36. London: Lawrence and Wishart, 1997.

Snow, David A., and Leon Anderson. *Down on Their Luck: A Study of Homeless Street People.* Berkeley: University of California Press, 1993.

Socia, Kelly M. "The Policy Implications of Residence Restrictions on Sex Offender Housing in Upstate NY." *Criminology & Public Policy* 10, no. 2 (May 3, 2011): 351–89. doi:10.1111/j.1745-9133.2011.00713.x.

——. "Residence Restrictions Are Ineffective, Inefficient, and Inadequate: So Now What?" *Criminology & Public Policy* 13, no. 1 (2014): 1–9.

——. "Too Close for Comfort? Registered Sex Offender Spatial Clustering and Recidivistic Sex Crime Arrest Rates." *Sexual Abuse: A Journal of Research and Treatment* 25, no. 6 (December 2013): 531–56. doi:10.1177/1079063212469061.

Socia, Kelly M., and Janet P. Stamatel. "Neighborhood Characteristics and the Social Control of Registered Sex Offenders." *Crime & Delinquency* 58, no. 4 (November 8, 2011): 565–87. doi:10.1177/0011128711420111.

Spradley, James P. *You Owe Yourself a Drunk: An Ethnography of Urban Nomads.* Boston: Little, Brown, 1970.

Stack, Carol. *All Our Kin: Strategies for Survival in a Black Community.* New York: Basic Books, 1974.

Stombler, Mindy. "'BUDDIES' OR 'SLUTTIES': The Collective Sexual Reputation of Fraternity Little Sisters." *Gender & Society* 8, no. 3 (September 1, 1994): 297–323. doi:10.1177/089124394008003002.

Strang-Vadebogart, Nancy. "Fuller Road Motel 33 Fuller Road Review Request for Waiver of Moratorium." Transcription of meeting notes, Colonie Planning Board, Albany County, N.Y., May 17, 2011.

Sykes, Gresham M. *The Society of Captives: A Study of a Maximum Security Prison.* Princeton, N.J.: Princeton University Press, 1958.

Tewksbury, Richard. "Collateral Consequences of Sex Offender Registration." *Journal of Contemporary Criminal Justice* 21, no. 1 (February 2005): 67–81. doi:10.1177/1043986204271704.

——. "Experiences and Attitudes of Registered Female Sex Offenders." *Federal Probation* 68, no. 3 (2000): 30–34.

Tewksbury, Richard, and Matthew B. Lees. "Perceptions of Sex Offender Registration: Collateral Consequences and Community Experiences." *Sociological Spectrum* 26, no. 3 (May 2006): 309–34. doi:10.1080/02732170500524246.

Tewksbury, Richard, and Elizabeth E. Mustaine. "Where Registered Sex Offenders Live: Community Characteristics and Proximity to Possible

Victims." *Victims & Offenders* 3, no. 1 (January 15, 2008): 86–98. doi:10.1080/15564880701752371.

Thacher, David. "Order Maintenance Reconsidered: Moving Beyond Strong Causal Reasoning." *Journal of Criminal Law & Criminology* 94, no. 2 (2004): 381–414.

Town of Colonie Building Department Files, n.d.

United States Census Bureau. *Income, Poverty and Health Insurance Coverage in the United States: 2010.* Washington, D.C., 2011. https://www.census.gov/newsroom/releases/archives/income_wealth/cb11–157.html.

United States Department of Housing and Urban Development. *HUD-VASH Best Practices—Version 1.0: A Working Document.* Washington, D.C., 2012.

United States District Court, Southern District of Florida. *United States of America v. Ghanashyambhai M. Patel and Joyitshana G. Patel, d/b/a Econo-Lodge Motel Defendants.* http://www.justice.gov/crt/housing-and-civil-enforcement-cases-documents-16. Accessed April 23, 2014.

United States Interagency Council on Homelessness. "Housing First." Accessed September 2, 2015. http://usich.gov/usich_resources/solutions/explore/housing_first/.

Valentine, Bettylou. *Hustling and Other Hard Work: Life Styles in the Ghetto.* New York: Free Press, 1978.

Vasquez, Bob Edward, Sean Maddan, and Jeffery T. Walker. "The Influence of Sex Offender Registration and Notification Laws in the United States: A Time-Series Analysis." *Crime & Delinquency* 54, no. 2 (October 26, 2007): 175–92. doi:10.1177/0011128707311641.

Venkatesh, Sudhir Alladi. *Off the Books: The Underground Economy of the Urban Poor.* Cambridge, Mass.: Harvard University Press, 2006.

Wakefield, Sara, and Christopher Wildeman. *Children of the Prison Boom.* New York: Oxford University Press, 2013.

Wann, Daniel L., and Nyla R. Branscombe. "Die-Hard and Fair-Weather Fans: Effects of Identification on BIRGing and CORFing Tendencies." *Journal of Sport & Social Issues* 14, no. 2 (September 1, 1990): 103–17. doi:10.1177/019372359001400203.

Weiss, Robert S. *Learning from Strangers: The Art and Method of Qualitative Interview Studies.* New York: Simon & Schuster, 1994.

Western, Bruce. *Punishment and Inequality in America.* New York: Russell Sage, 2006.

Western, Bruce, and Becky Pettit. *Collateral Costs: Incarceration's Effect on Economic Mobility.* Washington, D.C.: Pew Charitable Trusts, 2010.

White House. "Ending Veteran Homelessness," n.d. https://www.whitehouse.gov/issues/veterans/ending-homelessness.

Whyte, William F. *Street Corner Society.* Chicago: University of Chicago Press, 1943.

Willis, Gwenda M., and Randolph C. Grace. "The Quality of Community Reintegration Planning for Child Molesters: Effects on Sexual Recidivism." *Sexual Abuse: A Journal of Research and Treatment* 20, no. 2 (June 2008): 218–40. doi:10.1177/1079063208318005.

Wingate-Lewinson, Terri, June Gary Hopps, and Patricia Reeves. "Liminal Living at an Extended Stay Hotel: Feeling 'Stuck' in a Housing Solution." *Journal of Sociology & Social Welfare* 37, no. 2 (2010): 9–35.

Wolfgang, Marvin E., and Franco Ferracuti. *The Subculture of Violence: Towards an Integrated Theory in Criminology.* London: Tavistock, 1967.

Yukich, Grace. "Boundary Work in Inclusive Religious Groups: Constructing Identity at the New York Catholic Worker." *Sociology of Religion* 71, no. 2 (2010): 172–96.

Zandbergen, Paul A., and Timothy C. Hart. "Reducing Housing Options for Convicted Sex Offenders: Investigating the Impact of Residency Restriction Laws Using GIS." *Justice Research and Policy* 8, no. 2 (September 1, 2006): 1–24. doi:10.3818/JRP.8.2.2006.1.

Zevitz, Richard G., and Mary Ann Farkas. "Sex Offender Community Notification: Managing High Risk Criminals or Exacting Further Vengeance?" *Behavioral Sciences & the Law* 18 (2000): 375–91.

Zinn, Howard. *A People's History of the United States.* New York: HarperCollins, 1980.

INDEX

methodological issues, 231. *See also*
Boardwalk Motel study; research
migration: from Boardwalk, 199;
phases of, 60
Mike (Boardwalk resident), 17, 27, 117,
123, 156, 178, 187, 226, 234; move to
Park Place of, 44, 49
minimum wage, 216–17
motels: boom construction of, 2;
chain, 241n17; competition for,
2–3; culture of, 39; as last-ditch
housing, 3; marginalized clientele
of, 1; origins of, 2; private/public
partnership for, 211–12; reputation
of, 3; and residential instability,
xiv; as safe living environments,
213–14; as settlements, 211;
stigma of, 126; for vulnerable
populations, 208. *See also*
Boardwalk Motel

Narcotics Anonymous (NA), 83,
140
narratives, 127; boundary, 108;
creation, 126; desistance, 107;
identity in, 32; and public identity,
107; redemption script for, 108; of
registered sexual offenders, 105–6;
self-, 99; and stigma resistance, 99;
subjectivity of, 31–32; "truth" and,
108; of work, 111–19
Natalie (Boardwalk resident), 17, 44,
45, 49, 50, 58, 89, 119, 132, 133, 134,
137, 153–54, 178, 190, 200, 229; drug
use of, 85–86; and shutting down
Boardwalk, 186
National Coalition for the Homeless,
223
National Housing Survey (1981), 5–6
National Law Center on
Homelessness and Poverty, 223
Neal (Park Place resident), 147, 156,
229

Ned (Boardwalk resident), 131, 140,
227
Ness, Elliot, 3
"The New Colossus" (Lazarus),
223–24
Newman, Lloyd, xi
Nolan (Boardwalk resident), 34, 94,
137, 185, 226, 246n76
Noonan (Boardwalk resident), 19–20,
45, 57, 152, 160, 228
Nora (Boardwalk resident), 227

Obama, Barack, 220
Occupational Safety and Health
Administration (OSHA), 57
office, at Boardwalk Motel, 49–51
Origins of Totalitarianism, The
(Arendt), 223
"othering," process of, 126
*Our America: Life and Death on the
South Side of Chicago* (Isay), xi
owner of Boardwalk Motel, 58;
accommodation of, 199, 205;
and closing of Boardwalk, 190;
residents neglected by, 192

Pager, Devah, 63
Park Place Motel, 19, 20, 38, 41, 58,
77, 189; code compliance of, 40;
disadvantages at, 45; layout of,
44; location of, 44; reputation of,
46; shutting down of, 190, 204;
stabbing at, 46
parolees: at Boardwalk, 9, 19,
21, 29, 89, 195; challenges of
reentry for, 67; and drug dealing,
132–33; dual transition for, 65;
housing for, 62, 67, 202–4; job
requirements of, 133–34; jobs
for, 63, 64, 65; motel housing for,
209; problems of, 66; sources of
income for, 64; stigma attached
to, 65